D1207055

This work makes available in English translation a select body of Russian materials that portray the evolution of Soviet policies toward labor during the early years of Communist rule in Russia, 1917–1921. It documents one of the most striking paradoxes of the early history of Soviet communism: how, after starting its career by holding out before the Russian masses the vision of a workers' state free from oppression and exploitation of man by man, communism wasted no time in introducing a system of labor regimentation as cruel as any devised in modern history.

The narrative opens in the early months of the revolution when the utopian slogans of workers' control of industry and trade union management of production were the dominant factors in shaping Soviet policy toward labor. The author traces the gradual introduction of measures of labor compulsion, first in relation to the recalcitrant "bourgeoisie" and afterward to the working class itself. He devotes three chapters to the story of labor militarization, which the Communists believed would solve the major economic problems in a socialist state. Finally, he reviews the general crisis of communism and the repudiation of some of the more oppressive features of that system. Here are the records which illuminate the will and acts of the revolutionary leaders. They reveal the shifts, the contradictions, and the flexibility of deeds in the fanatical and ruthless application of a social philosophy, and at the same time give a vivid picture of the conflict, suffering, and death that accompanied the revolutionary upheaval.

These documents, carefully selected, annotated, and woven into a coherent narrative, include official records, Party resolutions, collected works of Bolshevik leaders, memoirs of participants, and the daily press. Most of these materials have never been published in English. The volume should be invaluable to the historian, the economist, and the student of politics as a compendium of sources, and to the general reader as a stirring and fascinating picture of the human drama of social revolution.

James Bunyan is co-author of *The Bolshevik Revolution, 1917–1918* (with H. H. Fisher) and author of *Intervention, Civil War and Communism in Russia, April–December, 1918.* He now is engaged in a study of Soviet economic organization and planning, 1917–1967.

THE ORIGIN OF FORCED LABOR IN THE SOVIET STATE 1917–1921

HOOVER INSTITUTION PUBLICATIONS

THE ORIGIN OF FORCED LABOR
IN THE SOVIET STATE
1917-1921
Documents and Materials

by
James Bunyan

Published in Co-operation with
THE HOOVER INSTITUTION ON
WAR, REVOLUTION AND PEACE
Stanford, California

THE JOHNS HOPKINS PRESS, BALTIMORE

PREFACE

We started with free employment and, through a number of stages, made the transition to mass labor mobilization, based on the principle of universal compulsory labor. This enabled us to enlist and distribute the labor force on an all-national scale and in the interests of the national economy as a whole, which was being organized on a new foundation. . . . Step by step the entire labor force of the country became encompassed by a single leadership and a single principle. The labor force of the Republic was nationalized and, having become the property (*sobstvennost*) of the state, was carrying out the orders and the objectives of the state. As this process of socialization of the labor force was taking place, a single organ was established to consolidate and to direct this colossal work . . . which paves the way to the communist organization of labor.

(A. Anikst, *Organizatsiya rabochey sily
v 1920 godu*, Moscow, 1920, p. 63)

The above quotation is from a report a high-ranking Soviet official presented to the Eighth Congress of Soviets that met at the end of December, 1920. The quotation epitomizes three years of Bolshevik policy toward labor and reveals one of the most striking paradoxes of the early history of Soviet communism: how communism started its career in Russia by holding out before the Russian masses the vision of a workers' state, free from oppression and exploitation of man by man, but culminated in a system of labor compulsion under which the Russian workers were ruled and exploited by a new bureaucracy under the leadership of the Communist Party. The process by which this transformation was brought about is the theme of our study.

A number of contemporary documents that are essential for an understanding of the development of Soviet

policies toward labor between 1917 and 1921, the forma-
tive years of Communist rule in Russia, have been selected,
translated and are presented here. The study starts with
the early months of the revolution, when the utopian slogans of workers' control of industry and the elusive promise of trade-union management of industrial production
were the controlling factors in shaping Soviet policy toward labor. Chapter II traces the gradual introduction of
measures of labor compulsion, first in relation to the
groups of the population that were classified by the Bolsheviks as the "bourgeoisie" and afterwards in relation to
the working class itself.

Chapters III, IV, and V, which are the focal part of the
study, tell the story of labor militarization—the new for-
mula that, for the Communists, held the key to the solution
of all economic problems in a socialist state. Chapter III
presents the theories that were used to justify the militarization of labor and it outlines the institutional framework
that kept the system in operation. Chapter IV deals with
the application of this system to the different segments of
the Russian population. Chapter V analyzes compulsory
labor in transportation, in which the validity of labor
militarization as an institution came most sharply into
question.

The last chapter, Chapter VI, reviews the general crisis
of communism, the repudiation of some of the most oppressive features of that system, and the efforts to reconcile conflicting views within the Communist Party on the
role of labor under socialism.

The first Communist experiment with forced labor
ended in disaster, but it was not without significance for
the future. When, in the late twenties, Stalin launched a
new drive to usher in the socialist economic order by means
of a forced industrialization of Russia, he adopted the

entire organizational framework of compulsory labor that Lenin and Trotsky had developed in 1920. Similarly, a regime of labor compulsion was imposed upon the Soviet-bloc countries that, after World War II, were compelled to adopt Soviet forms of political and economic organization; and the mass labor mobilization of China's "Great Leap Forward" of 1958–60 is but a greatly magnified version of Soviet labor policies of 1920.

For the "emerging countries," Russian experience during the early years of the revolution has a deep significance. It supplies concrete evidence of the widespread misery, tyranny, and cruelty that occur in fanatical application of easy panaceas to complex social and economic problems.

Most of the documents included in this study are quoted in full, but a few items were too long to be cited in their entirety, and the latter have been abbreviated, either by omitting unessential parts or by summarizing sections of a document. Except in cases of documents with numbered paragraphs, where it is obvious from the numbering that material has been omitted, asterisks are used to indicate omissions. Brackets are used to indicate summaries. A translation of Russian sources used in this work can be found in the Bibliography.

The introductory notes are designed to call the reader's attention to issues that deserve to be highlighted in a basic and well-balanced interpretation of the events as a whole. The author also intended, by means of these introductory summaries, to present a connected narrative of the principal developments in the application of Soviet labor policies.

The preparation of this study was aided by a grant from The Hoover Institution, Stanford University, and I wish to express my obligation to Dr. W. Glenn Campbell, director of The Hoover Institution, and to Dr. Stefan T. Pos-

sony for their interest. I am deeply indebted to the staff
of the Hoover library for its unfailing help in filling my
requests for needed material. Dr. Albert K. Weinberg
contributed generously his critical abilities during the revi-
sion of the first draft of the study, for which I am most
grateful. I am also grateful to Mr. Daniel J. McCarthy,
copy editor, who exercised great skill in a difficult editorial
task, and to Miss Penny James, of The Johns Hopkins
Press, who saw the manuscript through publication.

Palm Beach, 1967   JAMES BUNYAN

CONTENTS

ix

CHAPTER I

THE ROLE OF LABOR IN
THE SOVIET STATE

In the many pamphlets and articles he wrote in the summer and early autumn of 1917, Lenin attempted to deal in detail with the organization and function of the Russian working class in the socialist society that he confidently predicted would be established after the seizure of political power by the Bolsheviks. The substance of Lenin's thought on this problem revolved around the familiar Marxist idea that the fundamental features of a socialist economy were developing automatically even within the framework of capitalism, so that there was a straight-line road from capitalism to socialism. "Capitalist culture," Lenin observed, *"has created*[1] large-scale production, factories, railroads, postal services and telephones, etc. *On this basis*, the great majority of functions of the old 'state power' have become so simplified and can be reduced to such elementary operations of registration, bookkeeping, and checking, that they will be fully within the reach of all literate people, and it will be quite possible to perform these functions for an ordinary 'workingman's wage.' "[2]

To achieve this state of affairs was simple; all that was necessary was to replace the existing Provisional Government by the Soviets, "to break up the old bureaucratic machinery . . . to organize large-scale production on the basis of what capitalism has already created. . . . Such a beginning . . . leads to the gradual establishment of an order . . . that bears no resemblance to wage slavery, an

---

[1] All italics as in the original text.
[2] V. I. Lenin, *Sochineniya*, Moscow, 1928–37, XXI, 399. Unless otherwise stated, all quotations from Lenin are from the third edition of his collected works.

order in which the functions of supervision and accounting, which are becoming steadily simplified, will be performed by each in turn, . . . and will finally disappear as a *special* function of a special stratum of the population." [3]

To reassure the moderate elements among his followers that the transition to the new order would involve minimal disruption in the basic forms of economic relationships, Lenin affirmed that the *"transfer of power to the Soviets was the only way that would make future developments gradual, peaceful, and tranquil . . .* that *no one* would dare to offer resistance to the transfer of the administration . . . and control over the economy to the workers and the peasants who would *learn quickly,* by their own experience, how to divide the land, production, and bread." [4]

When the Bolsheviks seized political power and began to evolve their political, social, and economic policies, they soon discovered that there were many persons who dared to resist the Soviet regime. This resistance led to civil war and foreign intervention, and to the separation from Russia of some of its most productive agricultural and industrial areas. The Bolsheviks further discovered that, although the peasants were not slow in dividing the land, they resisted parting with their crops unless they received needed industrial products from the cities in return. This resistance resulted in the "bread war" between the Bolsheviks and the peasants, and in famine conditions in the Russian cities. [5] The Bolsheviks also discovered that the industrial workers had failed to learn how to organize large-scale production quickly and that the short-lived

[3] *Ibid.,* pp. 402–3.
[4] *Ibid.,* pp. 147–48.
[5] Materials relating to the early phases of the Russian civil war and to Bolshevik relations with the peasants will be found in James Bunyan and H. H. Fisher, *The Bolshevik Revolution, 1917–1918,* Stanford University Press, Stanford, Calif. (2d printing), 1961, and in James Bunyan, *Intervention, Civil War and Communism in Russia, April–December, 1918,* The Johns Hopkins Press, Baltimore, 1936.

policy of workers' control had resulted in much confusion and conflict and led to the total paralysis of plant management and to the complete disruption of the already badly functioning machinery of industrial production.

Except for some documents that disclose the early misgivings by some advocates of greater trade-union supervision of economic life, this chapter does not deal with the political and economic difficulties and disruptions that followed the Bolsheviks' assumption of power; the chapter, rather, sets forth the ideas and institutions that were the point of departure in an experiment that was destined to lead, as far as the position of labor in the Soviet state was concerned, to the very antithesis of what had originally been proclaimed in the Bolshevik program.

A. Bolshevik Blueprint of Workers' Control of Industry

"Workers' control of industry" was one of the principal slogans of the Bolsheviks in the preparatory period before the seizure of power by Lenin and his followers in November, 1917. In his brochure, *Will the Bolsheviks Retain State Power?*, Lenin's plea for the overthrow of the Provisional Government and for the establishment of a dictatorship of the proletariat was intimately connected with the idea of workers' control of industry. "If it is a question," Lenin argued, "of establishing a proletarian state, i.e., the dictatorship of the proletariat, then workers' control *is capable* of becoming universal in scope, all-embracing, omnipresent, and the most accurate and conscientious *accounting* of production and distribution. . . . Therein lies the essence of the proletarian, i.e., the socialist, revolution." [6]

On November 7, 1917, when the success of the Bolshevik coup d'état seemed almost a certainty and Lenin emerged

[6] Lenin, *Sochineniya*, XXI, 259.

from his hiding place to make his first appearance at the Bolshevik headquarters in the Smolnyy Institute, Lenin reiterated his belief that one of the aims of the revolution was to establish workers' control over production.[7] This belief also was proclaimed by the Second Congress of Soviets, on November 8,[8] but the formal decree on workers' control was not promulgated until November 27, 1917. This decree turned out to be one of the most crucial pronouncements of the new revolutionary regime. It resulted in far-reaching changes in the organization and management of Russian industry and in the functioning of the Russian economy as a whole.

Although it left the question of industrial ownership in a rather indeterminate state, the decree on workers' control authorized workers' supervision of production, of the purchase of raw materials, and of the sale of output—as well as workers' supervision of the financial transactions of every enterprise that employed hired labor. All business correspondence and all account books were to be open to the inspection of workers' committees. Under these conditions, little scope was left for private initiative in industry. By mid-summer of 1918, private operation of large- and medium-scale industry had practically come to an end. At the same time, industrial production had suffered a catastrophic decline.

THE STATUTE OF WORKERS' CONTROL

[Decree of the Soviet of People's Commissars, November 27, 1917][9]

1. In the interests of a systematic regulation of the national economy, workers' control over production, over the purchase and

---

[7] *Izvestiya*, No. 207, November 8, 1917.

[8] Bunyan and Fisher, *The Bolshevik Revolution*, 1934, p. 122.

[9] In *Sobranie usakoneniy i rasporyazheniy rabochego i krestyanskogo pravitelstva*, 1917, No. 3, Art. 35. This source is hereafter cited as *S.U.R.*

Soviet of People's Commissars (*Sovet Narodnykh Komissarov*) was the name assumed by the Soviet government on November 7, 1917. It is generally abbreviated *Sovnarkom*, and this abbreviation will be used throughout this study.

sale of end products and raw materials, over the storage of these, and over the financial affairs of the enterprise is introduced in all industrial, commercial, banking, agricultural, transport, consumers' and producers' cooperatives, and other enterprises which employ hired labor or put out work domestically.

2. Workers' control is exercised by all the workers of a given enterprise through their elected organizations, such as factory-shop committees, councils of elders, etc. Representatives of employees and technical personnel are also included in these committees.

3. A Council of Workers' Control is to be established in every large city, *guberniya*, or industrial region. This Council, being an organ of the Soviet of Workers,' Soldiers,' and Peasants' Deputies, is composed of representatives of trade unions, factory, shop and other workers' committees and workers' cooperatives.

4. Pending the convocation of a congress of Councils of Workers' Control, an All-Russian Council of Workers' Control is established in Petrograd, made up of representatives of the following organizations:

a. Five from the All-Russian Central Executive Committee of the Soviet of Workers' and Soldiers' Deputies;
b. Five from the All-Russian Central Executive Committee of the Peasants' Deputies;
c. Five from the All-Russian Council of Trade Unions;
d. Two from the All-Russian Union of Workers' Cooperatives;
e. Five from the All-Russian Bureau of Factory-Shop Committees;
f. Five from the All-Russian Union of Engineers and Technicians;
g. Two from the All-Russian Union of Agronomists;
h. One from every All-Russian Union of Workers with less than 100,000 members;
i. Two from every union with more than 100,000 members;
j. Two from the Petrograd Council of Trade Unions.

5. Commissions of trained inspectors (technicians, accountants, etc.) are to be attached to the higher organs of workers' control to be sent out either on the initiative of these higher organs or at the request of the lower organs of workers' control to investigate the financial and technical aspects of enterprises.

6. The organs of workers' control have the right to supervise

production, fix the minimum of output, and determine the cost of the product.

7. The organs of workers' control have the right to control all the business correspondence of an enterprise. Owners of enterprises are legally responsible for all correspondence kept secret. Commercial secrets are abolished. The owners are under obligation to show to the organs of workers' control all their books and statements for the current year and for past years.

8. The rulings of the organs of workers' control are binding on the owners of enterprises and can be annulled only by decisions of the higher organs of workers' control.

9. The owner or the directors of an enterprise are granted a period of three days in which to lodge complaints with the higher organs of workers' control against the decisions of the lower organs of workers' control.

10. In all enterprises the owners and the representatives of the workers and employees that have been elected to carry out the functions of workers' control are responsible to the state for the strictest order and discipline and the safety of the property. Persons guilty of concealing materials or products, of falsifying accounts, and of similar abuses are criminally liable.

11. Regional Councils of Workers' Control (Article 3) have the power to settle disputed points and conflicts that may arise between the lower organs of workers' control as well as to render decision on the complaints of the owners of enterprises. They also issue instructions (within the limits fixed by the All-Russian Council of Workers' Control) to conform to local conditions of production and supervise the activities of the lower organs of control.

12. The All-Russian Council of Workers' Control formulates general plans and instructions for workers' control, issues binding decisions, regulates relations between the Regional Councils of Workers' Control, and serves as the highest court of appeal for all matters connected with workers' control.

13. The All-Russian Council of Workers' Control coordinates the activities of the organs of workers' control in their dealings with other national-economic institutions. A statute defining the relations between the All-Russian Council of Workers' Control and other institutions engaged in the organization and management of the national economy will be issued separately.

14. All laws and circulars restricting the work of factory, shop

and other committees or councils of workers and employees are hereby annulled.

V. ULYANOV (LENIN)
*Chairman of the Soviet
of People's Commissars* (Sovnarkom)

A. SHLYAPNIKOV
People's Commissar of Labor

The All-Russian Council of Workers' Control, which—in accordance with paragraph 12 of the Statute on Workers' Control—was to formulate rules for the co-ordination of the activities of local control councils, does not appear to have become very active. It apparently drew up instructions for the guidance of the local control councils, but these instructions never became operative. They were not even issued as a separate document but appeared in the form of an appendix to the resolution on workers' control that was adopted on January 27, 1918, by the First All-Russian Congress of Trade Unions.[10] Indeed, the Council itself completely disappeared from the political scene. According to A. Ryazanov, a prominent Marxist theoretician and trade-union leader who in the early days of the revolution was in close contact with Bolshevik top policy makers, there was a plan—when the Supreme Council of National Economy was established on December 14, 1917[11] to have that body operate rather closely with the All-Russian Council of Workers' Control. For some reason, however, the Control Council was not allowed to meet,[12] which is not

[10] *Pervyy Vserossiyskiy sezd professionalnykh soyuzov, Stenograficheskiy otchet*, Moscow, 1918, pp. 370–72.

[11] The decree establishing the Supreme Council of National Economy is cited in Bunyan and Fisher, *The Bolshevik Revolution*, pp. 314–15. The Supreme Council of National Economy was in charge of industrial management in the U.S.S.R. until 1932, when it was abolished by Stalin. It was resurrected by Khrushchev in March, 1963, ostensibly for the purpose of returning to the Leninist organizational framework of industrial management (*Pravda*, Nos. 73 and 75, March 13 and 15, 1963). Khrushchev's successors abolished the Supreme Council of National Economy.

[12] *Trudy I Vserossiyskogo sezda sovetov narodnogo khozyaystva*, Moscow, 1918, p. 104.

surprising if one considers that the drive for local initiative and the spirit of the "creativity of the masses" were the dominant characteristics of the time, and were greatly encouraged by the Soviet government.

In the early months of the revolution, in order to secure as wide a popular support as possible, the Bolsheviks laid great emphasis on local authority (*vlast na mestakh*). In a decree published on November 18, 1917, the Soviet government called upon workers, soldiers, peasants, and all toilers to take all local power into their own hands. "Take and guard as the apple of your eye, all grain, factories, implements, products, and transport. All of these are from now on wholly yours." [13]

Under these circumstances it was only natural that the real executors of workers' control were the local factory-shop committees, and each committee acted in accordance with its own understanding and interpretation of the basic statute on workers' control. A good illustration of this is the case of the factory-shop committees of Petrograd. Early in January, 1918, a conference of these committees passed a resolution on the scope of workers' control and issued detailed instructions on the application of workers' control in plants and factories. As the next two documents show, both the resolution and the instructions go far beyond the original statute on workers' control that the Soviet government decreed on November 27, 1917.

THE SCOPE OF WORKERS' CONTROL

[Resolution of the Petrograd Council of Factory-Shop Committees, January 6, 1918] [14]

Workers' control of industry, being a component part of control

[13] *S.U.R.*, 1917, No. 2, p. 28, in Bunyan and Fisher, *The Bolshevik Revolution*, p. 279.
[14] A. Pankratova, *Fabzavkomy Rossii v borbe za sotsialisticheskuyu fabriku*, Glavpolitprosvet, Moscow, 1923, p. 243. *Fabzavkomy* stands for "Fabrichno-zavodskie komitety" (Factory-shop committees).

over the entire economy, is to be understood not in the narrow sense of mere inspection, but in the wider sense of intervention in the acts of the [plant] proprietor relating to capital investment, inventories of the enterprise, raw materials and semi-finished products, as well as active supervision over the proper and expedient fulfillment of factory orders, use of electric power and of the labor force, and the participation in the organization of production in accordance with rational principles. Workers' control is to be looked upon as the transition phase for the organization of the entire economy on Socialist principles, as the first essential step taken from below and paralleling the work going on in the central organs of the national economy.

THE APPLICATION OF WORKERS' CONTROL

[Instructions of the Petrograd Council of Factory-Shop Committees, January 6(?), 1918][15]

31. The Factory-Shop Committee is the basic nucleus for the application of workers' control.

32. The Factory-Shop Committee has the right to intervene at any time in the decisions and the activities of the plant owner or the administration if these decisions are contrary to the vital interests of the enterprise. In such cases the Committee has the right to issue its own orders which are compulsory not only for the workers and employees but also for the administration and the owner. The Committee has the right to institute uninterrupted supervision over the bookkeeping and the accounts of the enterprise and to audit its books and correspondence. The Committee, in cooperation with the administration, has the right to establish regulations for the internal life of the enterprise.

33. All orders and decisions of the Factory-Shop Committees, that were approved by the general meeting of workers and employees of a given enterprise and that are in line with the decisions of the higher organs of the National Economy, are compulsory upon the administration and the owners of the enterprise. These orders have to be carried out within three days after they were issued.

[15] *Ibid.*, pp. 356–60. The instructions are part of a resolution on the principles of organization of the factory-shop committees. The first thirty paragraphs deal with organizational matters.

34. Instructions and acts of the administration or of the owner relating to the operations of the enterprise cannot be put into effect without the knowledge and consent of the Factory-Shop Committee.

[Paragraph 35 provides for the confiscation of plants if an owner refused to follow the orders of the control committees. Paragraphs 36 and 37 state that the control committees are to carry out the policies of higher authorities.]

38. The activities of the Factory-Shop Committees are divided into the following basic functions:

- a. Control over the organization of production;
- b. Control over the supply of essential materials;
- c. Guarding the interests of workers and employees of the enterprise.

A. Control over the Organization of Production

39. The Factory-Shop Committee as represented by the Control Commission takes charge of the following:

- a. In the Technical-Economic Field:
  1. Works out the general scheme of the organization of the enterprise;
  2. Checks on the technological equipment and its utilization;
  3. Determines the cost of the end product;
  4. Makes an inventory of goods and watches after their preservation;
  5. Makes known the existing production orders and distributes them to the various shops.

- b. In the Financial Field:
  1. Checks periodically the financial condition of the enterprise;
  2. Determines at any given moment the available cash of the enterprise;
  3. Determines the outstanding payments and receipts of the enterprise;

4. Draws conclusions as to the availability or shortage of means for the conduct of the enterprise;
5. Looks after the correctness of expenditures of money by the enterprise and makes sure that the books and correspondence are in order;
6. Studies production orders and delivery conditions and, if they are not found to be in the interests of the enterprise, stops their execution pending the decision of the higher national economic organizations;
7. Audits the annual balances of the enterprise and the distribution of profits.

[Section *c* deals with the industrial demobilization that took place soon after the Bolsheviks initiated peace negotiations with the Germans.]

B. Control over the Supply of Essential Materials

40. [This section deals in considerable detail with the competence of workers' control in the field of supply.]

C. Watching over the Interests of Workers and Employees

41. The Factory-Shop Committee, through its Commission on Labor, exercises control of the following:
   a. Formulates rules for the internal organization of the enterprise;
   b. Hires and fires workers and employees;
   c. Grants leaves to workers and employees;
   d. Discharges members of the administration who are unable to establish normal relations with the workers;
   e. Gives its approval for the hiring of new members of the plant administration;
   f. Establishes norms of working time;
   g. Makes decisions in the case of minor conflicts between the workers and the plant administration.

[The resolution also deals with such problems as sanitation, culture and education, and sources of income to cover the operational expenditures of the control committees.]

The Instructions on the Application of Workers' Control, as issued by the Petrograd Council of Factory-Shop Committees, came in for a good deal of criticism at the First All-Russian Congress of Trade Unions, which met January 20–27, 1918. Commenting on these instructions, A. Lozovsky [16] observed:

I am somewhat puzzled by the clause which refers to the distribution of profits.[17] If a business is completely within the jurisdiction of the control committee, it is not clear why anyone should want to distribute profits. Where does the factory owner or the shareholder come in under this scheme? What sort of profits can they expect?

I should also like to call your attention to the aims which the factory-shop committee places before the control commission. Insofar as the control commission is concerned, the factory-shop committee is the owner (*khozyain*) of the enterprise. Its competence includes not only control, but also production. It prescribes the order of industrial output, checks on deliveries, studies the market, and looks for customers. In short, if this path is followed these instructions should have been concluded by the following clause: "The plant owner is herewith abolished." [18]

Lozovsky also criticized the fragmentation of workers' control in which each committee acted on its own initiative and without reference to interests other than those that affected the particular factory.

Other attacks on the theory and practice of workers' control were voiced at the Congress,[19] but the majority of the delegates took the decree on workers' control quite seriously and adopted a resolution in favor of its retention, with the recommendation that the control commissions be placed under the general supervision of the trade unions.

[16] Lozovsky, a prominent worker of the Russian trade-union movement and a member of the Bolshevik Party, who frequently criticized Bolshevik politics, was expelled from the Party on January 11, 1918, less than ten days before the opening of the All-Russian Congress of Trade Unions (see Bunyan and Fisher, *The Bolshevik Revolution*, pp. 637–38).

[17] See point 7, section 39*b*, of the preceding document.

[18] *Pervyy Vserossiyskiy sezd professionalnykh soyuzov*, pp. 192–93.

[19] Ryazanov was particularly bitter in his criticism of the factory-shop committees and workers' control councils (*ibid.*, pp. 233–38).

THE TRADE UNIONS TRY TO SET LIMITS
TO WORKERS' CONTROL

[Excerpts from the resolution of the First All-Russian Congress
of Trade Unions, January 27, 1918][20]

[The first paragraph of the resolution gives a general description of the alleged anarchy of capitalist production relationships. Paragraph 2 asserts that the Provisional Government continued the war in the interests of the dominant classes.]

3. Workers' control is one of the essential elements of [state] regulation of the national economy. Its purpose is to bring an end to the autocratic regime in the economic sphere in the same way as that regime has been brought to an end in the political sphere.

4. Workers' control, which is indissolubly connected with the general system of state regulation and which, in the provinces, is the champion of the general economic plan developed by the regulating organs [of the state], is one of the great conquests of the proletariat in its struggle for complete emancipation.

5. In order that workers' control may bring the maximum of benefits to the proletariat, it is necessary to reject once and for all any idea of pulverizing that control by giving the workers of any individual enterprise the right to make final decisions on questions affecting the very existence of the enterprise.

6. The workers of every enterprise and their elected organization—factory-shop committees—will be in a better position to carry on the work [of control] if they operate on the basis of a general plan formulated by the higher organs of workers' control and the regulatory organs of the economy.

7. In this colossal work which the organs of workers' control have assumed, the trade unions should take the most active part by championing the interests of the workers as a whole as opposed to the sectional and group interests of the workers of a given trade or enterprise.

8. The trade unions which are organized by industries should take part in the local and central organs of workers' control and should assume the role of ideological and organizational leadership. The trade unions should study every decision taken by the

[20] *Pervyy Vserossiyskiy sezd professionalnykh soyuzov*, pp. 369–70.

factory-shop committees in the field of control to make it clear to their delegates in plants and factories that control over production does not signify the transfer of the enterprise to the workers— that workers' control is not the same as socialization of production and distribution, but is only a preliminary step in this direction.

9. The trade unions, acting in close contact with the factory-shop committees and local Soviets of Workers' and Soldiers' Deputies, should champion the idea of centralizing the function of workers' control to correspond to the present-day methods of industrial organization and the structure of labor organization.

10. After they have established themselves as the backbone of the control organization within their own branch of production and have transformed workers' control into an instrument in the struggle for socialism, the trade unions will be able to play an enormous role in paving new paths for the trade-union movement of the entire world.

11. A proper organization of workers' control requires that local control commissions, or factory-shop committees that replace them, are placed under the supervision of economic control commissions established in connection with the trade unions of every branch of industry. To bring this about, every enterprise should send one or two delegates to take part in the work of the control commission and report to the trade union about the activities of the lower organs of control.

12. Economic control commissions attached to the industrial trade unions are composed of elected delegates of the union, enlarged by representatives of factory-shop committees and invited technicians, bookkeepers and statisticians.

13. The activities of control commissions attached to trade unions are checked and regulated by the local Council of Workers' Control organized in accordance with the Decree on Workers' Control of November 14, 1917.

14. Factory-shop committees and trade-union control commissions, in exercising local and central control, are guided in their activities by the instructions formulated by the All-Russian Council of Workers' Control. [These instructions are given in the form of an appendix to the above resolution (*ibid.*, pp. 370–72).]

Not much was done at this time to implement the part

of the resolution that related to trade-union supervision of the workers' control commissions. In those early days of the revolution, Lenin continued to cling to his faith in the socialist mentality of the average worker and his ability to manage affairs of the state. In his speech at the Third Congress of Soviets, January 24, 1918, Lenin gave expression to this faith and defended workers' control as one of the prerequisites for "the building of a socialist economy."

LENIN REAFFIRMS WORKERS' CONTROL

[Excerpts from a speech at the
Third All-Russian Congress of Soviets, January 24, 1918][21]

. . . The transition from workers' control to the confiscation of plants was also quite easy. When we were being accused that by introducing workers' control we were breaking up the process of production into separate shops, we merely brushed aside that nonsense. In introducing workers' control we knew that it would take a good deal of time for it to spread all over Russia. But we wanted to demonstrate that we recognized only one road—transformation from below—in order that the workers themselves be given a chance to develop new economic conditions from below. This development will take a good deal of time.

From workers' control we proceeded to the establishment of the Supreme Council of National Economy. It is this measure, together with the nationalization of the banks and the railroads, which is to take place in the next few days,[22] that will enable us to undertake the building of a new socialist economy. We fully realize the difficulty of our undertaking but we affirm that the only real Socialist is the one who undertakes this task, relying on the experience and instinct of the toiling masses. The masses will make many mistakes, but the main thing has already been accom-

[21] Lenin, *Sochineniya*, XXII, 215.

[22] The construction of this sentence in Russian is such that the clause "which is to take place in the next few days" relates both to the nationalization of the banks and the railroads. Lenin did not know, or forgot, that the banks were nationalized on December 27, 1917 (*S.U.R.*, 1917, No. 10, pp. 149-50), i.e., nearly a month prior to his speech at the Third Congress of Soviets. Nor was there need to nationalize the railroads: with the exception of a few minor side lines, they were already the property of the Russian state.

plished. They know that when they appeal to the Soviet Government, they will receive full support against the exploiters. There is not a single measure capable of easing their work which would not be fully and completely supported by the Soviet Government. The Soviet Government does not know everything, is not able to do everything on time, and is frequently confronted with difficult problems. Very often delegations of workers and peasants come to the Government and ask, for example, what they should do with a certain piece of land. Frequently, I myself felt embarrassed when I saw that their outlook was not entirely clear. And I would say to them: "You are the power, do all you want to do, take everything you need; we shall support you, but take care of production, take care that production is useful. Take up useful work. You will make mistakes, but you will learn." And the workers have already begun to learn; they have already begun to fight against the saboteurs. Education has been made into a fence which hinders the advance of the toilers. That fence will be pulled down.

. . . The workers and peasants [23] do not as yet have sufficient faith in their powers. Age-long tradition has created the habit of waiting for orders from above. They have not as yet become fully accustomed to the fact that the proletariat is the dominant class, that there are elements among them who were frightened and downtrodden and who imagine that they must go through the despicable school of the bourgeoisie. This most despicable of bourgeois superstitions has remained alive longer than all the rest, but it is perishing and will perish completely. And we are convinced that with every step taken by the Soviet Government there will appear more and more people who have freed themselves completely of the old bourgeois prejudice that the ordinary worker and peasant are incapable of managing the affairs of the state. They are capable of learning and they will learn if they take the management into their own hands! . . .

B. Early Misgivings About Workers' Control

Abolition of the plant owner, which Lozovsky thought was the logical conclusion to be drawn from the Instruc-

[23] Lenin, *Sochineniya*, XXII, 216.

tions on the Application of Workers' Control, was soon accomplished. Throughout the winter and spring of 1918, many plants were taken over by the Soviet government, and management of these plants fell into the hands of the committees of workers' control, which ran them without regard to the interests of anyone but themselves. This undoubtedly created the illusion in the rank and file of the industrial workers that a new social and economic order had come into being and that the workers now were masters of their own fate. This illusion, however, was short-lived. Difficulties soon developed when the vague and comforting abstractions about the dominant role of the proletariat, so assiduously fostered by Lenin and by other leading Bolsheviks, had to be translated into specific economic terms.

The Bolsheviks were forced to come to grips with these difficulties as the tempo of nationalization of industry quickened and reached its climax, in the summer of 1918, with the wholesale nationalization of Russia's large-scale industry.[24] From that time on, the state became the principal employer of labor, and its main interest—as with any employer of labor—was production and labor productivity.

---

[24] Various theories have been used to explain the Soviet policy of nationalization of industry. One theory interprets the nationalization decrees as punitive measures, in some cases to discipline the workers and in others to punish the plant owners for refusing to submit to workers' control. Another theory claims that nationalization was intended to prevent the Germans from acquiring an interest in Russian industrial plants. Still another theory, which attributes nationalization to the exigencies of the civil war, dates "war communism" in industry from June 28, 1918 (E. H. Carr, *The Bolshevik Revolution, 1917–1923*, Vols. 1–3 of *History of Soviet Russia* [7 vols; New York, 1951–60], Vol. 2, pp. 173, 176). There is no doubt that nationalization served a major purpose of the Communist program of introducing socialism in Russia. To usher in the socialist economic order, it was essential that both production and distribution be planned and controlled by the state, acting through the medium of a centralized administrative machinery. After the means of production and distribution were in the hands of the state, each citizen would become an employee of the state, doing what he was ordered to do for whatever reward the state chose to give him.

Even before the radical step of large-scale nationalization was taken, the First All-Russian Congress of Councils of National Economy, in its resolution of June 3, 1918, urged "the establishment of production norms for individual workers in plants, the correlation of wage scales with production standards, strict labor discipline enforced by workers themselves, the introduction of compulsory labor, the mobilization of technical specialists, and the organized redistribution of labor."[25] These measures, however, were difficult to achieve. As a speaker at the First Congress of Councils of National Economy stated: "Every attempt we make to introduce production norms is met with great opposition from the workers."[26] And *Izvestiya*, the official organ of the Soviet government, lamented the fact that "the revolution has created a chaos in the minds of a number of people. The ideas of socialism are quite often interpreted . . . as an opportunity to divide property . . . and the workers are now carrying away the machines . . . from the plants . . . thinking that these objects belong to them."[27] But the willfulness of the rank and file of the workers was only one factor in the developments that were leading to the decline of industrial production. The other factor was the critical food shortage in which the industrial workers found themselves soon after the Bolshevik coup d'état.

Soviet food and agricultural policies were closely bound up with industrial developments, and this gave rise to a vicious circle that the Bolsheviks were unable to break during the entire period under consideration. The shortage of available consumers' goods for exchange for agricul-

---

[25] The Proceedings of the Congress, as well as the resolution, are given in Bunyan, *Intervention, Civil War and Communism in Russia*, pp. 387–98.

[26] *Trudy I Vserossiyskogo sezda sovetov narodnogo khozyaystva, Stenograficheskiy otchet*, Moscow, 1918, p. 380.

[27] *Izvestiya*, No. 58, March 27, 1918.

tural products caused a food shortage in the industrial centers, and the food shortage in the industrial centers affected the health of the workers and made them even less able to produce commodities to exchange for agricultural products.

Another feature of the Bolshevik food policy that contributed to the decline of industrial production was the method of food distribution that was in force during the early period of the revolution. The system of food rationing that the Soviet government introduced was organized in such a way that compensation lost all relationship to the actual work performed and depended primarily on the worker's classification (i.e., heavy work or light work) that had been introduced for the purpose of rationing. This system, which provided no incentive to higher productivity, contributed to the steady decline in production.

It was not long after the beginning of the experiment in workers' control that some Soviet officials began to deplore the chaotic results of workers' interference in industrial management. The two documents that follow illustrate the criticisms of the system of workers' control, both as it appeared on the railways and as it led to a decline of labor productivity in general. The third document exemplifies the line that usually was taken by supporters of the system in answering such criticisms. The matters that were complained of were held to be the unavoidable result not of the attitude of the workers themselves but, rather, of the deterioration in their living conditions. The fourth document interprets workers' control from the point of view of *Novaya zhizn*, a paper founded by M. Gorki, which represented the position of the Socialist Internationalists, a small but sophisticated group that was highly critical of Bolshevik policies. In their view, it was the "November demogogy" of the Bolsheviks that created chaos in the minds of the workers and misled them into believing that workers' control was "their only way of salvation."

DISRUPTION OF THE RAILWAY SYSTEM

[Excerpts from a statement by A. Shlyapnikov, People's Commissar of Labor, at the Central Executive Committee, March 20, 1918][28]

. . . What is happening on the railways cannot be described as destruction, it can only be described as complete disorganization which is getting worse every day. It has reached a stage when we are no longer getting locomotives and cars. Let us take first the repair shops. Labor productivity is falling hourly. We asked why locomotives are not available. When we turned to the repair shops which repair the cars and locomotives we found a frightening picture. Workers in large plants, such as the Alexandrovsky R.R. Car Construction Plant with its locomotive repair shops, were engaged in fitting railroad cars for the use of the workers, their wives, children, and their household belongings.

On my way [from Petrograd] to Moscow, I stopped at a number of stations to find out how things stood on this most important road, and I telegraphed to all stations asking the representatives of committees or station-masters to prepare brief reports on what was going on in their respective divisions, stations, depots, and shops. The picture presented in these reports is a very sad one and it brings us face to face with the necessity of taking the most rigorous measures to re-establish labor discipline on the railways at any cost and before all else. The trains are often operating without lights, there is no signalling, the cars are never cleaned, etc. The usual excuse is that no kerosene or candles are available. However, I found out that both these items were available but were being pilfered in the most shameless manner.

Train crews, being not at all interested in the exploitation of the railways, frequently refuse to take charge of the trains. Because of this, both cars and locomotives may be available, but there are

---

[28] *Protokoly zasedaniy Vserossiyskogo tsentralnogo ispolnitelnogo komiteta 4-go sozyva, Stenograficheskiy otchet,* Moscow, 1920, pp. 43–44. Shlyapnikov's statement is of interest not only because of the information it supplies about the effects of workers' control on the operations of the railways but also because it comes from the future leader of the Workers' Opposition, which in 1920 and 1921 advocated a return to the system of workers' control of industry.

no engineers and no conductors. They either pretend illness or simply refuse to go. It sometimes happens that on certain trains which require a certain number of persons, a substitute has to be found [for someone] who is really ill, but the station-master is unable to exercise his authority, for as soon as he puts someone in place of the sick man the substitute tells him that he will not go without the consent of the Committee. Since it is impossible to get the Committee together on the spot, the train cannot be dispatched. . . .

By present-day [29] rules the workers are guaranteed their pay. The worker turns up at his job and spends some time at his bench. Whether he does anything or not, no one can say anything to him because the shop committee is powerless. If the shop committee attempts to control the shops, it is immediately disbanded and another committee is elected. In a word, things are in the hands of a crowd that, due to its ignorance and lack of interest in production, is literally putting a brake on all work. . . .

DECLINE IN LABOR PRODUCTIVITY

[Excerpt from an article by M. Tomsky, Chairman of the Central Council of Trade Unions, May 25, 1918] [30]

. . . The decline in labor productivity has reached catastrophic proportions. Industrial production is threatened with complete collapse. This is due to the fact that the worker produces *less value than he receives*, less than he requires for the bare necessities of life. Under these conditions the worker becomes a state pensioner, a parasite living at other people's expense. This state of affairs cannot last, and unless productivity is soon restored to normal conditions a general economic crisis and the collapse of production are inevitable. . . .

[Excerpt from a statement by Gastev at the First All-Russian Congress of Councils of National Economy, May 30, 1918] [31]

. . . At the present time the laboring masses function in the capacity of consumers and not as producers. This is due to the

---

[29] *Ibid.*, p. 46.
[30] *Professionalnyy vestnik*, No. 7–8, May 25, 1918, p. 7.
[31] *Trudy I Vserossiyskogo sezda sovetov narodnogo khozyaystva*, p. 380.

economic backwardness of our country. We do not tell the worker to maintain the same level of production, irrespective of the government he lives under. Basically what we are facing now is enormous sabotage by millions of people. I find it ridiculous to hear people talk about sabotage of the bourgeoisie, when the frightened bourgeois is picked as one engaged in sabotage. What we really have is sabotage on a nationwide scale, by the whole people, by the proletariat. We encounter enormous opposition on the part of working masses whenever we attempt to establish output norms. . . .

DETERIORATION OF THE WORKERS' STANDARD OF LIVING

[Excerpts from V. Nogin's speech at the First Congress of Councils of National Economy, May, 1918][32]

I am glad that I am speaking after Comrade Gastev. In answer to his speech of indictment, it is necessary to say a few words in defense of the working class, especially as it may help Comrade Gastev and those who think like him to descend to this sinful earth and consider the conditions under which the Russian worker lives at the present time. I should like to remind Comrade Gastev of a few facts with which he is probably familiar. He must surely know that the productivity of a human being is determined first of all by his nourishment. Comrade Gastev knows that if we take an average man weighing approximately four *puds* [144 pounds] he would need 2,300 calories just to sustain himself without performing any serious work. For light work he needs 2,600 calories; for average work 3,100 calories are needed, and for heavy work 3,600 calories. It is also known that by decreasing food intake labor productivity decreases much more rapidly than the decrease in food. Thus with 90 percent of normal food intake, labor productivity is only 72 percent. With 80 percent of food intake, productivity is only 45 percent. With 70 percent of food intake, productivity is only 17 percent, and with 60 percent of normal food intake, productivity equals zero.

What is the condition of the Russian worker in this respect? A complete answer would require an extensive study of the problem, which is not available. We can arrive at an approximate

[32] *Ibid.*, pp. 381–82.

answer to this question on the basis of data recently received at the Petrograd Commissariat of Labor. The data relate to wages, the increase in food prices, and the cost of a normal food ration (*paek*) which is customarily consumed by a Petrograd worker. They show that the wages of workers throughout the country, including the workers of Petrograd, have risen to an extraordinary degree. In some places the wages have reached a colossal figure. For example, tanners in Nizhniy Novgorod receive as much as 400 to 800, and even 1,000 rubles a week. These figures give the impression that the workers are unreasonable and are stretching their demands to incredible limits, that the workers are fully capable of meeting their [food] requirements and can, therefore, be expected to be more productive than they actually are. From this the inference is drawn that the decline in labor productivity is due to disorganization and demoralization.

A more careful examination of the data discloses the following picture: Wages in Petrograd have been rising rapidly and are now 945 percent in relation to 1914. The average daily wage of a Petrograd worker in the early part of May is known to have been as follows:

```
1914— 1 ruble,   7 kopeks
1915— 1   "      38    "
1916— 2 rubles, 94    "
1917— 5   "      33    "
1918—11   "      20    "
```

The cost [per day] of an average ration of a Petrograd manual laborer during the same period was as follows:

```
1914— 0 ruble,  26.1 kopeks
1915— "    "    32.4    "
1916— "    "    41.0    "
1917— "    "    85.8    "
1918—20 rubles,  5.0    "
```

This means that the increase in relation to 1914 is 7,700 percent. We are thus forced to the conclusion that at the present time the Petrograd worker is in no position to purchase the amount of food that would enable him to do the work that is required of him.

As regards a married worker, he was able to make monthly savings for his family needs, other than food, as follows:

1914—15 rubles, 0 kopek
1915—15   "   92 kopeks
1916—55   "   5   "
1917—94   "   64   "

In 1918 the worker has a deficit of 622 rubles, 25 kopeks. [Nogin then analyzed the relation of wages to the cost of living of the Moscow workers and ended with the general conclusion that the drop in workers' productivity was due primarily to their reduced food intake.]

HOW WORKERS' CONTROL OPERATED

[A review in *Novaya zhizn*][33]

Workers' control was among the slogans of the November Revolution. The future of the working class under workers' control was pictured in such rosy colors that the workers seized upon this idea as their only way of salvation.

Six months have now passed and it is possible to give an appraisal of the results of that control.

In the first place it should be stated that the majority of workers, especially in the provinces, owing to their ignorance of market conditions, functions of the banks, etc., were quite sincere in their belief that as soon as "control" started there would come to the surface lots of money which the sabotaging entrepreneurs were supposed to be hiding away. Naturally, their expectations were not justified by the facts. The following account of his search for money was given by a Communist worker: "I arrived at the factory and began to exercise control. I broke open the safety vault but could take no account of the money. There was no money to be found there." It is with some such naive faith and understanding of the role of industrial capital that a great number of workers undertook the "accounting and control" of Russian industry.

Let us see what were the results of this control.

Two general tendencies have asserted themselves during this period. Workers have either shown a tendency toward "nationalization," meaning by this the taking over [of] the enterprise into

[33] *Novaya zhizn*, No. 95, May 21, 1918.

their own hands; or they have entered into "contract" with the entrepreneur, soliciting [from the government] money and raw materials for the enterprise.

Control, nationalization, and seizure have proven in the majority of cases to be synonymous terms. Ordinarily the Control Commission begins its activity by assuming complete authority in a factory or shop, as if that factory or shop belonged to the workers. It interferes with the acts of the administration, annuls its orders, and upsets the entire economic plan of the enterprise.

[The rest of the article pointed out that, in exercising control, the masses had developed the psychology of small proprietors, which led them either to dominate the plant in which they worked or to try to secure favors for their factories. The article ended with the following observation:]

Some of the leaders are beginning to sober up from the orgy of the November demagogy. Frequently one hears voices urging the exercise of control not only over the bourgeoisie but also over the workers.

C. Effect of Nationalization of Industry on Workers' Control

The large-scale industry of Russia was nationalized on June 28, 1918, and this step was hailed at the time as the fulfillment of Karl Marx's prophecy of the "expropriation of the expropriators." [34] But the nationalization of the means of production created new problems for the Soviet government, for the question now was one not merely of controlling the operations of privately owned industry but of organizing and managing plants and factories that belonged to the state. The Supreme Council of National Economy, which was established for this purpose, was for some time engrossed in problems of internal organiza-

[34] See V. M. Molotov's article in *Novyy put,* No. 3, August 1, 1918, quoted in Bunyan, *Intervention, Civil War and Communism in Russia,* p. 399. The decree on nationalization of industry is on pp. 397–99.

tion.[35] When the blueprint for a centralized administrative apparatus for industry was drafted in the form of *Glavki* and *Tsentry*[36] and Main Administrations, these agencies and their representatives at the plant level could make no headway against the workers' control commissions that continued to run plants and factories in defiance of all established authority. Eventually, however, ways were found to curb the influence of the workers' control committees and to assert the authority of the Supreme Council of National Economy.

Workers' control over the railroads was brought to an end as early as March 26, 1918,[37] and, toward the end of 1918, workers' control councils were abolished in a number of leading branches of industry, such as machine and metal-working plants (October 18, 1918)[38] and leather and shoe factories (November 13, 1918), where control was transferred "to the regulating organs of industry," i.e., the Supreme Council of National Economy.[39] From then on, factory-shop committees and workers' control councils began to fade from the Soviet political and economic scene. By the close of 1918, the decision seems to have been taken to draw a sharp line between management and control. Management was to be within the jurisdiction of the Supreme Council of National Economy and the local Councils of National Economy. Control, on the other hand, was to be placed with the trade unions, and the existing work-

---

[35] *Ibid.*, p. 312.

[36] *Glavki* and *Tsentry* were subdivisions of the Supreme Council of National Economy and were in charge of administering specific branches of industry.

[37] Bunyan and Fisher, *The Bolshevik Revolution*, pp. 655–56. The decree that abolished workers' control over railroads was signed by Lenin, who less than three weeks earlier—on March 8, 1918—presented the Seventh Party Congress a draft of a new Party program that advocated "socialist organization of production . . . managed by workers' organizations (trade unions, factory-shop committees, etc.)." *Ibid.*, p. 549.

[38] Bunyan, *Intervention, Civil War and Communism in Russia*, p. 413.

[39] *Ibid.*, p. 415.

ers' control councils were to be subordinated to these unions. This decision is reflected in the two resolutions cited below; the first resolution was adopted at the Second All-Russian Congress of Councils of National Economy, and the second resolution was adopted by the Second All-Russian Congress of Trade Unions.

ASSERTION OF THE PRINCIPLE OF CONTROL
FROM NATIONAL LEVELS

[Resolution of the Second All-Russian Congress of
Councils of National Economy, December 27, 1918][40]

1. The imperialist policy of the bourgeoisie brought the country to a state of complete economic ruin: factories were closed, transportation was disrupted, and there was mass unemployment. Under these conditions the economic organizations of the working class, the trade unions, were faced with the task of intervening in the production process to prevent complete shut-down of factories and the imminent spread of unemployment.

2. With this in view, workers' control was introduced in the factories and plants before the October Revolution. Such control proved to be a mighty revolutionary weapon in the hands of the workers' organizations in their struggle for economic domination of the proletariat, in their fight against the rapacious bourgeoisie, and in their efforts to prevent the disruption of industry and sabotage by employers.

3. During the above period, the organs of workers' control sought, by intervening in the work of the factory, to take over the management of production. They assumed not only the functions of control but also those of the organization of production—not only the supervision but also the administration of factories.

4. At the present time, under the political and economic dictatorship of the proletariat and as a consequence of the nationalization of industries, new conditions were created for the initiative of the working class in the field of national economic organization. New institutions have been created for the organization and regu-

[40] *Trudy II Vserossiyskogo sezda sovetov narodnogo khozyaystva, Stenograficheskiy otchet*, Moscow, 1919, pp. 198–200.

lation of the national economy in which the representatives of trade unions participate. The working class has now acquired wide opportunities to take part in the administration of industrial enterprises.

5. In these circumstances the task of workers' control must be limited to monitoring factory production and to inspecting the activity of individual plant administrations, as well as [to] the activity of the administration of whole branches of industry. Workers' control is to be carried out in the following order of priority: it should follow rather than precede the work of administration.

6. The attainment of these objectives is of particular concern to the industrial trade unions. They must, therefore, participate most actively in exercising control on a national scale and must see to it that a system of workers' control is established that is integrated by a single plan, regulated by a single center, and capable of performing the task of gradually training the broad masses of the working class for direct participation in the management and organization of production.

7. At the present time control over production is the prerogative not only of the trade unions, but also of the Councils of National Economy and the People's Commissariat of State Control. Councils of National Economy, which are engaged in the organization of production, must not take over the functions of control of production, for this would mean that the management would be doing its own inspecting. The Commissariat of State Control, which so far has had no control over industrial enterprises, has no experience and lacks enough inspectors to exercise control over all industrial enterprises or to rely upon the independent workers' organizations. Therefore, control exercised by the Commissariat of State Control will be essentially bureaucratic and out of touch with workers' organizations.

8. The only adequate solution of the problem of organizing workers' control lies in transferring this control to the trade unions. The present machinery of State Control must not undertake an independent control of production. This control must be gradually replaced by the control machinery of workers' organizations. The control functions of the *Glavki*, *Tsentry*, and departments of the Supreme Council of National Economy must be transferred to the corresponding industrial trade unions.

[The rest of the resolution deals with the organization and functions of local and higher organs of workers' control. The provisions are similar to those of paragraph 6, sections 2–11, of the resolution of the Second All-Russian Congress of Trade Unions, which is quoted in the next document.]

SUBORDINATION OF COUNCILS OF WORKERS' CONTROL
TO TRADE UNIONS

[Resolution of the Second All-Russian Congress of Trade Unions, January 23, 1919][41]

The Second All-Russian Congress of Trade Unions, having heard the report on workers' control, resolves as follows:

1. Workers' control, which has served as a powerful revolutionary weapon in the hands of the workers' organizations in their struggle against the disruption of industry, against the sabotage practiced by employers, and in their fight for the economic supremacy of the proletariat, has led the working class to direct participation in the organization of production.

2. The economic dictatorship of the working class has created new conditions for the initiative of the wide masses of the workers. Through their trade-union associations the workers have been called upon to organize the national economy of the country and to participate in the management of production.

3. At the same time, the supremacy of the working class over the economic life of the country has not as yet reached its culmination point. A latent struggle is still going on within the new economic forms, which makes it necessary for the working masses to control the activities of the institutions charged with the management of production.

4. Under the conditions of transition from the capitalist to the socialist regime, workers' control must be transformed from a revolutionary weapon used in the struggle for the economic dictatorship of the proletariat into a practical institution aiding in the consolidation of this dictatorship in the field of industrial production.

5. Workers' control must be confined to supervising the work

[41] *Vtoroy Vserossiyskiy sezd professionalnykh soyuzov, Stenograficheskiy otchet, Gosizdat,* Moscow, 1921, pp. 112–14.

carried on by various enterprises and inspecting the activities of plant administrations as well as the administrations of entire branches of production. However, workers' control must not precede executive management, but rather follow it.

6. Workers' control is also charged with the task of training the masses of the working class in the skills of production organization and management.

With these objectives in view, the Congress resolves:

1) To confirm the resolution of the First All-Russian Congress of Trade Unions regarding the formation of organs of control, both locally and in the center, under the guidance of the workers' industrial trade unions.

2) Within every nationalized industrial, commercial, or transport enterprise the local control commission assumes the task of supervising the work of the enterprise and the activities of its management. For this purpose it gathers and systematizes all data relating to the operations of the enterprise and places the same at the disposal of the Control Department of its industrial union, before which it may also raise the question of inspecting the work whenever this is deemed necessary.

Note: In exceptional cases the local control commission has the right on its own responsibility to set the time for an inspection of an enterprise provided it immediately notifies the Control Department of the corresponding industrial union of the nature of such an inspection.

3) The local control commission is to be composed of: (*a*) representatives of the corresponding industrial trade unions; (*b*) persons elected by the general meeting of the workers employed in a given factory, their election to be confirmed by a committee of the corresponding industrial trade union. However, members of the local control commission appointed by the industrial union shall retain their office for a considerable length of time while members elected at the general meeting shall be replaced within short intervals of time. This is done with a view to training large masses of workers for the management and organization of industry and thereby ensuring a gradual transition to a system of

universal participation in industrial management by all workers.

4) The local control commission is responsible for its activities both to the general meeting of the workers of the factory and to the Control Department of its industrial trade union. In case of abuse of authority and negligence of duties, the local control commission is subject to severe penalties.

5) Representatives of the local control commission are to participate in the meetings of the factory management in a consultative capacity only. Executive rights in the administration of an enterprise remain with the management, which bears full responsibility for the work of the establishment.

6) Coordination of workers' control within the limits of any given industry is within the jurisdiction of the appropriate industrial trade union. The union creates a Workers' Control Department which is responsible to the administrative body of that union.

7) Control over the activities of the various committees of workers' control is entrusted by the Congress to the All-Russian Central Council of Trade Unions, which is authorized to organize a higher organ of workers' control composed of representatives of the industrial trade unions.

8) With a view to coordinating all functions of control and of eliminating duplication, the organizations of the People's Commissariat of State Control must work in contact with the controlling organizations of the industrial trade unions.

9) The higher organ of workers' control is to work out regulations of control as well as the form of their organization. Pending the publication of such regulations, the workers' control organizations in the nationalized enterprises should be guided by the present decree.

10) The statute relating to workers' control in nationalized enterprises is to be promulgated in the form of a decree of the Soviet of People's Commissars.

11) In non-nationalized enterprises, workers' control is to be carried out in accordance with the decree of November 27, 1917.

The decision to incorporate workers' control commissions into the central machinery of the trade unions was

bitterly opposed by the Mensheviks and the Social Democrats (Internationalists), who were led by the still unre-
pentant Lozovsky.[42] The resolution introduced in behalf
of the Social Democrats (Internationalists) gives a vivid
description of the chaotic conditions that prevailed during
the period of workers' control, when "a number of entangled and cumbersome control organizations [were]
interfering in each other's work." The resolution attributed this chaos to the policy of the Supreme Council of
National Economy and to the failure of the trade unions
to take advantage of the opportunities that had been open
to them during the early period of workers' control. The
confused conditions that the resolution criticized notwithstanding, the Internationalists advocated the extension of
workers' control to cover not only industrial establishments but every other Soviet institution as well. It en-
dorsed the transfer of control to the trade unions on
condition, however, that these unions remain completely independent of the Soviet government and of "the entire
Soviet bureaucratic machinery." The resolution also recommended the re-establishment of the All-Russian Council of
Workers' Control that had been created by the original
statute on workers' control.

THE SOCIAL DEMOCRATS (INTERNATIONALISTS) OPPOSE
SUBORDINATION OF COUNCILS OF WORKERS' CONTROL

[Resolution introduced by the Social Democrats (Internationalists)
at the Second Congress of Trade Unions, January 23, 1919][43]

I. Prior to the November Revolution, workers' control was a
battle cry of the revolutionary proletariat striving to change the

---

[42] In less than a year's time—in December, 1919—Lozovsky and his small
group of followers rejoined the Communist Party (L. Schapiro, *The Origin of
the Communist Autocracy*, London, 1955, p. 231).

[43] *Vtoroy Vserossiyskiy sezd professionalnykh soyuzov*, pp. 114–16.

correlation of forces existing between labor and capital in the production relationships of the capitalist world.

II. The November Revolution, which dealt the first blow to
the economic dictatorship of the bourgeoisie, has made it possible
for the proletariat to apply control over production in practice.

III. In the course of the first few months after the November Revolution, anarcho-syndicalist tendencies became apparent in
the practice of workers' control. At the same time the pulverization and decentralization of control has found its most ardent supporters among the members of the Communist Party, a fact which
found its expression in the decree on workers' control issued
November 27, 1917.

IV. The First Congress of Trade Unions summed up the
period of amateurish work [in this field], formulated a clear
theoretical basis for workers' control, and outlined an accurate and
practical policy for the establishment of the organizations of workers' control.

V. The year that has elapsed since the First Congress of Trade
Unions has supplied us with a good deal of experience which
must be taken into account by the present Congress in determining the future development of workers' control. That experience
has shown us the following:

1) That the local commissions of control were unequal to the
task of solving complicated problems of a national-economic
nature.

2) That the commissions of control considered mainly the interests of their own enterprises, often ignoring the interests
of the country as a whole.

3) That the constitution, the scope, the character, and the
methods of work of control commissions differed not only
in various branches of industries, but also in enterprises
belonging to the same branch of production.

4) That the economic institutions of the Soviet Government
have disorganized the entire work of control in that they
tried to remove workers' control from the jurisdiction of
the trade unions and to concentrate it in the Councils of
National Economy.

5) That the trade unions failed to defend their rights of preserving their own control machinery, which slipped out of
their hands, with the result that workers' control disap-

peared in certain branches of labor under the pretext that it was not needed in Soviet government institutions and in nationalized enterprises.[44]

VI. Simultaneously with the withering away of workers' control by trade unions, a process of formation of technical control departments attached to the *Glavki* and *Tsentry* took place. The organization of these departments proceeded without system or plan and without any contact with the economic organizations of the proletariat, with the result that they turned into purely bureaucratic institutions.

VII. Paralleling the commissions of control attached to the trade unions and the technical control departments of the *Glavki* and *Tsentry*, the institution of State Control has been resurrected, with its old prerevolutionary personnel, its old apparatus, and old methods of work. In this way there came into being, both in the center and locally, a number of entangled and cumbersome control organizations interfering with each other's work. Given the imprecision and lack of organization in the commissions of control attached to the trade unions, the initiative has passed to the technical control departments of the *Glavki* and *Tsentry*, and to the departments of State Control. These institutions are now advocating the complete subordination to them of all organs of workers' control.

VIII. The weakening of workers' control in the provinces also can be explained by the fact that during the past year the entire work of regulation and organization of industry has been concentrated exclusively in the Supreme Council of National Economy— the *Glavki*, *Tsentry*, and the Main Administrations of the nationalized industries.

IX. The trade unions, both in the center and in the provinces, failed to profit sufficiently from past years' experience, positive and negative, of the control commissions and were found wanting in adapting the control machinery which has arisen spontaneously to the changed conditions of industrial organization and goods exchange.

[44] The reference here is to the abolition of workers' control in the nationalized metallurgical plants on October 18, 1918. The resolution that sanctioned the abolition reads, in part, as follows: "The regulative organs of the State will have a decisive influence in the management of the amalgamated shops; the need for the previously existing special organs of workers' control is thereby removed" (Bunyan, *Intervention, Civil War and Communism in Russia*, p. 413).

X. The theory that workers' control has become obsolete is indicative of the effort to create an armored screen protecting Soviet industry and the entire Soviet bureaucratic machinery from the control of the workers' economic organizations. The trade unions cannot and must not allow such independence to be enjoyed by the Soviet regime.

XI. Workers' control should not only be retained, but should be expanded. It should go beyond the limits of control over production and extend its influence over all areas of the social and economic life of the country. The entire Soviet machinery which has been created by the November Revolution, and which to a great extent has become alienated from the workers, must be placed under their control.

XII. In view of the adoption of a policy of economic centralization and of trustification of entire branches of industry, the nature and the methods of work of control commissions must be changed. Workers' control should be exercised from the centers, while locally and in individual enterprises the control commissions should merely assume the functions of inspection and survey and should not interfere in the technical and managerial functions of the enterprise. Only in extreme and exceptional cases can the control commissions veto the orders of the plant management.

XIII. All technical control departments should be separated from the *Glavki* and *Tsentry* and transferred to the corresponding industrial trade unions which, together with the All-Russian Council of Trade Unions, will form an All-Russian Council of Workers' Control having the same number of departments as there are industrial unions.

XIV. In addition to workers' control over production, transportation, and distribution, there should be organized departments of inspection and control operating in state and public institutions, especially in financial and credit institutions which so far have not been served by the above-mentioned control departments.

XV. The work of control and inspection by trade unions over all food organizations is to be organized jointly with the workers' cooperatives.

[The resolution contains another five paragraphs, which pertain to the re-establishment of the All-Russian Council of Workers' Control and its relations with local councils.]

D. TRADE UNION MANAGEMENT PROVES AN ILLUSION

The breakdown of workers' control of industry was followed by a drive to transfer the responsibilities of control over production to the trade unions. This transfer, however, which was formally achieved at the Second All-Russian Congress of Trade Unions, was purchased at the price of harnessing the trade-union movement to the administrative machinery of the Soviet state.

Efforts in this direction were made at the First All-Russian Congress of Trade Unions, which met in January, 1918. There was a good deal of opposition to this move by some Bolsheviks, such as Ryazanov and Lozovsky. The principal opponents of the idea of government control over the trade unions, however, were the Mensheviks, who defended the principle of trade-union independence on the grounds that, under the conditions existing at that time, the relationship of employer and employee still existed in Russia and labor required protection from the state, which was becoming almost the sole employer of labor.[45]

The Bolsheviks at the Congress were opposed to trade-union independence and they succeeded in carrying through a resolution to the effect that "trade unions are organizations called upon to fight side by side with all the other revolutionary organizations of the working class for the dictatorship of the proletariat and the realization of socialism. . . . Trade unions, being class organizations of the proletariat, must take upon themselves the task of organizing production and restoring the shattered productive forces of the country." [46]

The resolution was widely interpreted as signifying a merger between the trade unions and government institu-

[45] *Pervyy Vserossiyskiy sezd professionalnykh soyuzov*, p. 122.
[46] Bunyan and Fisher, *The Bolshevik Revolution*, pp. 639–40.

tions, which was in line with good, orthodox Marxism to the effect that, in a socialist society, government must disappear and be replaced by purely economic organizations. The resolution, however, failed to make clear how the merger between the state and the trade unions was to be brought about—whether the merger meant the unionization of the state or the "governmentalization" of the trade unions. Under the circumstances, the resolution of the First Trade-Union Congress had no practical influence on the course of industrial organization in 1918, although the trade unions were given a large representation (thirty out of sixty-eight members) on the Plenum of the Supreme Council of National Economy (S.C.N.E.).[47] This representation, however, was largely symbolic. The Plenum, a kind of advisory council, was too large to play a role in the formulation of industrial policy. It met infrequently, and its business was transacted by the Presidium of the S.C.N.E., which consisted of nine members. The constitution of the S.C.N.E. does not even mention the possibility of including trade-union representatives in the membership of the Presidium.[48]

When the Second All-Russian Congress of Trade Unions met (January 16–25, 1919), the debate on the relationship between the trade unions and the Soviet government flared up with renewed vigor. As in the case of the First Trade-Union Congress, the clash was between the advocates of trade-union independence, who also demanded political freedom and freedom of speech, and the proponents of governmentalization (*ogosudarstvlenie*) of the trade unions (i.e., those who favored converting the trade unions into instruments of government labor policies). There was, however, a distinct note of caution in

---

[47] *Trudy I Vserossiyskogo sezda sovetov narodnogo khozyaystva*, p. 487.
[48] *Ibid.*, p. 487.

the Bolshevik resolution that was adopted by the Congress. It rejected the notion of fusing the trade unions with governmental institutions on the grounds that the Russian proletariat lacked the education and training required for industrial management and that the immediate task of the trade unions was to make up for this deficiency. The resolution affirmed the principle of trade-union subordination to the Soviet state but it failed to indicate the precise forms of that subordination or the methods of trade-union participation in industrial management.

The four documents quoted below illustrate the confusion and inconsistency that existed in the minds of the Communist leaders over the role of trade unions in industrial management. In his anniversary speech on November 6, 1918, Lenin maintained that workers who were organized in the trade unions were already participating in the administration of industry because some of the trade-union men sat in the *Glavki* and the *Tsentry*. On December 19, V. Milyutin, a member of the Presidium of the Supreme Council of National Economy, testified that by joining the *Glavki* and *Tsentry* the workers drifted away from the working masses who "have taken little part in administration." On January 20, 1919, speaking before the Second All-Russian Congress of Trade Unions, Lenin warned against giving the trade unions too much power because he thought the workers had not cleansed themselves "of the filth of the old world."

Finally, the resolution introduced by the Bolsheviks and adopted by the Congress (on January 21, 1919) included the statement that "the trade unions have made the transition from control over production to the organization of industry by taking an active part in the management of individual enterprises, as well as of the entire economic life of the country." This was a wholly unwarranted statement because, at most, it represented a promise rather than a reality.

LENIN ON THE TRANSITION FROM WORKERS' CONTROL TO WORKERS' MANAGEMENT OF INDUSTRY

[Excerpt from Lenin's speech at the Sixth All-Russian Congress of Soviets, November 6, 1918][49]

Comrades, our slogan at the beginning was workers' control. We were saying that despite all the promises of the Kerensky government, the capitalists continue to sabotage the country's production, destroying it more and more. We can see now that matters were heading for destruction and that workers' control was the first fundamental step which a socialist or workers' government had to take. We did not decree socialism immediately throughout industry because socialism can be established and consolidated only when the working class has learned how to administer, when the authority of the working masses has been firmly established. Without that, socialism is mere wishful thinking. We therefore introduced workers' control, knowing that it was a contradictory step, an incomplete step; but it was necessary that the workers should themselves undertake the great task of industrial construction, in a vast country, without the exploiters and in opposition to the exploiters. Those who, directly or indirectly, took part in this construction and those who experienced the oppression and brutality of the capitalist regime have learned a great deal. We know that little has been accomplished, we know that in a most backward and ruined country, where so many obstacles and stumbling blocks have been placed before the working class, a long time will be needed before that class can learn how to administer industrial production. We believe that what is most important and valuable is that the workers themselves have taken up the administration; that workers' control, which in all the most important branches of industry was bound to remain chaotic, fragmentary, and primitive, has given way to workers' administration of industry on a national scale.

The workers and the trade unions have changed their position.

[49] Lenin, *Sochineniya*, XXIII, 250–51.

Their principal task at the present time is to send their representatives to participate in the *Glavki* and *Tsentry* and to all the new organizations which have taken over a ruined and deliberately sabotaged industry from capitalism. They have taken it over without the assistance of those intellectuals who from the very outset used their knowledge and higher education—the result of mankind's store of knowledge—to frustrate the cause of socialism, rather than assist the people in building a socialized national economy without exploiters. These men used their knowledge for the purpose of putting a spike in the wheel, to hamper the workers who were least prepared for the work of administration. We can say that the main obstacle has now been removed. To do this was extremely difficult, but the sabotage of those gravitating toward the bourgeoisie has been broken. Despite the tremendous handicaps, the workers have succeeded in taking the fundamental step in laying the foundations of socialism. . . .

WORKERS' PARTICIPATION IN INDUSTRIAL MANAGEMENT

[Excerpts from Milyutin's speech at the Second All-Russian Congress of Councils of National Economy, December 19, 1918][50]

The problems of industrial management acquire particular significance in the face of new economic conditions and recent changes. Their solution must be based on past experience and in the light of new conditions. Our new economic program requires further consolidation and concentration, not only in respect to regulation, but also that of administering the production functions of individual branches of industry. We have already created colossal undertakings such as the Sormovo-Kolomna State Trust and the State Copper Trust. Consolidation of enterprises also has taken place in the textile industry. As soon as we have established combines and created production centers, we shall be in a position not only to regulate our economy, but also to manage production and distribution directly.

So far our departments have been more concerned with regulatory work rather than with administration. At the same time

[50] *Trudy II Vserossiyskogo sezda sovetov narodnogo khozyaystva*, pp. 12–13.

bureaucratic procedures have greatly increased. Even the presence of workers' representatives in these departments did not save them [from becoming bureaucratic]. After joining a regulatory agency, many of these workers have drifted away from the masses and turned into mere executors of specific tasks. They did not show any initiative, as they were expected to do. The working masses themselves have taken little part in administration. . . .

We have given up the kind of workers' control in factories and workshops which we advocated earlier, in the first period of our existence. We are beginning to organize workers' control on a higher level so that workers' organizations, and particularly the trade unions, can discharge more adequately their task of workers' control. . . .

LENIN'S NEGATIVE ASSESSMENT OF
THE RUSSIAN PROLETARIAN MASSES

[Excerpt from Lenin's speech at the Second All-Russian Congress of Trade Unions, January 20, 1919][51]

. . . Should the trade unions attempt arbitrarily to take over the functions of state power at this time, we would find ourselves in a mess. We have already suffered sufficiently from this mess.[52] For some time we have been fighting against the survivals of the accursed bourgeois regime, against the selfish, anarchic traits of the small holder, which have become so deeply ingrained in the workers' minds.

The worker has never been separated from the old bourgeois society by a Chinese wall. He has retained much of the traditional psychology of capitalist society. The workers are now building a new society without having transformed themselves into new human beings by cleansing themselves of the filth of the old world. They continue to stand up to their knees in that filth. We can only hope that they will cleanse themselves of this filth, but it would be utterly utopian to think that this can be done all at once; it would be utopian because, from a practical point of view, the

---

[51] *Vtoroy Vserossiyskiy sezd professionalnykh soyuzov*, p. 54.

[52] The reference is clearly to workers' control commissions that were operating industrial establishments in the name of the state.

kingdom of socialism would be removed into heaven. We do not build socialism in this way. We build socialism by standing firm on the soil of capitalist society and at the same time fighting against the weaknesses and the shortcomings which the toilers still have and which are pulling the proletariat down. . . .[53]

SUBORDINATION OF TRADE UNIONS TO THE SOVIET STATE

[Resolution of the Second All-Russian Congress of Trade Unions, January 21, 1919][54]

A year of political and economic dictatorship of the proletariat and the growth of the workers' revolution throughout the world have fully confirmed the correctness of the position taken by the First All-Russian Congress of Trade Unions which unreservedly cast its lot with that of the Workers' and Peasants' Government. [After criticizing the adherents of trade-union independence, the resolution continued:]

In the process of practical collaboration with the Soviet Government directed toward the strengthening and organization of the national economy, the trade unions have made the transition from control over production to the organization [of industry] by taking an active part in the management of individual enterprises, as well as of the entire economic life of the country.

The socialization of all means of production and the organization of society on a new socialist basis demand a persistent and protracted effort involving the reconstruction of the entire state apparatus, the creation of new organs of accounting, control, and regulation of all production and consumption, based on the organizational initiative of the broad toiling masses. This requires that the trade unions take a more active and energetic part in the work of the Soviet government (by direct participation in the work of all state organs, by organizing proletarian control over these bodies, by carrying out specific tasks which the Soviet government is facing) and by assisting in the reorganization of

[53] In *The State and Revolution,* which appeared in the summer of 1917, Lenin raised the same problem: whether the working class was fit to build the new social order. He then observed: "We want the Socialist revolution with human nature as it is . . ." (*Sochineniya,* XXI, 403).

[54] *Vtoroy Vserossiyskiy sezd professionalnykh soyuzov,* pp. 96–97.

various state institutions and [promoting] the gradual fusion of trade-union organizations with the organs of state authority.

However, it would be a mistake at the present stage of development of the trade-union movement, when its organizational structure has not yet taken sufficiently definite form, to convert the trade unions into organs of government immediately by fusing the two, or to have the unions take over willfully the functions of state organs.

The process of complete fusion between trade unions and the organs of government (the process of the so-called governmentalization) must come about as the inevitable result of their close collaboration and after the trade unions have trained the masses of workers in skills needed for the management of the state apparatus and of all regulatory economic organs. This, in turn, places before the trade unions the task of uniting the unorganized proletarian and semi-proletarian masses into strong industrial trade unions and of drawing them, under the control of proletarian unions, into the work of socialist construction and into the general work of solidifying their organizations by means of centralization, orderly development of the unions, and strengthening of trade-union discipline.

Directly participating in all branches of Soviet activity and cooperating in the establishment of governmental institutions, the trade unions must, by enlisting both their own organizations and the broad masses of the workers, train and prepare them for the management not only of production but also of the entire state machinery.

PARTY DOMINATION OF THE TRADE UNIONS

The conspicuous caution of the Bolshevik-sponsored resolution of the Second All-Russian Congress of Trade Unions, which pertained to the fusion of trade unions and Soviet economic institutions, was to a large extent influenced by the hostility of a number of influential trade unions toward the Bolsheviks. In some of the trade unions the Bolsheviks had a majority, in others they did not, and they used high-handed methods to obtain majorities. The

Petrograd Union of Printers, for example, was forcibly dispersed in 1918, and this also happened to the Union of Bank Employees.[55] Early in 1919, just before the meetings of the Second All-Russian Congress of Trade Unions, the Moscow Union of Employees also was dissolved, for reasons that have not been made public.[56] The Bolsheviks, therefore, were not sure of the attitude of the rank and file of the trade-union membership, even though they had majorities at the trade-union congresses.

An illustration of the methods used by the Bolsheviks in suppressing their opponents in the trade-union movement is the account of what happened to the Moscow Union of State Employees, which is given below. But the practice of Communist interference in the internal affairs of the trade unions was not confined to Moscow. Speaking before the Second All-Russian Congress of Trade Unions on January 20, 1919, Lozovsky read a number of telegrams from the provinces that described instances of interference in the work of the trade unions by local Communist officials. "The election of factory-shop committees," Lozovsky charged, "is forbidden. The same is true of trade-union boards of directors. Congresses of trade-union organizations, if they do not please the provincial blockheads, also are forbidden."[57]

The Soviet leaders, by carefully packing the trade unions, hoped to eliminate all critics of Communist labor policies, but effective control over the trade unions was never fully established during the period under consideration. Controversies over the proper function of the trade unions flared up at frequent intervals, and in the end they

[55] According to a speech by Kefali at the Second All-Russian Congress of Trade Unions (*Vtoroy Vserossiiskiy sezd professionalnykh soyuzov*, p. 28).
[56] *Ibid.*, p. 28.
[57] N-skiy, *Vtoroy Vserossiyskiy sezd professionalnykh soyuzov*, Moscow, 1919, p. 38.

precipitated a crisis in Soviet trade-union policy that nearly split the Party.

DISPERSAL OF THE UNION OF STATE EMPLOYEES

[From the Proceedings of the Conference of State Employees, February 25, 1919][58]

On February 25 [1919], at the initiative of the Central Council of Employees of the All-Russian Council of Trade Unions and the Moscow Council of Trade Unions, a conference of representatives of a number of trade unions of [state] employees was called for the purpose of establishing a consolidated union of all office employees and the election of a single administrative body.

The election campaign was marked by a good deal of interest and animation, and in the course of twelve days about 1,500 delegates were elected.

Two groups struggled for influence: the Communists and the champions of the independence of the trade-union movement. The Communists proposed that the conference begin with a debate on the aims of the trade-union movement. Speakers representing various points of view on the nature of trade unions presented their declarations. The Communists then moved that the declarations be put to vote. By an overwhelming majority the declaration of the independents was approved. This created a great commotion. The government party [Communists], numbering 200–250, left the conference hall singing the "International."

The conference continued in session and proceeded with the election of a board of directors, the great majority of whom were adherents of the [principle of] independence of trade unions from the government. The Central Council of Trade Unions registered the newly formed union of employees under the name "The Moscow Trade Union of Employees," and the new board of directors began functioning. But the board of directors was not allowed to operate. The Moscow Council of Trade Unions issued a statement to the effect that it did not recognize the new organization and that instead it recognized another union named "The Union of Workers of Soviet, Social, and Trade Organizations."

[58] *Delo naroda*, No. 2, March 21, 1919, p. 2.

SUDDEN CHANGE IN THE BOLSHEVIKS' ATTITUDE TOWARD
WORKERS' MANAGEMENT OF INDUSTRY

Two months after the meeting of the Second All-Russian Congress of Trade Unions, during which Lenin delivered a scorching attack on the proletarian masses—which were represented as standing up to their knees in the alleged filth of bourgeois society—the Eighth Party Congress assembled to draft a new Party program.

In his speech to the Congress, delivered on March 18, 1919, Lenin reverted once more to his old refrain about the inherent merits of the "independent initiative of the proletarian masses." He declared that, by virtue of the experience gained from workers' control, the proletariat was ready to take over the management of industrial production. He also greatly changed the attitude of reserve and suspicion toward the trade unions that had been so conspicuous in his speech at the Second All-Russian Congress of Trade Unions.

The resolution adopted by the Eighth Party Congress characterized the trade unions as "the organizational apparatus" that was to "achieve a de facto concentration . . . of the entire administration of the whole national economy"—an extraordinary assignment if we consider that the Supreme Council of National Economy was at that time making every effort to concentrate the administration of industry in its own hands. The resolution, however, served the purpose of placating the discontented elements in the trade-union movement with promises that were contrary to the emerging policies of the Bolshevik regime. These policies aimed at converting the trade unions into auxiliary organs of the state, with the primary function of keeping Russian workers and employees in well-disciplined mass organizations, while all initiative was being concentrated at the top.

LENIN ON WORKERS' MANAGEMENT OF INDUSTRY

[Excerpt from Lenin's speech at the Eighth Party Congress,
March 18, 1919][59]

. . . Let us take the question which has occupied us most of all,
namely, the transition from workers' control of industry to workers' management of industry. Hundreds of decrees and thousands
of resolutions of the Soviet of People's Commissars and practical
measures taken by local organs of the Soviet power have all contributed to our political experience in this field. All that, in fact,
remained for the Central Committee to do was to summarize. It
could hardly lead, in the true sense of the word, in such a matter.
One has only to recall how helpless, impulsive, and fortuitous were
our first decrees and resolutions on workers' control of industry.
It seemed to us to be the most easy thing. In actual practice,
however, workers' control brought about the realization that there
was a need for building but we utterly failed to answer the question of how to build. Every nationalized factory, every branch of
nationalized industry, transport, and particularly railway transport—that most typical expression of the capitalist system that is
constructed in the most centralized way, on the basis of large-
scale mechanization, and most essential to the state—all this em-
bodied the concentrated experience of capitalism and occasioned
us immeasurable difficulties.

Even now we are still far from having conquered these difficulties. We at first regarded these difficulties in an entirely abstract way, like revolutionaries who preached but really did not
know how to set about doing things. Of course, there was a large
number of people who accused us—and the Socialists and Social-
Democrats are accusing us to this day—of having undertaken this
task without knowing how to finish it. But these are ridiculous
accusations by lifeless people. Who has ever set about making a
great revolution knowing beforehand how it is to be completed?
Where could this knowledge be obtained? It could not be derived
from books. There are no such books. No, our decision could be
born only from the experience of the masses. And I count it to
our credit that amidst incredible difficulties we took upon ourselves the solution of a problem which until then was only half

[59] *VIII sezd Rossiyskoy kommunisticheskoy partii, Stenograficheskiy otchet,*
Moscow, 1919, pp. 16–18.

known to us, that we attracted the proletarian masses to work independently, that we achieved the nationalization of industrial enterprises, and so forth. We recall that at Smolny we passed as many as ten or twelve decrees at one session. That was a manifestation of our determination and our desire to arouse the spirit of experiment and independent initiative of the proletarian masses. We now have the experience. We now have passed, or are about to pass, from workers' control to workers' management of industry. In place of our former absolute helplessness, we now have a number of lessons from experience and, as far as it was possible, we have summarized that experience in our program. We shall have occasion to deal with this in greater detail in connection with the problem of organization. We would have been unable to fulfill this task had we not had the assistance and collaboration of the comrades from the trade unions.

[Lenin then launched an attack on Western trade unions, alleging that they were under the control of "yellow" representatives of the old socialism.]

Let us take the question of experts, a question which faces us at every turn, which arises in connection with every appointment, and which the leaders of our industry and the Central Committee of the Party are continually encountering. [We had disagreements on this question, but basically there can be no doubt as to its proper solution.] The idea that we can build communism by the hands of pure Communists, without the assistance of bourgeois experts, is a childish idea. We have been steeled in the struggle, we have the forces and we are united, and we must carry on our work of organization, making use of the knowledge and experience of the experts. This is an indispensable condition, without which socialism cannot be built. Socialism cannot be built unless advantage is taken of the heritage of capitalist culture. There is nothing communism can be built from except what has been left us by capitalism.

We must now build practically, and we must create the communist society with the hands of our enemies. This appears to be a contradiction, perhaps even an insoluble contradiction. But, as a matter of fact, the problem of building communism can be solved only in this way, and when we examine our experience, our daily confrontations with this question, when we examine the practical work of the Central Committee, it seems to me that in the main our party has solved the problem. It entailed tremendous difficulties, but that is the only way it could have been solved. The bourgeois experts must be so emcompassed by our organizational work that they will be compelled to fall in line with the proletariat, no matter how much they resist and fight at every step. We must put them to work as a technical and cultural force in order to preserve them and in order to transform an uncultured and barbarian capitalist country into a cultured communist country. And it seems to me that during the past year we have learnt how to build, that we have entered the right path and shall not now be diverted from that path. . . .

THE EIGHTH PARTY CONGRESS ON
TRADE—UNION MANAGEMENT OF INDUSTRY

[Excerpts from the Resolution of March 23, 1919][60]

5. The organizational apparatus of the socialized industry must be based, first and foremost, on a trade-union foundation. The trade unions must gradually free themselves of their narrow guild outlook and transform themselves into large-scale production associations embracing [at first] the majority and, in the course of time, every worker of a given branch of production.

Since, according to the laws of the Soviet Republic and existing practice, they are already participating in all local and central organs of industrial administration, the trade unions must achieve a de facto concentration in their own hands of the entire administration of the whole national economy considered as a single economic unit. By ensuring the closest possible tie between the central state apparatus, the national economy, and the large masses of the toilers, the trade unions will facilitate the widest possible participation of the toiling masses in the management of the economy. At the same time, the participation of the trade unions in the

---

[60] *VIII sezd Rossiyskoy kommunisticheskoy partii,* pp. 348–49. The quotations are from the Economic Section of the New Program of the Russian Communist Party (Bolshevik), adopted at the Eighth Party Congress, March 23, 1919. The first four paragraphs of this section relate to general economic problems; paragraphs 7 to 17 deal with the role of experts in industry and with specific sectors of the economy, such as agriculture, industry, transport, etc.

management of the economy will serve as an instrument in the fight against the bureaucratization of the Soviet economic apparatus and will make possible a genuine people's control over the results of production.

6. The planned development of the national economy, the maximum utilization of the whole available labor force, its precise distribution and redistribution, both among the various territorial regions and the various branches of industry, must form the immediate task of the economic policy of the Soviet government—a task which can be realized only in close cooperation with the trade unions. The mass mobilization of the able-bodied population by the Soviet government, with the participation of the trade unions, for the carrying out of certain public works must be applied in a much wider and more systematic way than has been done hitherto.

The dramatic reversal of the Bolshevik attitude toward the trade unions was due not so much to a change of Communist policy toward labor as to developments that were taking place outside the field of labor relations.

In the late winter and early spring of 1919, the civil war had increased greatly in intensity because of the initially successful drive of Kolchak's armies on the eastern front of the Russian civil war. These military difficulties dominated every other consideration in the domain of Bolshevik political and economic policy. Even in the field of labor relations, the crucial matter was to mobilize as many workers as possible for service in the Red Army, and the trade unions could make a major contribution to the mobilization of April 10, 1919,[61] and to encouraging voluntary Red Army enlistments by the rank and file of the trade-union

---

[61] According to Zinoviev, the trade unions helped mobilize their members for military service (*Izvestiya Tsentralnogo komiteta Rossiyskoy kommunisticheskoy partii*, No. 13, March 2, 1920, p. 2). See also Trotsky's speech at the Third Trade-Union Congress, *Tretiy Vserossiyskiy sezd professionalnykh soyuzov*, p. 87, and *Izvestiya glavnogo komiteta po vseobshchey trudovoy povinnosti* (No. 6, 1920, p. 10).

membership.[62] Thus the resolution of the Eighth Party Congress was a device for winning over the trade unions with the promise of transferring the management of industry to them. Actually, however, the Soviet government continued its drive for a centralized system of industrial management, and the Supreme Council of National Economy played a leading role in the drive. Control was sought not only over management but over production as well.[63]

Eventually, the functions of the trade unions were narrowed down to the determination of wage rates and the maintenance of discipline. For disciplinary matters, special tribunals were created on November 14, 1919, that gave the trade unions full authority over industrial workers.[64] By this time the drift toward labor compulsion had made deep inroads in the life of Russia's laboring masses.

[62] Zinoviev, "Partiya i professionalnye soyuzy," in *Izvestiya tsentralnogo komiteta Rossiyskoy kommunisticheskoy partii*, No. 13, March 2, 1920.

[63] Almost every issue of *Narodnoe khozyaystvo*, the official organ of the S.C.N.E., carried a review of the activities of this agency in 1919 and 1920. One section of this review, entitled "Reviziya, kontrol i obsledovanie" ("Inspection, Control and Investigation"), described the activities of the control commissions of the Supreme Council of National Economy; no reference was made to trade unions. In this way did the managers perform their own inspection. See paragraph 7 of the Resolution of the Second All-Russian Congress of Councils of National Economy, December 27, 1918 (above).

[64] See pp. 87–88 (below).

CHAPTER II

THE DRIFT TOWARD LABOR COMPULSION

In theory, forced labor originally was established on a class basis as a means for suppressing the resistance of the expropriated classes and for forcing their co-operation with the proletarian state. Forced labor also was looked upon, by the Bolsheviks, as an instrument for the degradation and penalization of the former bourgeoisie by the triumphant working class.

The ideas that underlay this initial use of forced labor were formulated by Lenin in a pamphlet entitled *Will the Bolsheviks Retain State Power?* which was written only about three weeks before the Bolshevik coup d'état of November 7, 1917. In this pamphlet Lenin observed that the capitalist state had created "universal compulsory labor which is nothing but military penal servitude for the workers. The proletariat takes its weapons from capitalism. . . . In the hands of the proletarian state . . . universal compulsory labor is a powerful weapon which, when applied by the workers to the capitalists and *the rich in general*, will supply an unprecedented force to bring the state machinery into motion, to overcome the resistance of the capitalists and to subordinate them to the proletarian state."[1] He made it clear that, when the Bolsheviks become the rulers of Russia, "this would be the basic, primary, and principal rule which the Soviets . . . will put into effect."[2]

When the Bolsheviks came into power, on November 7,

[1] Lenin, *Sochineniya*, XXI, 262.
[2] *Ibid.*, p. 263.

1917, they proceeded almost immediately to translate Lenin's ideas for the treatment of the propertied classes into official policy. A number of steps were taken to deprive the well-to-do groups of the population of their possessions and means of livelihood. These steps were followed by measures that were designed to subject the former propertied classes, including large sections of the professional classes, to compulsory labor. But Lenin's assumption that forced labor would have to be applied only to the capitalist and the rich soon had to be abandoned. In less than a year's time, Soviet labor legislation was gradually extending the methods of compulsion and pressure to the working class. At first, Soviet citizens were deprived of the right to terminate their employment on their own volition, and this was followed by the establishment of forced-labor and concentration camps for recalcitrant workers. Thus there was a drift toward a comprehensive system of labor compulsion under which each citizen became a servant of the state and performed such work as he was ordered to do by his communist rulers.

A. Compulsory Labor Imposed on the Bourgeoisie

During the early months of their rule the Bolsheviks were preoccupied with the extension and consolidation of their authority, with gaining control of the various departments of the government, and particularly with the "expropriation of the expropriators" (i.e., depriving the well-to-do citizens of their possessions and sources of income).[3] Because of these preoccupations, no systematic effort was made at first to apply a regime of forced labor

[3] Materials relating to this phase of Bolshevik activities are included in Bunyan and Fisher, *The Bolshevik Revolution*, pp. 315–17, 324–26, 542–43, 601–3, 610–14; and Bunyan, *Intervention, Civil War and Communism in Russia*, pp. 397–401, 423–29, 435–39, 441–42, 450–52.

to the groups of the population that were classified as the bourgeoisie.

A more aggressive policy toward the bourgeoisie was adopted shortly after the Soviet government decided, in the spring of 1918, to establish a regular army. This army was to be built on a class principle. As Trotsky expressed it: "Our army is a class army and will include primarily workers and poorer peasants. . . . We do not arm the bourgeoisie, for we want to wipe them off the face of the earth."[4] Because the bourgeoisie could not be eliminated overnight, Trotsky proposed to use the formerly propertied classes for menial work as rear-service battalions. A memorandum Trotsky presented to the Soviet of People's Commissars (on June 26) advocated the imposition of a regime of compulsion on the "parasitic elements" of the population, and he also pleaded for measures that would force all of the most disagreeable and dirty work upon the bourgeoisie. Former army officers who did not enlist in the Red Army, and thus were classed with the bourgeoisie, were to be sent into forced-labor camps, and, in cases of refusal, were to be placed in concentration camps.

The "class principle" of food rationing, which was first introduced in Moscow and Petrograd in September, 1918, and which then spread throughout the country, was combined with the regime of compulsory labor that was imposed on the bourgeoisie. By an order of the People's Commissariat of Food (October 19, 1918), this type of rationing became compulsory in all areas under Soviet control. There were variations in the application of the class principle of food distribution, but generally there were three categories of rations. The highest ration (*payok*) went to workers who were engaged in physical

[4] Excerpt from Trotsky's speech at the Fourth Trade-Union Conference, quoted in Bunyan, *Intervention, Civil War, and Communism in Russia*, p. 268.

labor;[5] next in order came Soviet officials; and the lowest ration went to those who were classified as the bourgeoisie (children under sixteen and invalids were in the first category).[6]

According to one source, those who were classified as bourgeoisie were allowed one-eighth of a (Russian) pound of bread every other day; and Zinoviev, the Chairman of the Petrograd Commune, made it known that the reason for allowing the meager ration for members of the formerly well-to-do groups was "to ensure that the bourgeoisie do not forget the smell of bread."[7]

TROTSKY'S PROPOSALS FOR HANDLING THE BOURGEOISIE

[Excerpt from a memorandum for the *Sovnarkom*, June 26, 1918][8]

. . . I propose that the Soviet of People's Commissars approve the following measures:

1. Simultaneously with the mobilization of the workers and peasants, the city and village bourgeoisie of the same age groups shall be mobilized and organized into rear-service battalions to do menial work (cleaning barracks, camps, streets, digging trenches, etc.). The best elements of the bourgeoisie who show in practice loyalty to the working class would be transferred to the regular formations.

3. Every bourgeois family, any member of which fails to enter the rear-service battalions, shall be fined from 3,000 to 100,000 rubles, and the head of the family shall be kept under arrest until the fine is paid. A law to this effect should be prepared by the Commissariats of Justice and Internal Affairs.

4. Pending the introduction of compulsory labor, it is neces-

[5] Those who were engaged in heavy physical labor were entitled to a supplementary ration (L. Kritsman, *Geroicheskiy period velikoy Russkoy revolyutsii*, Moscow, 1924, p. 110).

[6] Lenin, *Sochineniya*, XXIII, 543.

[7] A. Izgoev, "Pyat let v sovetskoy Rossii," in *Arkhiv Russkoy revolyutsii* (I. V. Hessen, ed.), Berlin, 1921–34, X, 28.

[8] L. Trotsky, *Sochineniya*, XVII Part 1, 290–91.

sary to take, as a preliminary measure, an accurate census of all parasitical elements; i.e., all those who do not discharge any socially necessary function in the Soviet Republic. These elements, perverted by their past mode of life, are the chief source of discontent, sabotage, perversion, disloyalty, and treachery. The sacred task of defending the Soviet Republic, surrounded by enemies, demands from the toilers strict surveillance over the parasitical classes which should be placed in such conditions of life (food, living quarters, etc.) as would make them actually feel the iron clutches of the workers' and peasants' dictatorship. . . .

[Excerpt from Trotsky's speech of June 29, 1918][9]

. . . For centuries the workers and peasants have been cleaning the dirt of the ruling classes, but now let [the former ruling classes] clean [the dirt] which we are leaving behind, until such time as they join the working class in the pursuit of a common goal. We must place them in such conditions that they will lose the desire to remain bourgeois. Let us take an accounting of the bourgeoisie. We appeal to you, comrades, to do this. Let every bourgeois house be marked as one in which so many families live who lead a parasitic mode of life and we shall post yellow tickets on these houses.

October 5, 1918, brought the first decree that authorized labor conscription of members of the bourgeoisie, and thus legalized a practice that had been going on for several months. According to this decree, members of formerly well-to-do classes were to be registered and issued labor books, and failure to register and obtain a labor book carried heavy penalties. In this way the groups that were classified as bourgeois were made available for any assignment the Bolshevik authorities chose to give them. The decree affected such groups as former directors of stock companies, merchants, brokers, middlemen, persons belonging to the liberal professions (if they did not perform

[9] *Ibid.*, p. 293.

"socially useful" functions), former army officers, and attorneys.[10]

A vivid description of the methods used in the call-up of these groups for compulsory labor is given in the following two documents. The first is from a memoir of a former official of the Petrograd office of the Commissariat of War; the second is an excerpt from Boris Pasternak's celebrated novel, *Doktor Zhivago*.[11] As the two documents show, many of those who were conscripted for forced labor pursued humble walks of life and had no taint of bourgeois background.[12]

DRAFTING THE BOURGEOISIE FOR FORCED LABOR

[Account of a former official of the Petrograd
Military Commissariat][13]

About the middle of October, 1918, the commander of the Sixth Army on the northern front sent in a request to the Petrograd military commissariat for 800 workers for road construction and trench digging. The commissariat decided to employ on this work persons liable to compulsory labor. [The job of mobilizing the needed labor was placed in the charge of the Chief of the Compulsory Labor Section, Comrade Ryazhkin.]

As it turned out later, the "mobilization" was carried out as follows. A number of citizens, mainly from the former merchant class, were invited to appear at Soviet headquarters, allegedly for the purpose of registration for possible labor duty at some future

[10] *S.U.R.*, 1917–18, No. 73, Art. 792. This decree is quoted in Bunyan, *Intervention, Civil War and Communism in Russia*, p. 409.

[11] This novel contains many verbal "candid camera shots" that were taken by a keen observer of the Russian revolutionary scene. Some of the scenes in this novel are descriptions of happenings that can be verified by contemporary documents.

[12] A similar impression is left in the memoirs of A. Peshekhonov, Minister of Agriculture in the Provisional government. Excerpts from his memoirs are quoted in Bunyan, *Intervention, Civil War and Communism in Russia*, pp. 233–35.

[13] M. Smilg-Benario, "Na sovetskoy sluzhbe," in *Arkhiv Russkoy Revolyutsii*, III, 155–56.

date. When these citizens appeared for registration, they were placed under arrest and sent to the Semenovsky barracks[14] to await their dispatch [to the front]. Notwithstanding this "clever" method of mobilization, the Soviet authorities failed to obtain the necessary 800 men. Thereupon Ryazhkin and other members of the local Soviet, making use of the previously issued instructions by Zinoviev, adopted the following "remarkable" procedure. Three days before the dispatch of the men to the northern front, Nevsky Prospekt[15] was surrounded. All persons who happened to be there, and who had no party cards or certificate from some government institution, were arrested and marched to the Semenovsky baracks. Among those thus "mobilized" were also a number of women; these were released on the following day. On the third day all the men were sent to Vologda, where they were to be taken over by a representative of the Sixth Army.

Not one of the thus strangely mobilized men was allowed to settle his family affairs, to say goodbye to his relatives, or to obtain suitable clothing and footwear. . . .

Some time later,[16] the commander of the Sixth Army, Gittis, demanded an additional 500 men, also for work at the northern front. The military commissariat again turned the request over to the Department of Compulsory Labor of the First City Precinct. Comrade Ryazhkin promised to produce the required number of men within seven days. As we heard later, the second group was mobilized by the same "simple" manner as the first. . . .

In the evening,[17] on the day of their departure from Petrograd, the men were lined up in the yard of the Semenovsky barracks and surrounded by a strong guard. Before starting the march to the Nikolaevsky Station, the commander of the guard announced in a loud voice: "Anyone attempting to leave the line will be shot immediately." When the group started, [the men saw that] their wives and children were awaiting them in the street. Heart-rending cries were heard, and the women tried to rush to their husbands, but were repulsed by the soldiers. One young student noticed his father among the marching men. Kneeling down be-

[14] The Semenovsky barracks had been the quarters of a famous Tsarist regiment.

[15] Nevsky Prospekt was the principal street in Petrograd (Leningrad).

[16] Smilg-Benario, "Na sovetskoy sluzhbe," III, 159.

[17] *Ibid.*, p. 163.

fore the commander of the guard, with tears in his eyes he begged permission to take his father's place. The commander, apparently moved by the self-sacrifice of the young man, granted his request and the son departed in place of his father. Like a herd of cattle the men were marched to the Nikolaevsky Station, still unaware of their destination or of the nature of the work they were to do. . . .

. . . The journey lasted two days [18] and one night. When they arrived in Vologda, the following conversation took place between the commander of the guard and the local station-master:

"What is this crowd you have brought here?"

"These are the Petrograd bourgeoisie who have come to work at the front."

"What do we want them for? We have nothing to eat ourselves."

The commander of the guard smiled bashfully.

"It looks funny to you," shouted the station-master, "but we have to find quarters for this rabble. It would have been much better to have them finished off in Petrograd. You only burden us with extra work."

The men were then lined up and marched through the streets of Vologda. Passers-by stopped to look at them; some with mockery, others with pity. Street urchins ran after the prisoners shouting: "Here come the Petrograd bourgeoisie, here come the White Guards."

The prisoners soon reached their destination, the notorious Vologda prison. Cold, damp cells were the first shelter given these physically and mentally broken people. They were treated like dangerous criminals. Under such circumstances there is little wonder that some of them, already during the first night, became insane and a few committed suicide.

Their stay in the Vologda prison was not long. A few days later the exiled men were sent to various sectors of the front where, under the fire of English guns, they were put to digging trenches. They were divided into groups of ten, with each member responsible for the acts of all others. They were told by their superiors that in case one of them escaped, the other nine would be shot.

[18] *Ibid.*, pp. 164–65.

Some were assigned to digging trenches, others to work on the railway line and building barracks for soldiers. Some were ordered by Red Army men to remove, under fire of the English, machine guns abandoned in battle. . . .

The work and the perils connected with it were not the worst evil suffered by the exiles; hunger and cold were far worse. Lightly clad, wearing thin-soled shoes, these men were forced to work out of doors in bitter frost. No suitable clothing from the military stores was provided for them, and all their pleadings were left unanswered. When their friends and relatives sent or brought them warm clothes, the military authorities refused to deliver them to the front line [where they were working], saying that the mail service at the front was not for the bourgeoisie. . . . Nor were they able to buy additional food from the peasants, who were being intimidated against selling anything to the *burzhui*. Yet, in the majority of cases, these men did not belong to the bourgeoisie. . . .

TYPES OF THE "BOURGEOISIE" CONSCRIPTED
FOR FORCED LABOR

[Excerpts from Pasternak's *Doktor Zhivago*][19]

. . . There were several labor conscripts in freight car fourteen. They were guarded by Private Voronyuk. Three of the men stood out from the rest. They were Prokhor Kharitonovich Pritulev, who had been cashier in the government liquor store in Petrograd—the caster,[20] as he was called in the car; Vasya Brykin, a sixteen-year-old apprentice in an ironware store; and Kostoed-Amursky, a gray-haired revolutionary, active in the cooperative movement, who had been in all the forced-labor camps of the old regime and was now discovering those of the new.

The conscripts, who had all been strangers when they were rounded up in various places, were gradually getting to know each other. It turned out that Pritulev, the cashier, and Vasya, the apprentice, came from the same part of the country, Viatka

---

[19] The translation was made from the original Russian of Pasternak's novel, which was published by the University of Michigan Press, Ann Arbor, 1959 (pp. 224–27).

[20] A mispronunciation of the Russian word *kassir*, which means "cashier."

Guberniya, and also that the train would be going through their native villages.

Pritulev came from Malmyzh. He was a stocky man with cropped hair, pockmarked and hideous. His gray jacket, black with sweat under the arms, fitted him snugly like a fleshy woman's bodice. He would sit for hours as silent as a statue, lost in thought, scratching the warts on his freckled hands until they bled and suppurated.

One day last autumn, while going down the Nevsky, he walked into a militia roundup at the corner of Liteyny Street. He was asked to show his papers and was found to hold a ration card of the fourth category, the kind issued to non-workers, on which no food was ever issued. On the basis of this evidence, he was detained, with many others who were arrested for the same reason, and taken under escort to barracks. The group assembled in this way was to be sent to Vologda like the one preceding it, which was dispatched to dig trenches on the Archangel front. However, it was diverted on its way and sent instead to the Eastern Front via Moscow.

Pritulev had a wife in Luga, where he had worked before the war. She heard indirectly of his misfortune and rushed off to Vologda to look for him and obtain his release from the labor army. But the unit had not gone there, her labors had been in vain, and she lost track of him.

In Petrograd, Pritulev lived with a certain Pelagia Nilovna Tyagunova. At the time he was arrested at the Nevsky he had just said goodbye to her, preparing to go in a different direction to keep an appointment, and looking down Liteyny Street he could still see her back disappearing among the crowd.

She was a plump woman with a stately carriage, beautiful hands, and a thick braid which she tossed from time to time, with deep sighs, over her shoulder. She was now with the convoy, having volunteered to accompany Pritulev. It was difficult to understand what it was that attracted women to such an ugly man, but certainly they clung to him. . . .

Vasya's story was quite different. His father had been killed in the war and his mother had sent him to Petrograd to be apprenticed to his uncle.

The uncle kept an ironware shop in Apraksin Yard. One day last winter the uncle had been summoned by the local Soviet to answer a few questions. He mistook the door and walked into the office of the commission in charge of compulsory labor for the bourgeoisie. The room was full of people. When a sufficient number of those called up had assembled, Red Army soldiers arrived, surrounded the men, and took them to the Semenovsky barracks for the night, and escorted them to the Vologda train in the morning.

The news of so many arrests spread throughout the city and the prisoners' families came to say goodbye to them at the station. Among them were Vasya and his aunt. His uncle begged the guard to let him out for a minute to see his wife. The guard was the same Voronyuk who was accompanying the group in car fourteen. Voronyuk refused without a guarantee that he would return. The uncle and aunt offered Vasya as a hostage. Voronyuk agreed. Vasya was brought in and his uncle was let out. This was the last he ever saw of his aunt or uncle.

When the fraud was discovered, Vasya, who had suspected nothing, burst into tears. He threw himself at Voronyuk's feet, kissed his hands, and begged him to let him go, but to no avail. The guard was inexorable, not because he was cruel but because discipline was very strict in those troubled times. The guard answered for the number of his charges with his life, and the numbers were checked by roll call. That was how Vasya came to be in the forced-labor corps.

The cooperative society worker, Kostoed-Amursky, who had enjoyed the respect of his jailors under both Tsarism and the present government and who was always on good terms with them, repeatedly spoke to the head of the convoy about Vasya's predicament. The officer admitted that it was a terrible misunderstanding, but said there were formal difficulties in the way of examining the case until they arrived. He promised to do his best at that moment.

Another decree on compulsory labor, although expressed in rather general terms and aiming only in part at the formerly well-to-do classes, was published toward the end of October, 1918. This decree, however, made no provision for its enforcement and was merely a declaration of the Bolshevik principle of the universal liability to labor.

It was made Part I of the Soviet Labor Code of 1918. Special regulations for the application of compulsory labor to the bourgeoisie were issued by the People's Commissariat of Labor on December 11, 1918.

GENERAL PRINCIPLES OF COMPULSORY LABOR

[Decree of the Central Executive Committee, October 31, 1918][21]

1. All citizens of the R.S.F.S.R., with the exception of those specified in Articles 2 and 3, are subject to compulsory labor.

2. The following are exempt from compulsory labor: (*a*) persons under 16 years of age; (*b*) persons over 50 years of age; (*c*) persons who are incapacitated as a result of injury or illness.

3. The following are temporarily exempt from compulsory labor: (*a*) persons who as a result of illness or injury are temporarily incapacitated for a period necessary to their recovery; (*b*) pregnant women, for a period of eight weeks before and eight weeks after confinement.

4. Students in all institutions of learning will perform compulsory labor at school.

5. Permanent or temporary incapacity must be established by a medical examination performed by the Bureau of Medical Examiners.

Note 1: Rules for establishing incapacity to work are herewith appended [at the end of the Labor Code].

Note 2: Persons subject to compulsory labor and not engaged in socially useful work may be summoned by local Soviets of Deputies for public work on conditions determined by the Sections of Labor [22]—in agreement with local trade-union councils.

6. Work takes the form of: (*a*) organized gangs; (*b*) personal services; (*c*) performance of special work.

7. Compensation of labor in Soviet state institutions is to be based on wage rates approved by the central Soviet government as represented by the People's Commissariat of Labor.

8. Compensation of labor in all Soviet enterprises and in

---

[21] *S.U.R.*, 1918, Nos. 87–88, Art. 905. This decree appeared as Part I of the Soviet Code of Labor Law.

[22] Departments of the People's Commissariat of Labor.

nationalized, social and private establishments is to be based on wage rates established by trade unions in concurrence with the directors or owners of the establishments and with the approval of the People's Commissariat of Labor.

Note: In case no agreement can be reached with the directors and owners of establishments, wage rates are to be set by the trade unions, subject to the approval of the People's Commissariat of Labor.

9. Personal services and special work are compensated on the basis of wage rates established by the trade unions, subject to the approval of the People's Commissariat of Labor.

YA. SVERDLOV
*Chairman of the Central
Executive Committee*

REGULATIONS FOR THE APPLICATION OF COMPULSORY LABOR TO THE BOURGEOISIE

[Decree of the People's Commissariat of Labor,
December 11, 1918][23]

Pending the publication of a general decree establishing norms of compulsory labor on a national scale, the People's Commissariat of Labor proposes to all local Executive Committees, in applying the decree of October 5, 1918 (*S.U.R.* 1918, No. 73, Art. 792),[24] adherence to the following rules:

1. Labor conscription has been introduced for the purpose of using the idle labor force for socially useful work, and it must not be interpreted as punitive measures applied to the non-working elements.

2. Subject to compulsory labor are individuals listed in the Decree on Labor Books; i.e., individuals:

    a. Living on unearned income;

    b. Having no definite occupation; and

    c. Not registered at the labor exchanges.

3. The following are exempt from compulsory labor:

    a. Persons under 16 and over 50 years of age;

[23] *S.U.R.*, 1918, No. 90, Art. 919.

[24] This reference is to the decree on Labor Books for Non-Workers, which is cited in Bunyan, *Intervention, Civil War and Communism in Russia*, p. 409.

b. Students who can produce special certificates issued by the departments of the People's Education, entitling the holder to exemption from labor conscription;

c. Persons who can produce certificates from medical bureaus attached to Hospital Insurance Offices, or from the medical commisison of the Medical Sanitary Section of the Soviet of Deputies, concerning their incapacity for work;

d. Pregnant women after six months of pregnancy, and for eight weeks following childbirth;

e. Housewives who have no servants, provided their families consist of more than two persons.

4. Within the category of compulsory labor are included all kinds of work, the importance of which is determined by a commission composed of representatives of the local Council of National Economy, of the Municipal Department of the local Soviet of Deputies, the Section of Labor of the local Soviet of Deputies, and the local Council of Trade Unions.

Note 1: Work of the military establishment which is in the nature of emergency work, such as the digging of trenches, work connected with evacuations, the shipment of military supplies, etc., if it cannot be carried out by rear-service detachments at the disposal of local authorities may be included in the category of compulsory labor work and undertaken irrespective of the decision of the aforesaid commission.

Note 2: Supervision over individuals called up for compulsory labor devolves upon a collegium appointed by the commission and consisting of representatives of the Section of Labor and of the Trade-Union Council.

[Articles 5 to 7 deal with wages, work hours, and social insurance for those called up for compulsory labor. Payment was to correspond to prevailing wage scales; the eight-hour work day was to be observed; and all social-insurance regulations were to be applied.]

8. Detailed notations must be entered into the labor books of those performing compulsory labor, showing the character and the amount of work performed, as well as notations by the commission indicating how the work was carried out.

9. The commission responsible for organizing the work of

non-workers [25] (Sec. 4) is charged with the preparation of detailed reports for the information of the institutions that are represented in the commission, showing the extent to which the decree on Labor Books [for non-workers] was being realized in life and how much work the bourgeoisie had performed during the month covered by the report. In case the decree is found inapplicable in a given area, a detailed explanation of the reasons for the inapplicability should be presented.

S. Schmidt
People's Commissar of Labor

B. Beginnings of Coercion of the Working Class

Lenin's assumption that the resort to forced labor would be confined only to the capitalists and the rich soon had to be modified. In the early spring of 1919 the methods of compulsion began to be applied to the working class, in whose name the Communist dictatorship had originally been established. There were several reasons for this change of policy.

First, the application of compulsory labor to former capitalists did not turn out to be the "powerful weapon" that Lenin had predicted would "supply an unprecedented force to bring the state machinery into motion." [26] Forcing the bourgeoisie to dig trenches or to clean snow from the streets did not contribute much to the effectiveness of the administrative machinery of the Soviet state. It did produce, however, a situation that forced large numbers of the formerly well-to-do classes to flee from the areas under Bolshevik control and to join forces with those who had taken arms against the Bolshevik dictatorship. This gave an added impetus to the civil war, deepened the political

[25] Individuals who are listed in article 2 of this decree.
[26] See p. 52 (above).

and military crises of the country, and called for greater sacrifices by the population under Bolshevik control.

Second, Communist policies in agriculture, industry, trade, and finance had struck a crippling blow at Russia's economy and had resulted in a sharp decline of the industrial labor force and in an even greater decline in the productivity of labor because of undernourishment and the general disorganization of city life. Contemporary memoirs and press reports paint a dark picture of workers' discontent, food shortages, strikes, and the open expression of dissatisfaction by the rank and file.[27]

In the winter months of 1918–19, cold probably was as great a cause of human misery as hunger; and epidemics took a heavy toll in human life. Everyone who had had an opportunity to leave the larger cities had done so, even if he had no relatives in the rural areas to go to.[28]

As the nation's economy continued to decay and as a new ruling class began to emerge—one that had a stake in the success of the socialist experiment—a disciplinarian trend began to assert itself, at the same time searching for new forms of labor management and of submission to labor discipline. Symptomatic of this trend is the following, anonymously written article in *Izvestiya*. The article did not state anything strikingly new but it helped harden various attitudes that were already in evidence—attitudes that led to the introduction of measures that extended coercion to the workers, and in a spectrum that ran from punitive lockouts to "freezing" miners to their jobs and establishing forced-labor camps for those who violated

[27] See esp. M. Gorki's article in *Novaya zhizn*, June 1, 1918; I. Maysky's memoirs, *Demokraticheskaya kontrrevolyutsiya, Gosizdat*, Moscow, 1923, (pp. 19–20) ; and *Pravda*, February 26, 1920.

[28] According to the *Statisticheskiy yezhegodnik, 1918–1920* (Moscow, 1920), the population of Moscow decreased from 2.2 million in February, 1917, to 1.3 million in August, 1920 (II, 332). The population of Petrograd decreased from 1.2 million in June, 1918, to 574,000 in August, 1920 (*ibid.*, p. 342).

labor discipline. The process proceeded gradually, and it involved giving up many basic convictions by those who had been brought up on the Marxian idealization of the proletariat.

Lenin, however, shared none of the hesitations of some of his associates, even if—as was shown in the previous chapter—he drifted from extremes of hostility toward labor to affirmations of faith in the future of the working class. His basic motives were tactical and looked toward the surest way of attaining his end: establishing the Party's firm control over the industrial labor force.

A PLEA TO ESTABLISH AN ECONOMIC DICTATORSHIP

[*Izvestiya*, March, 1919][29]

We are not going to look into the reasons which brought about the decline in labor productivity following the revolution. In the West, too, revolutions have led to a decline in labor productivity. We might conclude then that this is inevitable under any political, and especially economic, disruption in the life of the state.

The initial efforts in the struggle against the decline in productivity did not go beyond the resort to persuasion, comradely discipline, and the establishment of definite production norms. But who drafted these norms? The proletarians themselves. On this score we must admit the bitter truth: the proletariat did well in looking after its own interests, and in a great majority of cases it established norms which were ludicrously low. When this is taken into account, it becomes clear that our proletarians were not merely eager to look after their own interests but they also inflicted cruel punishment upon themselves, for there is not the slightest doubt that even under the present conditions of famine, and of fuel and raw-material shortages, much more could have been produced than has actually been the case. If, immediately after the October Revolution, piece work and bonuses had been introduced, the scarcity of manufactured goods would never have reached its present proportions and much more food could have been obtained from the rural districts.

[29] No. 65, March 26, p. 3.

The proletariat revealed extreme shortsightedness soon after it took over the management of the most important industries of the country. The proletariat is absolutely incapable of understanding the interests of the state, or even the interests of its own class, or of a single factory. All that the proletarians are interested in is their pay, and they are not in the least concerned whether that pay corresponds to the work done by them, or to the expenses incurred for fuel and raw materials, etc. The bitter truth must be told: the proletarian masses (workers and employees) do not care a whit how much they produce because they have learned by experience that their government will raise their wages as soon as prices go up. Why should the proletarians worry if the government takes care of them? The restoration of the economy requires sacrifices on the part of the proletariat. Without such sacrifices, ruin is inevitable.

On every front a struggle which calls for sacrifice for the sake of an ideal is now being waged. Some fighters understand this ideal and sacrifice everything for it. Others, however, required the application of severe disciplinary measures. This has been the situation at the front. But what about the people behind the front line? The rear is undermining the front because it disorganizes the national economy.

Economics remains economics and it has its own inexorable logic. It is quite immaterial who manages the economy; the only thing that matters is whether the management is in capable and diligent hands. Short of this, an economy is certain to perish, irrespective of whether it is in the hands of the bourgeoisie, of the peasantry, or the proletariat.

Following the coup d'état [of November, 1917], the proletariat became the master of several branches of industry and of the transportation system. But on the whole it proved insufficiently capable, energetic, or disciplined to check the further disruption of industry or transportation.

Yet, we have succeeded in improving the situation at the front. Why can't we do the same in the rear? It does not require such exceptional skill or wisdom. [The writer believes that this can be accomplished by selecting the most important branches of the economy, providing them with the necessary manpower and resources, and allowing the workers an improved ration so as to increase their productivity.]

The political dictatorship of the proletariat requires economic dictatorship as well. If this could not be understood right after the revolution, it is time that it be realized now. Discipline must be introduced in every enterprise, and a dictator responsible to the management of that enterprise must be appointed. Without such measures as piece work, bonuses, fines, dismissals, and dictatorial powers of specialist-administrators, the economy of the country, as the experience of the past year and a half has shown us, will not recover, and no revolution in the West will help it to recover. [Europe is exhausted and depends for its food on America and Australia.]

If the Soviet government fails to reestablish economic discipline, communism in Russia is bound to collapse, for the simple reason that a complete breakdown of the economy (including transport) in the cities and the rural areas will be inevitable. The bourgeoisie will then return and will reestablish its own discipline in its own interests. Is it not better for the proletariat to introduce discipline in the name of socialism rather than have it established in the name of capitalism? The proletariat of Russia is placed under such conditions that it has no other choice left because the country's economy has reached the final stage of disintegration and the revolution in the West has not as yet broken out. Exceptional measures and efforts are needed to restore the economy and keep our railways running. Only the introduction of an economic dictatorship behind the front line, like the one established at the front, can do this. . . .[30]

LOCKOUT IN THE REPAIR SHOPS OF
THE ALEKSANDROVSKY RAILROAD

[Announcement of the People's Commissariat of Railways,
March 31, 1919][31]

In the morning of March 31, a poster appeared on the gates of the principal shops of the Aleksandrovsky Railroad, with the announcement that the shops were being closed by order of the People's Commissariat of Railways. The reason for closing was the sharp drop in labor productivity.

[30] An editorial note at the end of this article stated that the editors were not responsible for the views of the writer, whose name is not mentioned. It might have been written by Trotsky or by one of his followers.
[31] *Vestnik putey soobshcheniya*, 1919, No. 12, p. 11.

When the workers arrived and read the announcement, they began to gather in small groups and to discuss the situation. The state of mind of the workers can best be described by expressions heard in the crowds: "So that's what we have come to!"

On April 1 a new recruitment of workers will begin.

"FREEZING" MINE WORKERS TO THEIR JOBS

[Decree of the Council of Workers' and Peasants' Defense, April 7, 1919][32]

In order to secure fuel supplies for the Russian Socialist Federated Soviet Republic, the Council of Workers' and Peasants' Defense has resolved:

1. All employees and workers in state or nationalized mining enterprises are forbidden to leave their work on their own initiative, without permission of the authorities in charge of such enterprises.

2. All persons working in the above mining enterprises, who attain military age as of March 15 of this year shall be considered as mobilized in the Red Army, but shall remain at their place of work.

3. Employees and workers who fail to discharge their duty will be held responsible for their actions before the revolutionary court.

V. ULYANOV (LENIN)
Chairman of the Council
of Workers' and Peasants' Defense

On April 15, 1919, *Izvestiya* carried a decree that had been issued by the Central Executive Committee and that established forced-labor camps for workers who were found guilty of having violated the provisions for labor discipline. Other penal-labor institutions were set up in the form of concentration camps, which were reserved primarily for the political opponents of the ruling party. These camps were under the control of the All-Russian

[32] *S.U.R.*, 1919, No. 14, Art. 163. On April 12 another decree was issued, which prohibited a person who was employed in a Soviet institution from transferring on his own initiative to another institution (*ibid.*, No. 18, Art. 204).

Extraordinary Commission to Fight Counterrevolution. The date of the establishment of these concentration camps is not available, but they are referred to in a decree pertaining to the procedures of the All-Russian Extraordinary Commission, which was adopted by the Central Executive Committee on February 17, 1919,[33] and in a subsequent decree that was published May 17, 1919.[34] As time went on, these concentration camps also were used for "particularly obstructive workers who repeatedly refuse to submit to disciplinary measures."[35]

THE ESTABLISHMENT OF FORCED-LABOR CAMPS

[Decree of the Central Executive Committee, April 15, 1919][36]

1. Forced-labor camps are herewith established and placed under the jurisdiction of the administrative sections of *Guberniya* Executive Committees.

Note 1: The initial organization and supervision of the forced-labor camps devolve upon the *Guberniya* Extraordinary Commissions [*Chekas*], who will transfer these camps to the administrative sections upon notification from the central government;

Note 2: Forced-labor camps in *uezds* can be opened only with the permission of the People's Commissariat of Internal Affairs.

2. Subject to confinement in the forced-labor camps are individuals or categories of individuals concerning whom there is a decision by the administrative sections of the Extraordinary Commissions [to Fight Counterrevolution], by the Revolutionary Tribunals, by the People's Courts, and by other Soviet institutions empowered by decrees and orders to make such decisions.

3. All inmates of these camps should immediately be assigned to work on demand by Soviet institutions.

4. Deserters from camps or from work are subject to severe penalties.

5. For the purpose of administering all forced-labor camps throughout the territory of the R.S.F.S.R., a Central Administra-

---

[33] *Ibid.*, No. 12, Art. 130.
[34] *Ibid.*, No. 20, Art. 235.
[35] See the Decree on Workers' Disciplinary Courts, quoted on p. 88 (below).
[36] *S.U.R.*, 1919, No. 12, Art. 124.

tion for these camps is established, to be attached to the People's Commissariat of Internal Affairs and [to operate] in agreement with the All-Russian Extraordinary Commission to Fight Counterrevolution.

6. Administrators of forced-labor camps are selected by local *Guberniya* Executive Committees, subject to confirmation by the Central Administration of the camps.

7. Funds for the equipment and upkeep of the camps are allocated, on the basis of estimates by the Commissariat of Internal Affairs, through the *Guberniya* Executive Committee.

8. Medical and sanitary supervision of the camps is the responsibility of the local health department.

9. Detailed regulations and instructions are to be worked out by the People's Commissariat of Internal Affairs within two weeks after the publication of this decree.

M. KALININ
*Chairman of the All-Russian
Central Executive Committee*

Detailed regulations for the operation of the forced-labor camps were published on May 17, 1919, in the form of a decree of the Central Executive Committee. It is a long document and consists of forty-nine clauses that go into minute detail on the organization and operation of the camps. In the document that follows, only a few of the regulations that relate to the inmates of the labor camps are quoted.

REGULATIONS CONCERNING FORCED—LABOR CAMPS

[Excerpts from the Decree of the Central Executive Committee,
May 17, 1919][37]

1. The organization of forced-labor camps is within the competence of *Guberniya* Extraordinary Commissions to Fight Counterrevolution. The Housing Department of the Executive Committee is to provide needed quarters.

2. Upon its establishment the camp is transferred, with the approval of the Department of Forced Labor of the Commissariat

[37] *Ibid.*, No. 20, Art. 235.

of Internal Affairs, to the jurisdiction of the [local] Executive Committee.

3. Forced-labor camps with a capacity of not less than 300 prisoners are to be established in every *Guberniya* center.

Note: Camps in *uezd* centers may be established only with the special permission of the Compulsory Labor Department.

4. The general administration of forced-labor camps within the territory of the R.S.F.S.R. is within the jurisdiction of the People's Commissariat of the Interior.

[Paragraphs 5 to 19 provide detailed regulations for camp administration; paragraphs 20 to 24 deal with sanitary and medical provisions; paragraphs 25 to 30 define the categories of people subject to confinement and restate the provisions of the Decree of April 15, 1919 (cited above, p. 72).]

31. All prisoners should be sent to work immediately upon arrival at the camp and should be engaged in physical labor during the entire period of their confinement. The nature of their work is determined by the camp administration.

Note: For some individuals, physical work may be replaced by intellectual work.

32. The eight-hour work day is to be applied to the prisoners. Overtime and night work are permitted but the regulations of the Labor Code (*S.U.R.*, 1918, Nos. 87–88) must be observed.

33. The food ration of the prisoners must be equal to the food norms of individuals engaged in physical labor.

34. Compensation for the prisoner's labor is to conform to trade-union rates established for similar work in the regions where the camp is located. Deductions from the prisoner's earnings are to be made to cover the cost of his maintenance (food and clothing), expenditures on living quarters, and the cost of administration and guarding the prisoners. The total amount of such deductions must not exceed two-thirds of the prisoner's earnings.

35. Expenditures for the upkeep of the camp, including administration costs, are to be fully covered by the labor of the prisoners if their numbers correspond to the full capacity of the camp. Responsibility for any deficit is placed upon the administration and the prisoners in accordance with the provisions of special instructions.

36. The nature of disciplinary penalties and the order of their imposition upon the prisoners are defined in special instructions.

37. The first attempt at escape is to be punished by a tenfold increase of the original prison term. With the second attempt the guilty prisoner is to be handed over to the Revolutionary Tribunal, which has the right to impose the highest measure of punishment [i.e., the death penalty].

38. As a precaution against possible escape, group responsibility may be established.

V. AVANESOV
For the *Chairman of the Central
Executive Committee*

Another step in the move toward compulsory labor was taken on June 25, 1919, with the issuance of a decree that compelled every worker to obtain a labor book. At first this law applied only to the population of the capitals, but later it was extended to the entire population of Russia.

In September, 1917, Lenin had expressed the view that the labor books Russian industrial workers were given by their employers, and which were used merely for accounting purposes, were "indisputably a document of capitalist hired slavery, an indication that the workingman is the property of this or that parasite. The Soviets will introduce the labor book for *the rich* and *then* gradually for the whole population. . . . It will be transformed into a token that in the new society there are no more 'workers' " [38]

It is not easy to follow Lenin's reasoning that the issuance of labor books by the Soviet government, rather than issuance by private employers, indicated that there were no more "workers." In the circumstances under which they were issued, labor books amounted to a general registration of the urban population (over sixteen years of age) for the purpose of restricting their freedom of

[38] Lenin, *Sochineniya*, XXI, 263.

movement and placing them at the disposal of governmental agencies.

LABOR BOOKS FOR WORKERS

[Decree of the Central Executive Committee, June 25, 1919][39]

1. All citizens of the R.S.F.S.R. who have reached the age of sixteen are under obligation to have labor books as evidence that their holders are engaged in productive activity. These books are to be used as personal identity documents throughout the R.S.F.S.R. and also as documents entitling the owners to receive food-ration cards as well as social-security benefits in case of loss of working capacity or unemployment.

Note 1: Military personnel of the Red Army and Navy are required to have labor books under the same provisions as others.

Note 2: [This note states that children under sixteen years of age are to be listed in the labor book of their mother, or, if there is no mother, in the labor book of their father.]

2. Labor books are issued by the Departments of Administration of the Executive Committees.

3. Labor books are issued only upon the presentation of the passport, which is to be retained [by the Department] after the [labor] book has been issued.

[Paragraphs 4 to 8 deal with procedural matters connected with the issuance of labor books and the information that employers have to enter into the labor books.]

9. In case the owner of a labor book changes employment, a note to this effect is to be entered in the labor book both by the institution which he has left and the one he has entered.

10. Authorities in charge of food distribution are required to enter notations in the labor books when issuing a food ration.

L. SEREBRYAKOV
*Acting Chairman of the All-Russian
Central Executive Committee*
V. ULYANOV (LENIN)
Chairman of the Sovnarkom

[39] *S.U.R.*, 1919, No. 28, Art. 315.

C. Depletion of the Ranks of Labor

The sporadic measures of labor compulsion that the Soviet government enacted during the first part of 1919 failed to bring about improvement in the country's industrial manpower position. On the contrary, conditions on the labor front were steadily deteriorating and were clearly heading toward a full-scale manpower crisis. An important cause of this crisis was a food shortage so acute that many regions, and especially the big cities, lived in the shadow of famine. This resulted in a flight of workers from the industrial centers—in search of food—and in the decline of labor productivity of those who remained on their jobs.

There were appeals to trade unions for help to bring back skilled workers from the villages and to develop wage policies that would contribute to an improvement of labor productivity. Measures also were taken—toward the end of 1919—to tighten labor discipline in plants and factories by establishing Workers' Disciplinary Courts. These courts were placed in charge of the trade unions, which more and more came to be looked upon as government agencies for the enforcement of labor discipline.

THE SHRINKAGE OF THE INDUSTRIAL LABOR FORCE

[Circular letter of the Central Committee of the Metal Workers' Trade Union, September 30, 1919][40]

In recent months the labor market has been experiencing a critical labor shortage, especially of skilled workers. The Section of Registration and Distribution of the Labor Force, attached to the People's Commissariat of Labor, has failed thus far to satisfy even the requirements of the war-production industries, so vital at present to the State.

[40] *Byulleten narodnogo kommissariata truda,* 1919, Nos. 11–12, pp. 28–29.

According to the information of the Section of Registration and Distribution of the Labor Force, there are large numbers of skilled workers in the villages. These workers moved to the country mainly on account of the food crisis in the large industrial cities. The problem now is how to get these needed workers out of the countryside. To do this is rather easy at this time, since the demand for labor comes from localities, such as Simbirsk, the Urals and the Izhevsk plant—localities well supplied with food. Also, the season of agricultural work is drawing to an end.

The Section of Registration and Distribution of the Labor Force has already taken a number of measures for the enlistment of the essential categories of workers who fled to the villages. The trade unions are vitally interested in reestablishing state industries as well as in preventing the shrinkage of the city proletariat. The trade unions must therefore assist in every possible way in the task of bringing back the skilled workers from the villages.

[The letter concludes with a number of suggestions of how trade-union locals can assist the Commissariat of Labor in the recruitment of skilled workers.]

The flight of workers from large industrial centers was mainly the result of a rapidly deteriorating food situation that was brought about by Soviet food and distribution policies. The establishment of a government food monopoly and the abolition of private trade made the city consumer entirely dependent on what he could receive from the socialized system of distribution.

In theory, the state took upon itself the obligation to supply the entire population with bread and other articles of prime necessity. The decree of the Central Executive Committee, of May 27, 1918, charged the Commissariat of Food with the duties of "provisioning the population with articles of prime necessity, of organizing on a national scale the distribution of these articles, and of paving the way for the nationalization of trade." [41] Distribution was made in the co-operative stores that were under the control of the Commissariat of Food. The amount of products received by a person depended, again in theory, on his class qualifications. Actually, the population was getting only a fraction of its food requirements, as the documents that follow indicate. By far the larger part of the food supplies came from the illegal trading that was going on in every part of the country. The illegal market converted many workers into traders who were forced to exchange personal belongings for whatever they could get by way of food supplies.

When the food situation became particularly acute, the government permitted workers to go to the food-surplus areas to obtain food supplies, but some of these workers preferred to stay on in the villages and engage in agriculture.

HOW THE POPULATION IS FED

[From the Proceedings of the All-Russian Congress of Statisticians, April 25, 1919] [42]

A. G. Lositsky presented interesting data on the question of how the people were fed during March of this year. So far figures have been received from four *guberniyas*—Yaroslav, Ivanovo-Voznesensk, Tver, and Novgorod. The general consumption of an adult male in calories may be expressed in the following figures:

Ivanovo-Voznesensk *Guberniya* ....2,151 calories
Yaroslav *Guberniya* 2,048   "
Tver *Guberniya* 1,836   "
Novgorod *Guberniya* 1,651   "

[41] *S.U.R.*, 1918, No. 38, p. 471, quoted in Bunyan, *"Intervention, Civil War and Communism in Russia,"* p. 466. Private trade was abolished by a decree of the *Sovnarkom* of November 21, 1918 (*ibid.*, p. 435–39).
[42] *Narodnoe khozyaystvo*, 1919, No. 6, p. 81.

Every male engaged in normal work requires 3,055 calories, while those engaged in intensive work require 3,448—so that the adult city population receives at present much less food than is required by a normally developed organism. Comparing these data with the food consumption of Moscow workers during the years 1909–11, it appears that the [present] consumption of bread is 51 percent, meat and fish 61 percent, fats 20 percent, potatoes 230 percent of the previous years. In terms of calories the present diet is 53 percent of that of the past. As may be seen from these figures, the diet has not only decreased quantitatively but has also changed qualitatively, toward roughage and monotony.

During the debates a number of other interesting facts became known. The daily ration of several categories of Petrograd workers is 1,680 calories. By weighing Petrograd workers there has been established an average loss in their weight of 20 percent. This was not true of bakers, whose weight has increased. As regards the Moscow population, investigation disclosed the following results: the third category consumes daily 1.2 *funts* [43] of bread; workers, 1.08 *funts*; Soviet employees, 0.8 of a *funt*. In this way the bourgeois part of the population (third category) is the best fed, while Soviet employees are among the worst fed. On an average, the Moscow population consumes 1.02 *funts* of bread, of which only 37 percent is received on ration cards.

BREAD RATIONS OF THE MOSCOW POPULATION
AT THE END OF 1919

[Announcement of the Moscow Consumers' Society,
December 2, 1919] [44]

The Moscow Consumers' Society hereby informs the population of Moscow that, beginning with December 2, the distribution of bread will take place every other day in the following amounts:

1. Coupon No. 20, First category and children's series B and V—three-fourths of a *funt* of bread.

---

[43] A *funt* is about nine-tenths of a pound.

[44] *Byulleten moskovskogo potrebitelskogo obshchestva*, No. 90, December 2, 1919, p. 2. The Moscow Consumers' Society was at that time completely under government control.

2. Coupon No. 20, Second category—one half of a *funt* of bread.

The illegal markets, which to some extent helped supplement the meager rations of the city population, diverted large numbers of workers from their normal occupations in industry and turned them into traders, thereby reducing still further the available labor force. Trading on the illegal markets tended to be a full-time occupation because, for workers who lived in large cities, it necessitated journeys to distant provinces. These journeys, furthermore, did not always result in success. As the following document indicates, government agents, known as "requisition cordons," were on the lookout for such traders and confiscated food that had been obtained on the illegal markets.

THE ILLEGAL MARKETS AND THE CURTAILMENT
OF THE LABOR FORCE

[Reports from provincial newspapers][45]

The influx into the provinces of Moscow inhabitants who are trying to obtain food has stimulated the development of moneyless transactions between city and village. In Tula *Guberniya* there has even been established a provisional norm of exchange: a bushel of potatoes for one and a half *funts* of salt, or one *funt* of sugar, or two *funts* of kerosene, or one half of a *funt* of tea; [or] one *pud*[46] of rye flour for two quarts of kerosene, or ten *funts* of salt. The village needs salt most of all. Thus a peasant exchanged a colt (3–4 weeks old) for seven *funts* of salt. [The report then cited prices in rubles, on the illegal markets in Tula and Vyatka *guberniyas*.]

Isvestiya of Vladimir *Guberniya* writes: "The bread which the peasant concealed [from the government] is now making its way

[45] *Ekonomicheskaya zhizn,* No. 38, February 19, 1919, p. 4.
[46] A *pud* is 36 pounds.

to the cities. However, it is not being sold for money, but exchanged for goods. The best dressers of the village demand for a *pud* of rye flour a fur coat or a white wedding dress with a pleated skirt. Not one of those village scoundrels has ever asked for a book in exchange for flour. City inhabitants are suffering great privations."

This exchange does not always proceed painlessly. The food committee of Kovrovsky *uezd* issued an announcement to the citizens inviting them to report the names of the villages and the peasants where manufactured goods were being accepted in exchange for food. These articles will be confiscated and returned to their owners.

In Kursk *Guberniya* strict measures are being taken in relation to "bagmen." [47] The food-requisition cordons of the Fifth Moscow Food Regiment operating at the station of Dmitriev confiscated about 700 *puds* of baked bread. Similar requisitions, according to newspaper reports, are taking place on the Syzran–Vyazma, Ryazan–Ural, and other railroads.

With the establishment of relations with the Ukraine, delegates from various parts of starving Russia are pouring into the Ukraine in search of food. Some of these delegates are conducting independent goods exchanges. Thus representatives from Tula are negotiating with the Kharkov Council of National Economy on the subject of exchanging Ukrainian bread for articles manufactured at Tula. . . .

The ranks of the industrial labor force were even further depleted by the influx, in large numbers, of factory workers into the administrative agencies of the Soviet state, which during the period under study were growing by leaps and bounds.

The Bolsheviks greatly encouraged this influx on the grounds, as Lenin expressed it, that state administration "will be fully within the reach of all literate people." [48]

[47] "Bagmen" were persons who engaged in the purchase of food from the peasants in violation of the Decree on Bread Monopoly, according to which only the state could acquire the peasants' surpluses.

[48] Lenin, *Sochineniya*, XXI, 399.

Eventually, some of these workers developed into efficient administrators. For the time being, however, and in the great majority of cases, the new administrators who came from the ranks of labor only hindered effective management. As A. Rykov's statement (below) indicates, the influx of workers into Soviet administrative agencies resulted mainly in a great increase in paper work. It also accelerated the rate of decrease in the size of the labor force.

INFLUX OF WORKERS INTO THE SOVIET BUREAUCRACY

[From Rykov's speech at the All-Russian Congress of *Guberniya* Departments of the Committee of State Construction, June 20–26, 1919][49]

. . . We created an enormous bureaucratic machinery of Soviet officials, and more than half of our time is being spent on going to various committees. We have already missed the construction season and are in danger of losing new seasons. The number of officials on the Committee of State Construction—both the central apparatus and its local departments—is unbelievably large. This is the largest bureaucratic organization of the republic. It should be reduced by more than 50 percent. Construction will only gain by this, since every employee has some kind of paper glued on to him. This state of affairs completely distorts the very idea of the Soviet state, which is based on the principle of labor. Labor is the relation of man to nature and not to paper. But we have interposed between work and nature a hundredfold more fences than existed previously during the bourgeois regime. Instead of staffing the offices with men, it would be better to transfer 80 percent of the [office] employees to work toward the alleviation of the fuel crisis which has assumed such threatening dimensions. Workers have less experience than specialists, so that every effort to replace a specialist by workers makes the situation so much the worse. . . .

[49] *Narodnoe khozyaystvo*, 1919, No. 8, p. 76.

D. Decline of Labor Productivity

Labor shortages were not the only factor that contributed to the sharp drop in industrial production in 1919. Another factor, no less important, was the decline in labor productivity. Malnutrition undoubtedly exercised a major influence in bringing about this decline, but other factors operated in the same direction. Foremost among these was the Soviet system of wage payments. Workers received part of their wages in kind (i.e., a food ration) and part in money.[50] The money part of a worker's wage was of no great significance to him because of the catastrophic drop in the purchasing power of the ruble. But the worker's food ration, which was of great importance to him, bore no relation to the actual work performed and depended solely on his rationing classification (i.e., heavy worker, light worker, or office employee). This system provided no incentive for higher productivity.

Improvement in this field was deemed to require the re-introduction of such features of the capitalist system as piece work and bonuses for additional output. According to an article in *Narodnoe khozyaystvo* (cited below), a number of trade unions were in favor of introducing these measures and were engaged in drafting production norms and wage agreements that were based on the production norms. The persistent food shortages and the further depreciation of the paper currency, however, made these wage agreements merely a theoretical exercise.[51] Bonuses in kind were not available, and bonuses in money were not of much use. Because there was no link between the level of living and the level of production, the wage agreements

[50] *Desyatyy sezd RKP(b)*, Moscow, 1933, p. 430. For a detailed account of the rationing system, see N. M. Vishnevsky, *Printsipy i metody organizatsion-nogo raspredeleniya produktov*, Moscow, 1920.
[51] See Preobrazhensky's comments on this point (pp. 179–80, below).

were not much help as incentives to higher labor productivity.

PROBLEMS OF LABOR PRODUCTIVITY

[A review in the Official Organ of the Supreme Council of National Economy, 1919][52]

. . . The decline in labor productivity which in some industries has reached 60 percent and more, as compared with pre-revolutionary times, creates a danger to the very existence of the Soviet regime, a danger no less threatening than the enemies against whom the Red Army is fighting at the present time. That is why it is so important to consider some of the problems involved in recent wage policies. The problems are as follows: the system of premiums, piece work, and the position of specialists.

In the past the system of premiums functioned for the benefit of the plant administration, which tried to squeeze a maximum of production from the workers. But now the question is one of making the premium system a legitimate element of the wages of the workers. The trade unions are presently debating this problem because the system of premiums is a real factor in raising labor productivity which has fallen so low. The Union of Metal Workers in particular is a convinced champion of the premium system. The Union decided to undertake an intensive study of the theoretical and practical aspects of the various types of premium systems in order to ascertain the most suitable from the point of view of labor efficiency. Apparently this system has already been established in certain industries.

[After reviewing the various types of bonuses proposed by different unions, the article continues:]

The Union of Metal Workers is also a pioneer in propagating the idea of piece work wages, again with the idea of raising the productivity of our industry. As is well known, the system of piece work was looked upon before the revolution as one of the most refined means of exploiting the workers. However, when

[52] *Narodnoe khozyaystvo*, 1919, No. 7, pp. 80–81.

applied by the toiling masses themselves, this system loses to a considerable extent its character of exploitation and becomes, on the contrary, an effective means for the raising of the productivity of labor. At the present time, when labor inspection and a code of laws relating to the protection of labor are in existence, one does not need to fear that piece work will assume the same character as in the pre-revolutionary period. That is why the Second All-Russian Congress of Trade Unions took piece work as the basis for its wage policy. The Union of Metal Workers has arrived at the same position and other unions are gradually freeing themselves from a negative attitude toward piece work wages.

Let us now consider the momentous question of the wage rates of the so-called "specialists." This question has already given rise to a lot of polemics which has not subsided even at the present moment.

Everybody is familiar with the complaints that the specialists demand excessively high compensation and give up jobs for others with better pay, or take employment in several institutions without giving sufficient attention to any one. Two attitudes have clashed [on this issue]. Representatives of one attitude advocate the application of the egalitarian principle to the higher technical personnel. Thus, the People's Commissar of Labor, Schmidt, points out that equality is required in the first instance by the socialist consciousness. "It is not permissible [he said], that the workers who have fought for the Soviet government and have won should receive less than others for an equal expenditure of energy" (*Ekonomicheskaya zhizn* [1919], No. 108, May 22). "The system of sharp wage differentials deprives the workers of essential necessities. There can be no doubt that such a policy will repel completely the proletarian masses from the Communists" (*ibid.*, No. 125, June 12).

However, the adherents of an egalitarian policy in relation to specialists remain apparently in the minority. Our industry is too poorly supplied with creative and organizational forces. The higher technical personnel should be attracted to work by all possible means. Economizing in this field will serve no rational purpose. The trade unions which approach the industrial question in an intelligent way, or are confronted in a practical way with problems of industrial management, are supporting energetically a higher remuneration for specialists. . . .

In addition to drafting wage agreements and establishing production norms for workers, the trade unions also were charged with the responsibility for maintaining work discipline in industrial establishments. With this in view, Workers' Disciplinary Courts were created by a decree of November 14, 1919, to enforce compliance with the wage agreements and the production norms.

It is doubtful that these courts had any impact on the course of events. A month after the decree, the fateful decision was taken to militarize the Soviet economy, to by-pass the trade unions, and to establish direct and immediate control over labor so as to enable the Soviet government to mobilize and allocate the nation's labor resources with great speed and maximum flexibility.

THE ESTABLISHMENT OF WORKERS' DISCIPLINARY COURTS

[Decree of the *Sovnarkom*, November 14, 1919][53]

In view of the extremely difficult military, food, and fuel situation in the Soviet Republic, and in order to improve labor discipline and productivity to the greatest possible degree, as well as to achieve the most rational utilization of all productive forces of the country, the Soviet of People's Commissars hereby decrees the introduction of the following statute:

1. The present statute shall be applied in the entire territory of the R.S.F.S.R. and is compulsory upon all Soviet, nationalized, cooperative, and private enterprises and institutions

2. Disciplinary courts are established for the purpose of raising and strengthening production discipline, dealing with all infringements of wage agreements in enterprises and institutions, and with violations of internal plant regulations, as well as with failures to adhere to trade union decisions concerning labor and trade-union discipline.

3. The courts are attached to the local departments (*Guberniya*, *uezd*, and *rayon*) of the trade unions and are to be composed

[53] *S.U.R.*, 1919, No. 56, Art. 537.

of one delegate each from the local or central plant administration, the trade union, and the general assembly of workers of the establishment where the court is to operate.

[Paragraphs 4 to 8 relate to operational procedures. The court was to have a chairman and a secretary. Its sessions were to be conducted on regular schedules, after working hours, and were to be open to the public. Appeals from lower courts could be made to higher disciplinary courts, which operated at the *guberniya* level.]

9. The court may impose the following penalties: (1) public reprimand, (2) temporary suspension—up to six months—from participation in trade-union elections or from being elected, (3) demotion with reduced pay for a period not to exceed one month, (4) assignment to hard, socially useful labor with corresponding rates of pay. Particularly obstructive workers who repeatedly refuse to submit to disciplinary measures will be subject, as non-workers, to discharge and confinement in concentration camps.

[Paragraphs 10 to 13 deal with the duties of the Commissariats of Labor and Justice and the All-Russian Council of Trade Unions in organizing the court.]

14. Administrative and technical personnel, in charge of plants, enterprises and institutions, if guilty of infringements of wage agreements, negligence, and failure to utilize the available personnel and resources of an enterprise or institution, may, upon the decision of the Chairman of the Supreme Council of National Economy, the Special Representative of the Council of Defense in charge of Red Army and Navy supplies, or the *Sovnarkom*, be held criminally liable and subject to arrest or confinement in concentration camps.

V. Ulyanov (Lenin)
Chairman of the Sovnarkom

CHAPTER III

MILITARIZATION OF LABOR: THE DECISION AND ITS INSTITUTIONAL FRAMEWORK

By the end of 1919 it had become abundantly clear that the flight of workers from the industrial centers of Russia and the sharp decline in labor productivity were the principal obstacles to the development of the socialist economic order. The first stage of the Bolshevik blueprint for "laying the foundations of socialism"—the nationalization of industry—was nearing completion, and an elaborate network of administration, with more than sixty complete systems of production control—all subordinate to the Supreme Council of National Economy—was ready to take full charge of industrial production. Labor, however, was the critical bottleneck in the realization of the Communist's economic goals, and there was need of a strategy that would provide a way through this critical bottleneck.

Resort to material incentives was precluded by the severe shortages of food and other consumers' goods. Nor was there a willingness to follow a course of slow, incremental improvement by which food and other necessities could be furnished to induce skilled workers to return to the cities and to offer incentives to higher productivity in labor. Flushed by their victories in the civil war and impatient to resolve the manpower crisis, the Bolshevik leaders apparently were emboldened to widen the sporadic measures of labor compulsion that had been enacted during 1919.

It was against this background that the strategy of labor militarization was evolved, and this strategy ushered in a new phase in Russia's internal revolution—with accompanying pressures on the masses of the people for the speedy realization of the Communist economic and social order. The decision was made to centralize the entire economy.

In agriculture, the "great campaign" was inaugurated to convert the peasant population into proletarians who worked on the land and grew the products—in the quantities that would be determined by the general economic plan of the nation. In industry, a vast mobilization of labor, on military lines, was undertaken. The industrial plan was formulated in an elaborate set of regulations that had been decreed toward the end of January, 1920—in the form of "theses" the Party Central Committee had adopted. In these theses the sporadic and piecemeal levies on labor that had been enacted during the previous period were greatly extended and consolidated under one agency, known as the Central Committee on Universal Compulsory Labor—the *Glavkomtrud.*

Successive decrees of the *Sovnarkom* and the *Glavkomtrud* broadened the application of forced labor to encompass almost the entire population of Russia. The militarization campaign was accompanied by a deluge of propaganda and exhortation. Government decrees provided severe penalties against persons who were charged with failing to carry out the compulsory-labor regulations. Such persons were called "deserters on the labor front." The leading role in formulating the policy of labor militarization was played by Leon Trotsky.

A. The Principles of Labor Compulsion

Toward the close of 1919, when the Russian civil war was drawing to an end, Trotsky, who still held the position of People's Commissar of War and Chairman of the Military Revolutionary Council of the Republic, was sum-

moned by Lenin to Moscow to address himself to what
were then the most critical problems facing the Soviet government: the utter ruin of the country's economy, and
particularly the critical shortage of industrial manpower.
By the middle of December, 1919, Trotsky had produced
an elaborate plan by which he hoped to lead Russia "out of
the present great destruction of its productive forces and
economic chaos." [1]

Trotsky's plan, which consisted of twenty-four proposi-
tions or "theses," was not a well-integrated document but
it was so provocative that it annoyed many persons, particularly in the trade-union movement and in the Supreme
Council of National Economy. Although it was intended
primarily for consideration by members of the Party Central Committee, the theses appeared in *Pravda* on December 17, 1919, with an editorial note that invited discussion. [2]

Trotsky's basic idea consisted of applying military
methods in the economic field and of turning the entire
population of Russia into a vast army of labor. The workers were to be "militarized"; that is, tied down to jobs
they could not leave without the permission of high authorities. Any shirking of duty or unauthorized absence
from work was to be punished on the same basis as desertion from the army.

Pravda's editorial note that invited discussion of Trotsky's theses precipitated a deluge of letters that attacked
or supported his proposals. Some of these letters appeared
in *Pravda* and others appeared in *Ekonomicheskaya zhizn*,
the official organ of the Supreme Council of National
Economy. The great majority of the letters opposed

[1] L. Trotsky, *Sochineniya, Gosizdat*, 1927, XV, 11.
[2] According to Trotsky, the theses were published without his knowledge, by
Bukharin, who—as a member of the Party Central Committee—received a copy
of the theses and had immediately sent it to be published in *Pravda*, of which
Bukharin was editor-in-chief (*ibid.* p. 36).

the militarization aspect of Trotsky's program, and representatives of the Supreme Council of National Economy and leaders of the trade unions were especially critical.[3] When—on January 12, 1920—Trotsky's proposals came up for informal consideration by the Communist faction of the All-Russian Central Council of Trade Unions, Lenin was the only speaker (except for Trotsky) who defended military methods for handling the labor problem. From the sixty or seventy members who were present at the meeting of the faction, Trotsky's program of militarization received only two favorable votes.[4]

The first document that follows is Trotsky's exposition of his theory of compulsory labor, as it appeared in his book, *Terrorism and Communism*. The second document is a greatly enlarged and modified version of his original theses,[5] which were accepted by the Party Central Committee and then promulgated as official Soviet policy on January 22, 1920.

TROTSKY'S EXPOSITION OF THE PRINCIPLES OF COMPULSORY LABOR

[Excerpts from Trotsky's *Terrorism i Kommunizm*][6]

. . . The fearful strain of the civil war is slackening. Economic needs and problems are coming more and more into prominence.

[3] Rykov thought that Trotsky's principal errors consisted of treating the problems of labor as if they were military problems, and that Trotsky made no mention of the trade unions or the Commissariat of Labor as having any relation to labor questions (*Ekonomicheskaya zhizn*, December 30, 1919).

[4] Trotsky, *Sochineniya*, XV, 530. At this meeting Lenin was rather outspoken toward Trotsky's critics. He referred to Rykov, Lomov, and Larin as stupid ignoramuses who did not know how to read and he accused them of starting "contemptible petty quarrels" for which there was absolutely no excuse (*ibid.*). Rykov was Chairman of the Supreme Council of National Economy, and Lomov and Larin were members of the Presidium of that body.

[5] According to Milyutin, a special commission was appointed to enlarge and rewrite Trotsky's theses (*Devyatyy sezd Rossiyskoy kommunisticheskoy partii, Stenograficheskiy otchet, Gosizdat*, Moscow, 1920, p. 122).

[6] Trotsky, *Sochineniya*, XII, 127.

History is bringing us face to face with our basic problem—the organization of labor on new social foundations. . . .

The principle of compulsory labor [7] is absolutely beyond dispute for a Communist. "He who does not work, shall not eat." Since everyone has to eat, everyone has to work. Labor service is inscribed in our constitution and in the Code of Labor. But until now it remained a mere principle. Its application had only a partial and incidental character. But now, when we are face to face with the problem of economic reconstruction, the question of labor service confronts us in its full concreteness. The only proper and practical solution of the economic difficulties is to view the population of the entire country as a reservoir of labor power— almost an inexhaustible source—and to introduce strict order into the registration, mobilization, and utilization of that labor power. . . .

The introduction of compulsory labor is inconceivable without the use, in one form or another, of the methods of militarization of labor.

The foundations for the militarization of labor [8] are the forms of state compulsion without which the replacement of the capitalist economy by a socialist system will forever remain an empty sound.

Why do we speak of *militarization?*

Of course this is only an analogy, but an analogy which is very rich in content. No social organization, except the army, has ever considered itself justified in subordinating citizens to itself in such a measure and in subjecting them to its will to such an extent as the state of the proletarian dictatorship considers itself justified in doing. Only the army, just because it was deciding the question of the life and death of nations, states and governing classes, was granted the powers to demand, from each and all, complete subordination to its mission, aims, regulations, and orders. The army's success in achieving those demands depended on the extent to which the tasks of military organization coincided with the requirements of social development.

The question of the life and death of Soviet Russia is at present being decided on the labor front. Our economic as well as our trade-union organizations have the right to demand from their

[7] *Ibid.*, pp. 129–31.
[8] *Ibid.*, p. 135.

members all that selflessness, discipline, and obedience, which hitherto only the army has required.

. . . There can be no other way[9] to Socialism except by the authoritative regulation of the economic forces and resources of the country and the centralized distribution of the labor force in accordance with the general state plan. The workers' state considers itself empowered to send every worker to the place where his work is needed; and not one serious-minded Socialist will ever deny the right of the workers' state to lay its hand upon the worker who refuses to discharge his work orders. And here is where the trouble with the Mensheviks comes in. Their path of transition to Socialism is a milky way—without the bread monopoly,[10] without abolition of the market, without the revolutionary dictatorship, and without the militarization of labor.

Without compulsory labor, without the right to command and demand execution [of orders], the trade unions will become a mere form devoid of all substance. The Socialist state, which is in the process of construction, requires trade unions not for the struggle for better conditions of labor—this is the task of the social and state organization as a whole—but for organizing the working class for the ends of production, to educate, discipline, distribute, "tie down" certain categories and individual workers to their places of work for fixed periods—in a word, hand in hand with the state to lead the workers authoritatively into the framework of a single economic plan. To advocate under such conditions "freedom" of labor, means to stand for futile, feeble and uncontrolled searches for better conditions, [to endorse] unsystematic and chaotic movements of workers from one plant to another, in a starving country, under conditions of terrible disruption of the transport and food-supply machinery. . . . [Omission in the text.] What else but complete disintegration of the working class and complete economic anarchy can result from the absurd attempt to reconcile the bourgeois freedom of labor with proletarian socialization of the means of production?

---

[9] *Ibid.*, pp. 136–37.

[10] The bread monopoly, one of the pillars of Soviet agricultural policy, brought the Bolsheviks into conflict with the peasants and led to the "bread war." The bread monopoly was inaugurated by decree of the *Sovnarkom*, which authorized the government to requisition all grain surpluses of the peasants over and above the established "consumption norm." The decree also prohibited private trade in grain and grain products. See Bunyan, *Intervention, Civil War and Communism in Russia*, pp. 460–62.

THE MANPOWER CRISIS AND HOW TO SOLVE IT

[Theses adopted by the Party Central Committee,
January 22, 1920][11]

1. The sharp economic decline of the country, resulting from the imperialist war and the counterrevolutionary attacks on the Soviet state, finds its direct expression in excessive shortages or disruption of such basic factors of production as technical equipment, raw materials, and, first and foremost, fuel and labor power.

2. There is no reason to expect any immediate importation from abroad of any quantity of machinery, of coal, or of skilled workmen, and this is not only because of the blockade, about which no predictions can be made at the moment, but also because of the extreme economic exhaustion of Western Europe.

3. Therefore, the principal lever capable of improving the national economy is the labor force, its organization, distribution, and rational utilization.

A. The Industrial Proletariat

4. The industrial proletariat, in whom political power is principally concentrated, must from now on devote its entire attention and every effort to the organization of the economy and take part directly in the process of production.

5. For this purpose it is necessary to reassemble the disrupted ranks of skilled and trained workers by recalling them gradually from the army, the food detachments,[12] Soviet institutions behind the front, Soviet farms and communes, and, first and foremost, from the ranks of speculators.

6. The release and concentration of professionally trained workers must be attained by the combined operation of measures designed to improve their food-supply conditions and their general standard of life; by a more accurate registration of these workers and greater trade-union influence upon them; and, finally, if necessary, by measures of administrative coercion.

[11] Trotsky, *Sochineniya*, XV, 107–14.

[12] Food detachments, better known as Food Requisition Detachments, were groups of armed city workers who were organized either by trade unions or by individual factories and sent to food-surplus regions to requisition grain from the peasants. The organization of these detachments was authorized by the Soviet government on August 6, 1918. See Bunyan, *Intervention, Civil War and Communism in Russia*, pp. 476–77.

7. The implementation of these measures, as well as the entire effort of industrial development, is conditioned upon the organizational consolidation of the trade unions, by placing at their disposal an adequate staff of responsible and reliable workers, capable of enforcing principles of iron discipline.

8. Simultaneously, extensive measures must be taken for the professional training of the younger generation, fourteen years of age and over, in order to secure the necessary reproduction of skilled workers. With this in view, the Commissariat of People's Education must create an organization, powerful and authoritative, in which representatives of all the institutions concerned must take part.

B. Unskilled Labor Force

9. Under present economic conditions the employment in industry and in transport of unskilled workers, i.e., the peasants, is made necessary to a degree far greater than ever before.

  a. The country's mechanical equipment is worn out and can be replaced only by human labor;

  b. The country's fuel position is critical and must depend on such labor-consuming work as wood procurement;

  c. Cultivation of Soviet farms will require large numbers of peasants;

  d. Clearing streets and roads of snow, loading and unloading freight, construction, etc., will require large numbers of unskilled labor.

10. The present conditions of the country are of such a character that industry, transport and economic life generally cannot obtain the necessary labor force without the introduction of *compulsory labor.*

C. Universal Compulsory Labor

11. Socialist construction repudiates the liberal capitalistic principle of "freedom of labor," a principle which in bourgeois society signifies freedom for some to exploit others, and freedom for others to be exploited. Insofar as the fundamental problem of social organization is to overcome the external physical conditions

hostile to man, socialism demands that all members of society should be *compelled* to take part in the production of material values; at the same time socialism aims at the establishment of the most rational, i.e., the most economical and generally the most attractive form of socialization of labor. The principle of universal compulsory labor, firmly established in the Fundamental Laws of the Russian Socialist Federated Soviet Republic, must now be applied on a wide and all-embracing scale.

12. The full realization of the principle of universal compulsory labor, within the framework of a general economic plan, can only be accomplished by perfecting the entire administrative and economic apparatus of the state, and by the universal introduction of labor books, showing the exact place of each citizen, male or female, in the economic system, as well as in the national defense system of the Soviet Republic.

13. The transition to the general application of compulsory labor must take place at once, in forms which may be lacking in precision but which are capable of securing the necessary labor force for the socialized economy.

14. With this in view it is necessary to determine the number of workers who are needed at present and who, depending on the amount of available foodstuffs and machinery, can be put to work immediately to solve the most critical problems of the present time (1920).

15. At the same time a special decree must be issued to specify which economic needs and requirements should be classified as local and regional, to be taken care of by means of local compulsory labor.

16. The organization of compulsory labor, which is to cover both sexes, must take into consideration the peculiarities of the various regions; and the distribution of manpower between national and local compulsory work should, as far as possible, be carried out uniformly throughout the country, in order to lessen the harm to the peasant economy.

17. In the immediate future compulsory labor is to be applied mainly to those age groups least affected by mobilizations for military service. As far as possible, women should be brought into this work.

18. Local machinery for carrying out compulsory labor of both national and regional importance should be built on a combination

of local departments of the Commissariat of War, the Administrative Department of the Executive Committee, and the Labor Section [of the Commissariat of Labor].

19. This local organization (Committee for Universal Compulsory Labor), which will be immediately subordinate to the Executive Committee, will receive orders for requisite labor, both from the center for carrying out national plans, and from the local Executive Committee for the economic needs of its district. The task of the Committee for Universal Compulsory Labor is to coordinate local demands with requirements arising from the center, which, as a rule, should be given first priority.

20. At the center, a committee for compulsory labor is to be established, composed of representatives of the Registration and Distribution Section of the Commissariat of Labor, of the Commissariat of the Interior, of the Mobilization Department of the All-Russian General Staff, and the Central Statistical Administration. For the immediate future the Central Committee [for Compulsory Labor] will be of an interdepartmental nature and will be attached to the Council of Defense. All state institutions, both central and local, are under obligation to carry out the orders of the Central Committee that relate to questions of compulsory labor.

D. Militarization of the Economy

21. In a society which is in a transitional phase of its development and which is burdened with the inheritance of a distressing past, the passage to a planned organization of socialized labor is inconceivable without compulsory measures being applied to the parasitic elements, to the backward sections of the peasantry, and even to the working class itself. The weapon of state compulsion is military force. Therefore the militarization of labor, in one form or another, is inescapable in a transitional economy based on universal compulsory labor. The element of compulsion is bound to be more sparingly applied in proportion as the socialist economic system becomes more developed, as the conditions of work become more favorable, and as the education level of the growing generation improves.

22. The militarization of the economy, in the given conditions

of Soviet Russia, is to be understood in the sense that problems affecting the economy (labor intensity, careful handling of machinery and tools, conscientious use of materials, etc.) must be treated by workers and state institutions as if they were problems of military combat. The entire urban and rural population must recognize that the prevention of labor desertion, self-seeking, unpunctuality in work, carelessness, laziness, and abuse are problems of life and death to the country as a whole. These shortcomings must be brought to an end as rapidly as possible, even if the most severe measures are necessary.

23. To this end a propaganda campaign must be undertaken [to create a wide popular interest in the economic life of the country]. The leading roles in this work should be assigned to the Party and the trade unions.

24. Formal militarization of individual enterprises or whole branches of industry, which are especially important at the present time, or are particularly in danger of disruption, will in each case take place by special decree of the Council of Defense and will have as its primary aim the temporary "freezing" of workers to their enterprise, as well as the introduction within the enterprise of strict discipline, giving the administration wide disciplinary powers, if the restoration of the enterprise can be achieved in no other way.

25. The summoning of large masses of unskilled and unorganized workers to perform compulsory labor in such fields as food and fuel gathering, construction, loading and unloading, etc., requires, especially at the outset, a form of organization which approaches the military type.

26. The essentials of labor organization and the necessary discipline, both internal and external, required for the hundreds of thousands, even millions of people, mobilized for compulsory labor, can be supplied only by leading, class-conscious, determined, and energetic workers, especially those who have gone through the school of war and are accustomed to handling masses and leading them under the most difficult conditions.

27. Basically, the establishment of compulsory labor involves the same problems of organization and of principle as underlie the establishment of the Soviet State as a whole and the creation of the Red Army: to make sure that the less class-conscious and

more backward peasant masses are placed under natural leaders and organizers from among the most class-conscious proletarians, who are in most cases professionally trained. Inasmuch as the army represents the most important experiment in a mass Soviet organization of this type, its methods and procedures (with all necessary modifications) must be carried over into the field of labor organization by utilizing the experience of those workers who will be transferred from military to economic work.

E. Labor Armies

28. Military units, including large army formations, which are being released from combat duty, should be given labor assignments. This will serve as a transition stage in the introduction of universal compulsory labor, and is the reason for the conversion of the Third Army into the First Labor Army, an experiment which will be extended to other armies.

29. The essential conditions in the employment of army units and whole armies for labor are the following:

a. The tasks imposed on the labor armies must be strictly limited to the simplest types of work, such as gathering and accumulating food supplies.

b. Organizational relationships must be established, with the relevant economic organs, to prevent the disruption of the economic plans of these organs and the disorganization of the centralized economic machinery.

c. Close contact and comradely relations must be established with the workers of the region, and, if possible, food rations of the two groups should be equalized.

d. An ideological struggle must be carried out against the prejudices of the petty intelligentsia and trade unionists who regard the militarization of labor and the employment of military units in the production process as a return to the Arakcheev regime.[13] It is necessary to explain the inevitability and the progressive character of military compulsion aimed at economic improvement on the basis of universal compulsory labor, and to clarify the progressive character of the gradual rapprochement between the organ-

---

[13] For the Arakcheev regime, see n 19 (below).

ization of labor and the organization of defense in a socialist society.

F. Food Supply

30. In framing economic plans and programs, the first and
most important problem in mobilizing and employing and establishing the Soviet regime in newly occupied regions is the *concentration in the hands of the Soviet State* of several hundred million
funts of bread, meat, fish, fats, i.e., of a food reserve sufficient to
meet the needs of the industrial proletariat, of Soviet employees,
and of the peasants mobilized for compulsory labor in the current
year. The creation of food-supply bases in the most important
industrial regions will serve as a firm guarantee for the realization
not only of the current economic plan, but also of the whole
process of socialist construction.

[The last paragraph, No. 31, stresses the importance of establishing "public feeding" so as to release large numbers of female
labor for employment.]

The first open forum for the presentation of the "theses"
of the Party Central Committee was the Third All-Russian
Congress of Councils of National Economy, which met in
Moscow toward the end of January, 1920.[14] Trotsky delivered a long speech before the Congress, on January 25,
in which he defended the measures proposed by the Party
Central Committee for dealing with the labor situation.
He pleaded for the right of the "workers' state" to require
the conscription of skilled and unskilled labor alike, and
for the compulsory transfer of workers from one activity
to another. He then outlined his own scheme for the militarization of the economy, in which industrial management
would become the prerogative of an elite that would be
recruited largely from the military.

[14] A behind-the-scenes discussion of Trotsky's proposals took place at the
meeting of the Communist members of the All-Russian Central Council of
Trade Unions on January 12, 1920 (see p. 92, above).

TROTSKY'S BLUEPRINT FOR SOVIET
INDUSTRIAL ORGANIZATION

[Excerpts from Trotsky's speech at the Joint Session of the Third
Congress of Councils of National Economy and the Moscow Soviet of
Workers' and Peasants' Deputies, January 25, 1920][15]

. . . The task of the present moment is to draw our economy
closer to military procedures. The military establishment must
come in line with the economic establishment. A military region
is to be established wherever there is an industrial region. With
the contraction of the military fronts, we shall gradually make the
transition to a militia system.

What is a militia system? It means that the population of a
given area is incorporated into the ranks of a regiment, a brigade,
or a division, where these units are located. In this way ready-
made cadres and ready-made commanding staffs are made available.

Who will make up these staffs?

The posts of commander should be occupied by our Red
[Army] technicians, the new engineers, the members of the factory or plant administrations. These [also] will be our colonels,
divisional commanders, generals, battalion and company commanders. Our army officers' schools should be located in the
principal industrial centers, so that everyone attending these
schools will become an officer and leader of the corresponding
industrial region.

The agricultural periphery should come under the undivided
leadership of the industrial centers. In this way a given region,
with the industrial plants at the center, will become at one and
the same time an industrial region, a militia region, and a militia
division.

As our army becomes adjusted to economic conditions, our
economy will absorb those elements of militarism which are of
vital importance—precision in the execution of orders, treating
economic orders as if they were battle orders. This is our most
urgent necessity; otherwise we face economic ruin.

[Trotsky then pointed out that under existing conditions there
was an easy way of bringing the army and labor in closer contact

[15] Trotsky, *Sochineniya*, XV, 69–70.

by transforming military units and entire armies into labor armies. In certain areas there were armies which had accomplished their military tasks, and he continued.]

Such is the present position of the Third Army.[16] It numbers (I can now mention the figure) not less than 150,000 men, and has 7,000 Communists and 9,000 sympathizers. Such an army is a highly class-conscious army, and there is no wonder that, since there was no combat assignment, it has offered itself for labor employment in the area where it is stationed.

[After outlining the conditions for the Third Army's employment—a restatement of paragraph 29 of the theses (see p. 100, above)—Trotsky addressed himself to the organization and operation of the labor army.]

A worker with wide experience [17] in various branches of industry will be appointed Chief of Staff of the labor army. His assistant will be the former Chief of Staff, an officer of the General Staff with similar experience. The Operations Division of the army is now called the Operations Division of Labor. It is in charge of executing and preparing all operational orders relating to labor, as well as preparing labor communiques. Formerly this Operations Division used to transmit orders: "Take such and such a village," or "Advance so many *versts* in a certain direction." Now the orders of this division will be labor orders: "To procure so many cubic *sazhens* of firewood in such and such a district."

Just think, comrades, what an enormous advantage this organization will have, with a centralized telegraph and telephone communications system at its disposal! Every regiment has its own telephone equipment and can establish direct contact with the brigade staff, through the brigade staff with the division staff and army staff. Here you have a large number of working units, scattered over large areas, all trained to carry out orders, to receive orders along established channels, and to report accomplishments on the same day.

In place of the Reconnaissance Department, a Statistical Department has been organized, in which the same personnel are

[16] *Ibid.*, p. 71.
[17] *Ibid.*, pp. 73–74.

retained and adapted to the new work. The Communications Department, referred to above, remains unchanged. It has an enormous task before it, to maintain contact between all the labor detachments and institutions and the [General] Staff, so that the results of every day's work are known at 2200 o'clock of the same day.

. . . Since we find it [18] necessary to make the transition to compulsory labor on a large scale, we shall not be able to utilize the trade unions in drafting hundreds of thousands and millions of peasants for production. They can be mobilized only by the use of military methods. They will have to be organized into military formations, such as labor detachments, labor companies, and labor battalions. To the extent that we will be dealing with masses who have not gone through trade-union training, it will be necessary to form organizations of a military character. We already have these organizations in our armies. They should, therefore, be used for and adapted to economic tasks. This is being done now.

The utilization of labor armies, in the opinion of liberal prattlers, is fraught with the danger of restoring the regime introduced by Arakcheev.[19] We are justified in discarding completely this prattle. We say that the avant-gardes of the working class have taken the rule of the country in their own hands and have the right to impose the laws of compulsory labor upon the backward part of the laboring masses. Tomorrow, or the day after, when the fruits of this labor will be seen, even the most backward peasants will understand—and the best part of the peasantry understand it now—that compulsory labor was a necessary law. . . .

[18] *Ibid.*, pp. 76–77.

[19] The Arakcheev regime, or *Arakcheevshchina* in good Russian, was a system of labor employment that was established during the reign of Alexander I by his Minister of War, A. Arakcheev. Under this system, military units quartered in certain parts of Russia were, in addition to their military duties, engaged in production work, mostly in agriculture. The system was introduced in 1810, and, in the course of its development, local inhabitants were combined with select groups of the military units to form what came to be known as a Military Colony (*voennoe poselenie*). In these military colonies the military system of organization remained in force. Individual military settlements were combined into regional organizations. According to Platonov, "the object of these colonies was to replenish the regular army easily, cheaply, and efficiently. Neither of these objectives was attained. . . . The settlers . . . were poor farmers and worthless soldiers." (S. F. Platonov, *A History of Russia*, New York, 1925, p. 331).

EARLY OPPOSITION TO TROTSKY'S MILITARIZATION PLAN

The stenographic records of the Third Congress of Councils of National Economy have never been published and the attitude its members took toward Trotsky's advocacy of universal compulsion in labor management is not known. The resolutions of the Congress, however, were made public, and they provide a few glimpses into the frame of mind of the Congress on this crucial issue of labor militarization. Three of these resolutions are cited below.

In the first, only brief mention is made of the theses of the Party Central Committee. It was merely stated, in one short sentence, that the "theses" of the Central Committee of the Russian Communist Party "were accepted unanimously." This method of handling an important party document was not in conformity with the established ritual that was followed in Soviet congresses. Usually, a resolution that was introduced by the Communist group and adopted by the congress was cited in full. This time, however, it was merely stated that the resolution was unanimously approved, even though it was generally known that Rykov, the Chairman of the Supreme Council of National Economy—as well as a number of Presidium members of this body—was opposed to the policy of labor militarization.

Another breach of Soviet protocol was the fact that the resolution on labor discipline was adopted in connection with Rykov's report rather than that of Trotsky, who spoke for the Party Central Committee. The resolution itself (cited below) is rather mild in comparison with the harsh measures advocated by Trotsky. The resolution on the organization and management of industry shows, moreover, that a majority of the All-Russian Congress of

Councils of National Economy was clearly opposed to the Draconian measures that Trotsky advocated. In opposition to Trotsky's proposals, the Congress recommended that the organizational machinery of industrial management, on both its highest and its lowest levels, should be formed in close co-operation with the trade unions. It also recommended that economic organizations be protected against interference from political and administrative agencies that were devoid of any relation to economic problems (a clear reference to the Commissariats of War and Internal Affairs and to the *Cheka*, which were placed in charge of labor mobilization).[20] Another recommendation was that the system of extraordinary commissions and of commissars with special powers be abolished because they only interfered with the economic development of the country.

These recommendations had little effect on Bolshevik policies toward labor during 1920. The trade unions were largely ignored. The Commissariats of War and Internal Affairs, together with the *Cheka*, were the principal agencies through which Soviet labor policies were applied. And extraordinary commissions and political commissars with special powers were extensively used in enforcing compulsory labor policies.

RESOLUTION OF THE THIRD ALL-RUSSIAN CONGRESS
OF COUNCILS OF NATIONAL ECONOMY

[Adopted January 26, 1920][21]

The theses of the Central Committee of the Russian Communist Party relating to the mobilization of the industrial proletariat, compulsory labor, militarization of the economy, and the employ-

---

[20] See paragraph 20 of the theses (p. 98, above).
[21] *Rezolyutsii tretego Vserossiyskogo sezda sovetov narodnogo khozyaystva,* Moscow, 1920, p. 22.

ment of army formations for economic tasks were accepted unanimously.

LABOR DISCIPLINE

[Resolution of the Third All-Russian Congress of
Councils of National Economy, January 26, 1920][22]

The decisive defeat of the Whiteguard Armies and the reunification with Soviet Russia of the basic sources of raw materials and fuel make it possible, by relying on the increased strength of Soviet economic organizations and the trade unions, to reestablish the economic position of the republic.

The continued development of the republic of Soviets and the satisfaction of the urgent needs of the workers and peasants will depend wholly on future successes in organizing the economy and raising labor productivity. In order to attain these goals, it is necessary to take decisive measures for the organization of labor and for increasing its productivity in the following ways:

1. Adopting radical measures for provisioning labor with food and other articles of prime necessity. At the same time, the food conditions of technical personnel should also be improved.

2. Introducing strict labor discipline in every branch of production. With this in view, the activity of the trade unions should be increased and the functions of the Disciplinary Courts, established by the decree of the *Sovnarkom*, of November 16, 1919, intensified.

3. Consistently and systematically applying compulsory labor to the entire population and utilizing army forces for productive labor.

4. Recovering skilled workers from the army and the rural areas and employing them in productive work.

5. Increasing the cadres of skilled workers by establishing special schools and courses.

6. Gradually introducing labor books, beginning with the most responsible categories of labor (skilled workers, technicians and engineers).

7. Undertaking a more careful registration of engineers and technicians and using them in their special fields.

[22] *Ibid.*, p. 23.

ADMINISTRATION OF NATIONALIZED INDUSTRY

[Excerpts from the Resolution of the Third All-Russian
Congress of Councils of National Economy, January 26, 1920][23]

7. The organizational machinery of industrial management
must lean upon the industrial trade unions, which are one of the
most important organizing forces of the national economy. The
organic connection which is developing in the more important
branches of industry between the economic administrative organs
and the trade unions should be extended to other branches of the
national economy. The following regulations are to be observed:
[In the four subsections under paragraph 7, procedures are given
for the formation of management boards on the various levels of
the industrial hierarchy, viz., All-Russian, *Guberniya*, regional,
and plant.]

8. The most important problem of the country's economic
policy should be decided upon at the joint sessions of the Supreme
Council of National Economy and the Presidium of the All-
Russian Central Council of Trade Unions. Individual trade
unions have the right to exercise control over the conditions existing in individual branches of industry or individual plants and
to discuss with the *Glavki* and *Tsentry* all essential problems relating to production. Individual trade unions are also entitled to
receive reports from the *Glavki, Tsentry*, and plant administrations relating to their work and may request needed information.

9. Business management of industry, as well as all administrative functions, belong exclusively to the Main Administrations,
departments and other organs of the Supreme Council of National
Economy. Trade-union representatives within the *Glavki* and
other agencies of economic administration are subordinate to the
Presidium of the Supreme Council of National Economy.

11. Administration of nationalized industry is to be based on
the principle of collegiality. The participation of trade unions and

[23] *Ibid.*, p. 11–14. Only the parts of the resolution that deal with the relation
between the Councils of National Economy and the trade unions were translated. The first six paragraphs are a defense of economic centralization, which
is characterized as "the basic instrument of national-economic management by
the victorious proletariat."

the laboring masses in the economic life of the country can be secured only on the basis of the principle of collegiality. The collegium of a plant administration must not exceed 3–5 individuals; of a Main Administration, 5–7 individuals. One-man management, in specific cases, may be introduced only with the consent of the appropriate trade union.

14. Economic organizations should be protected against interference in their administrative-executive functions by departments, organizations, and political and administrative agencies which have no relation to economic activity. Orders which have not received the approval of the Supreme Council of National Economy or the *Guberniya* Council of National Economy are not binding upon enterprises under their jurisdiction.

The institution of extraordinary commissars in charge of production and with special powers should be liquidated, since such methods of production management can only retard economic construction and the development of the productive forces of the R.S.F.S.R.

B. The Institutional Framework of Compulsory Labor

The first steps taken by the Soviet government toward implementing its policy of labor militarization were to legalize the system, by a decree of January 29, 1920, and to institutionalize it a few days later by establishing an interdepartmental committee to take charge of the mobilization and distribution of the entire labor force of the country. This committee was known as *Glavkomtrud*,[24] and it had subordinate committees in almost every administrative subdivision of the Soviet state. In its operations, *Glavkomtrud* employed the existing machinery of military mobilization for the recruitment of civilian labor.

---

[24] From *Glavnyy komitet po vseobshchey trudovoy povinnosti* ("Central Committee on Universal Compulsory Labor").

LEGALIZATION OF COMPULSORY LABOR

[Decree of the *Sovnarkom*, January 29, 1920][25]

Taking its stand on the Fundamental Law of the R.S.F.S.R.[26] and the Code of Labor Laws,[27] which require that those capable of working be drawn into socially useful work, in the interests of the socialist society, the Soviet of People's Commissars has resolved to introduce the following measures for the purpose of securing in the shortest possible time the required labor for industry, agriculture, transport, and other branches of the national economy:

1. In conformity with [the principle of] compulsory labor to enact the following:
    a. To call upon the entire working population to perform, in addition to their normal occupations, various kinds of compulsory labor, of an occasional or regular nature, such as procurement of fuel, agricultural work (both in state farms and sometimes in peasant farms), construction work, road repair, snow clearing, hauling, and so forth. (*Note:* In the performance of the above duties, livestock and vehicles are also subject to mobilization if this is found necessary.)
    b. To utilize Red Army and Navy units for the purpose of work.
    c. To withdraw skilled workers from the army and to transfer workers from agriculture and *kustar* [handicraft] enterprises to work in state enterprises, institutions, and other economic establishments.
    d. To enlist persons without regular occupations into useful public work.
    e. To reallocate the available labor in accordance with requirements.

2. The Council of Workers' and Peasants' Defense is charged with the general direction of compulsory labor measures.

3. [The Council of Workers' and Peasants' Defense] is to establish a central committee of universal compulsory labor [*Glavkomtrud*] which is to be subordinate to the Council of Defense and which is to include representatives of the People's Commis-

---

[25] *S.U.R.*, 1920, No. 8, Art. 49.
[26] The reference is to the Soviet constitution of July, 1918.
[27] Published October 31, 1918 (*S.U.R.*, 1918, Nos. 87–88, Art. 905).

sariat of Labor, the People's Commissariat of Internal Affairs, and the People's Commissariat of War. In the provinces there should be established *Guberniya, Uezd*, and—if necessary—City Committees on Compulsory Labor. These are to be subordinate to the corresponding Executive Committees [of Soviets] and are to include representatives of the Commissariat of War, the Administrative Section [of the Commissariat of Internal Affairs], and the Labor Section [of the Commissariat of Labor].

4. The Council of Defense is charged with the duty of proclaiming mobilizations for compulsory labor, which have an all-national significance, and which are listed in paragraph 1 of the present decree. The Council of Defense should also empower the *Guberniya* Executive Committees, the City Executive Committees, and the *Uezd* Executive Committees to proclaim mobilizations for compulsory labor for local needs and in accordance with special instructions of the Central Committee on Compulsory Labor.

Note: Orders issued by the Council of Defense, as well as orders of the Executive Committees, are published locally in the form of orders of the *Guberniya*, City, or *Uezd* Committees on Compulsory Labor.

5A. *Guberniya*, City, and *Uezd* Committees [of Compulsory Labor] are authorized to hand over to the People's Court those guilty of:

a. Evading registration for and appearance to perform compulsory labor;

b. Deserting from work, as well as inciting others to do likewise;

c. Using false documents, as well as fabricating such documents for the purpose of evading compulsory labor;

d. Supplying, in official capacity, deliberately false information for the same purpose;

e. Damaging tools and materials deliberately;

f. Organizing work carelessly and using mobilized labor unproductively;

g. Complying in the above acts and concealing those guilty.

5B. In especially malicious cases and in cases of repeated offenses the Committees on Compulsory Labor have the right to hand over the culprits for trial before the Revolutionary Tribunal.

5C. In cases of minor infractions of labor discipline the Committees on Compulsory Labor have the right to punish the offenders—by assigning them to punitive labor units or imprisoning them for periods of not longer than one week, by decision of the *Uezd* Committee, and for two weeks by decision of the *Guberniya* Committee.

V. ULYANOV (LENIN)
Chairman of the Sovnarkom

STATUTE OF COMMITTEES ON COMPULSORY LABOR

[Decree of the *Sovnarkom*, February 3, 1920][28]

1. For the purpose of establishing a system of universal compulsory labor and of consolidating the activities of the various agencies engaged in this field of work, a Central Committee on Universal Compulsory Labor, as well as *Guberniya, Uezd*, and, whenever necessary, City Committees on Compulsory Labor, are herewith created. These Committees are charged with full responsibility for the actual introduction of every variety and form of compulsory labor.

2. The Central Committee is directly subordinate to the Council of Defense and consists of three members—one each from the Commissariat of Internal Affairs, the Commissariat of Labor, and the Commissariat of War. The membership of the Central Committee is appointed by the Council of Defense [and] the membership of local Committees by the corresponding Executive Committees of Soviets.

3. The *Guberniya*, City, and *Uezd* Committees are directly subordinate to the *Guberniya*, City, and *Uezd* Executive Committees of Soviets, and each committee consists of three members— one representing the Commissariat of War, one the Administrative Department [of the Commissariat of Internal Affairs], and one the Labor Section [of the Commissariat of Labor].

Note: The Central Committee and the local Committees of Compulsory Labor are to include representatives of the Central Statistical Administration and its local organs, who will act in a consultative capacity only.

4. The Central Committee of Universal Compulsory Labor has the following duties:

[28] *Ibid.*, 1920, No. 8, Art. 50.

a. Coordinating plans developed by production and economic organizations generally for supplying the various branches of the economy with labor, with the aim of enlisting the population in the performance of compulsory labor and the proper distribution of the available labor force.

b. Determining procedures for the application of the various forms of compulsory labor; developing for local Committees instructions relating to questions of compulsory labor; and presenting plans relating to these decisions to the Council of Defense.

c. Utilizing the administrative machinery of the various departments for the purpose of carrying out compulsory labor as well as coordinating the activities of the various departments in this field.

d. Solving all problems arising in the course of enforcing compulsory labor.

5. *Guberniya,* City, and *Uezd* Committees on Compulsory Labor have the following duties:

a. Issuing announcements in the form of special orders based on decisions of the Council of Defense and the Executive Committees [of Soviets] relating to the introduction of one or another form of compulsory labor.

b. Studying labor-force requirements for local needs, setting priorities to meet these needs, and distributing the labor force recruited in accordance with the provisions for compulsory labor.

c. Utilizing the apparatus of local organs for the purpose of introducing compulsory labor, as well as coordinating the activities of these local organs.

d. Solving local problems connected with the introduction of compulsory labor.

e. Inflicting punishment, by administrative action, within the limits provided for in paragraph 5 of the Decree of the Central Executive Committee of January 29 of this year.[29]

6. All orders of the Central Committee on Compulsory Labor are binding on local (*Guberniya,* City, and *Uezd*) Committees. Orders of the *Guberniya* Committees are binding on City and *Uezd* Committees.

[29] See the preceding document.

7. In case of disagreement of local Executive Committees with the orders of the Central Committee on Compulsory Labor, the Executive Committees can lodge complaints with the Council of Defense, but in no case can they stop the execution of these orders.

V. ULYANOV (LENIN)
Chairman of the Sovnarkom

FELIX DZERZHINSKY, CHAIRMAN OF THE "CHEKA," APPOINTED CHAIRMAN OF THE CENTRAL COMMITTEE ON COMPULSORY LABOR

On February 19, 1920, the *Sovnarkom* resolved to increase the membership of the Central Committee on Compulsory Labor from three to five: a chairman and four members. Two members from the Commissariat of War, one member from the Commissariat of Internal Affairs, and one member from the Commissariat of Labor. Serebryakov and Danilov were to represent the Commissariat of War; Vasilev, the Commissariat of Internal Affairs; and Anikst the Commissariat of Labor.[30] Felix Dzerzhinsky was made chairman. His appointment, in all likelihood, was made in the expectation that the reputation he had gained as chairman of the dreaded Extraordinary Commission to Fight Counterrevolution would frighten people into taking the new Compulsory Labor Committee seriously.

In addition to the Committees on Compulsory Labor, Commissions on Compulsory Labor also were established. These were attached to factories and plants, and their principal duties were to supervise the conscripted members of the industrial labor force.[31] Front and Army Commit-

[30] *Izvestiya glavnogo komiteta po vseobshchey trudovoy povinnosti*, No. 1, March, 1920, p. 16.
[31] *Ibid.*, p. 72.

tees on Compulsory Labor also were set up by decree of the Council of Defense (April 21, 1920).

The document that follows is a review of the early operations of *Glavkomtrud*, and it was issued for the benefit of the delegates of the Ninth Party Congress, which was in session between March 29 and April 4, 1920.

EARLY ACTIVITY OF "GLAVKOMTRUD"

[From a report by A. Anikst, prepared for the delegates of the Ninth Party Congress, March, 1920][32]

The application of compulsory labor requires a well-organized and -ramified apparatus. This apparatus was established as a combination of representatives of three institutions which are directly involved in the problem. These institutions are: (1) Sections of Labor of the Commissariat of Labor, whose subsections—Registration and Distribution of the Labor Force—were already engaged in the registration and distribution of the labor force, mostly skilled labor; (2) Administrative Departments [of the Commissariat of the Interior] which, in the capacity of organs of compulsion, were already in charge of introducing compulsory labor for the rural population; and (3) War Commissariats which were experienced in carrying through mobilizations of large masses of the population.

The combination of the three institutions within the Committee of Compulsory Labor (with the assistance of the statistical departments) is the amalgamated machinery which, with the assistance of the trade unions, is charged with the duty of carrying out the policy of universal compulsory labor. The differentiation of functions of the component parts of this machinery has been defined by an order of *Glavkomtrud*, which outlined the general direction of the work. Special variations within this combination are inevitable, but they do not change the essentials of the task, which requires that the component parts be completely subordinated to the Committee on Compulsory Labor, thus ensuring the

---

[32] A. Anikst, *Stati i doklady za 1918–1920 po organizatsii raspredeleniya rabochey sily*, Moscow, 1921, p. 102.

unity of will [in the work of these organizations]. In this kind of work there is no room for interdepartmental friction. It requires a purely matter-of-fact attitude and *Glavkomtrud* will have to make every effort to develop its work along these lines.

By way of expanding its machinery, *Glavkomtrud* is trying to penetrate into the dense masses of the village population by utilizing the local administrative organs and by establishing city, *uezd*, and *guberniya* Committees of Compulsory Labor. Another important step is the establishment of Commissions of Compulsory Labor for every [industrial] enterprise and institution, which will ensure the extension of compulsory labor to hired personnel.

People not engaged in socially useful labor are in a special category. Conscription for compulsory labor for this group is in the hands of a special commission (consisting of representatives of the Extraordinary Commission to Fight Counterrevolution and the Administrative Departments [of the Commissariat of the Interior]) and the Department of Justice. The aim is to utilize this group of the population on a wide scale.

ARMY AND FRONT COMMITTEES FOR COMPULSORY LABOR

[Decree of the Council of Labor and Defense, April 21, 1920][33]

Supplementing the Decree of the *Sovnarkom* on Universal Compulsory Labor (*S.U.R.*, 1920, No. 8, Art. 49),[34] the Council of Labor and Defense decrees :

1. The Central Committee on Universal Compulsory Labor has a right, in agreement with the Revolutionary Military Council of the Republic, to organize Front and Army Committees on Universal Compulsory Labor, under the chairmanship of a member of the corresponding Revolutionary Military Council and with the participation of representatives of the People's Commissariat of Labor and the People's Commissariat of Internal Affairs

2. The Committees of Universal Compulsory Labor, attached to the Revolutionary Military Council of a front and of separate armies (with the status of a front), are under the jurisdiction of the Central Committee on Universal Compulsory Labor.

[The remaining four clauses of this decree give an outline of

[33] *S.U.R.*, 1920, No. 30, Art. 149.
[34] See pp. 110–12 (above).

the hierarchy of Front Committees for Compulsory Labor and the order of subordination.]

V. Ulyanov (Lenin)
*Chairman of the Council
of Labor and Defense*

C. The Ninth Party Congress Approves Compulsory Labor

The problems of compulsory labor, after this system had been in full operation for almost three months, came up for detailed consideration and approval at the Ninth Party Congress, which met from March 29 to April 4, 1920. Lenin gave full endorsement to the policy of compulsory labor and castigated the "bourgeois democrats" who expressed indignation against compulsion. He assured his audience that "the proletariat has the right to resort to compulsion in order to maintain itself at all costs."

Trotsky restated his position on labor militarization, which he had developed at the Third Congress of Councils of National Economy,[35] and pleaded for a regime under which "every worker feels himself a soldier."

Several critics opposed the militarization aspects of the resolution which had been introduced on behalf of the Party Central Committee. Thus V. Osinsky, although he did not object to the principle of militarization in the economic sphere, warned against excessive militarization and "the blind acceptance of military models." He took particular exception to Trotsky's notion that every worker must feel himself a soldier. "We object," Osinsky said, "to a mechanical militarization of the Party and the Soviets . . . , to the subordination of civilian to military agencies." Osinsky, moreover, charged that unpublished

[35] See pp. 102–4 (above).

clauses in Trotsky's theses advocated the replacement of Party organizations with special political departments, of the *Glavpolitput* type,[36] and that Stalin—who was placed in charge of the Ukrainian Labor Army—had already established such political departments in the Donets coal basin.

Rykov, Chairman of the Supreme Council of National Economy, expressed the view that labor armies cannot play a decisive role in improving economic conditions and that better results in industrial revival could be achieved by partially demobilizing the army and thus making more food and clothing available for workers.[37]

These and other dissenting voices hardly affected the outcome of the Ninth Party Congress. The resolution that was adopted fully approved the theses of the Party Central Committee, which called for a general mobilization of labor for compulsory work, the organization of production along military lines, and the employment of army formations for civilian labor tasks.

LENIN ENDORSES THE MILITARIZATION OF LABOR

[Excerpt from Lenin's speech at the Ninth Party Congress,
March 29, 1920][38]

. . . I now pass to the most important consideration of principles which induced us to direct the toiling masses with such determination to use the army for the solution of the basic current problems. The old source of discipline—capitalism—is undermined; the old source of unification has disappeared. We must create a different kind of discipline, a different source of discipline and unity. Compulsion provokes the indignation, howls and outcries of the bourgeois democrats, who make great play of the words "freedom" and "equality," but do not understand that free-

---

[36] See p. 123 (below).
[37] *Devyatyy sezd Rossiyskoy kommunisticheskoy partii*, p. 113.
[38] *Ibid.*, p. 16.

dom for capitalists is a crime against the toilers. In our fight against falsehood we are introducing labor service, thereby uniting the toilers. We are not afraid of using compulsion for nowhere has a revolution ever been effected without compulsion, and the proletariat has the right to resort to compulsion in order to maintain itself at all costs. When these bourgeois gentlemen, these compromisers, the German Independents, the Austrian Independents, and the French followers of Longuet, argue about the historical factor they always forget a factor like the revolutionary determination, steadfastness and inflexibility of the proletariat. At a moment when the capitalist countries and the capitalist class are disintegrating, at a moment of [capitalist] crisis and despair, the only decisive factor is the political factor. Talk about minority and majority, about democracy and freedom, decides nothing, whatever the heroes of the past historical period may say. It is the class-consciousness and firmness of the working class that count here. If the working class is prepared to make sacrifices, if it has shown that it is able to strain every nerve, the problem will be solved. . . .

"EVERY WORKER A SOLDIER"

[Excerpts from Trotsky's speech at the Ninth Party Congress, March 30, 1920][39]

Comrades! History is bringing us face to face with the task of organizing labor. Basically the organization of labor is the organization of a new society, because historically every form of society is the form of labor organization. We are organizing or are beginning to organize labor on a new socialist basis. In the past, society consisted of a compulsory organization of labor in the interests of the minority, which had the power to exert compulsion over the overwhelming majority of the laboring masses. But now, for the first time in history, we are attempting to organize labor in the interest of the toiling majority itself. This, of course, does not imply the elimination of compulsion, which will continue to play a great role during a rather extended historical period.

[Trotsky went on to develop his theory of human nature, ac-

[39] *Ibid.*, pp. 79–81.

cording to which man is essentially a lazy being, and his belief that the purpose of social organization is to impose limits on laziness and to force people to work.]

In approaching the problem of economic reconstruction on a communist basis, we are directly confronted with the question of militarization. A good many articles, meetings and discussions are devoted to this problem of militarization. A number of comrades, including well-known workers in the trade unions, express the view that they are not against militarization as such but cannot understand its meaning.

Comrade Smirnov and others agree with the necessity of mobilizing the peasants. But, Comrade Smirnov says that in industry and in the case of skilled labor there is no need for military organization, since the trade unions are already performing the task of organizing labor. Such an approach to the problem indicates a complete lack of understanding of the nature of the turning point in our national economy, which is taking place at the present time. To be sure, the difference between the proletarian labor force organized in trade unions and the peasant labor force functioning as a military organization is tremendous. The militarization in the first instance will have to be carried out quite differently than in the second. Nonetheless, to reduce the question of the organization of skilled labor to the mere existence of trade unions, and to think that trade unions, which are still organized in the form in which we inherited them [from the past], would solve the labor problem as it concerns skilled workers is to show a complete lack of understanding of the problem.

Under capitalism skilled labor was bought in the open market at a fixed price and was shifted from place to place in accordance with [the law of] supply and demand. This was called hired or free labor. The trade unions have grown out of the need of free labor to unite and to better its conditions by strikes and other forms of struggle. But who is now the distributor of the labor force and who shifts it to places where it is needed in the interests of the socialist economy? The trade unions, on orders of economic organizations. What are the methods used to ensure that a worker who was sent to place A actually went to place A? The worker no longer moves from factory to factory, from plant to plant of his own free will, as he is presumed to have done under capitalism. Now he is being shifted and he has to shift in accordance with a single economic plan, on orders from central economic organizations. Consequently the workers are now "tied down" to the factories and plants. While some workers view this condition as a service and obligation dictated by the need of improving the national economy, others cannot make sense of it; still others, the most backward workers, consider it all naked compulsion, and resist it. That there are such workers is clearly shown by trade-union statistics. In the most important branches of industry there are listed 1,150,000 workers, but actually only 850,000 are on hand. Where are the other 300,000? They have gone. Where to? Maybe to the village, perhaps to other branches of industry, or they may have joined the ranks of the speculators. A soldier would say that we have 300,000 deserters for every 800,000 effectives. What is to be done about it? In the army there is a special apparatus to force a soldier to carry out his duty. In one form or another the same should be used in the sphere of labor. If we are serious about a planned economy, centrally directed, then labor must be distributed, shifted and ordered in the same way that soldiers are. This is the basis of labor militarization, without which it is ridiculous to talk about organizing industry on a new basis. . . .

The militarization of labor is unthinkable without the militarization of trade unions, without the introduction of a regime under which every worker feels himself a soldier of labor who cannot dispose of himself freely. If an order is given to transfer him, he must carry it out. If he does not carry it out, he will be a deserter who is punished. Who looks after this? The trade union. It creates the new regime. This is the militarization of the working class. . . .

THE DEMOCRATIC CENTRALISTS OPPOSE EXTREME FORMS
OF LABOR MILITARIZATION

[Excerpts from Osinsky's speech at the Ninth Party Congress, March 30, 1920][40]

. . . First of all, I would like to justify the amendment which we are introducing on the question of militarization.

[40] *Ibid.*, pp. 99–100.

What is happening now at the Congress is the clash of a number of cultures, since our work of [socialist] construction has given rise to a number of cultures. We have created a military-Soviet culture, a civilian-Soviet culture, and the trade-union movement has created its own sphere of culture. Each of these cultures has its own approach to events and has created its own routine. Comrade Trotsky has posed the question from the point of view of a man who came from the sphere of military culture; we are approaching it from the point of view of the civilian sphere; and, finally, the trade-union comrades have posed it in a rather peculiar and inferior way, since they have been arguing all along that the working class needs to be protected against militarization, that labor should be free, etc.

I should like, in the first place, to make it clear that we approached the problem of militarization before anybody else had taken it up, but we approached it from another angle. I mention this not because I wish to glorify anybody. The question of applying combat and military forms of organization and administration was first raised by us. I, therefore, reject outright the assumption that we oppose militarization as such. . . . We are against stretching the concept of militarization too far; we are against the blind imitation of military models.

We believe that our Party centers interpret militarization in a much wider and a more definitive sense. Previously, in Trotsky's January theses, it was stated: "The militarization of the economy means that economic questions (labor productivity, careful handling of machinery and tools, conscientious use of materials, etc.) must be treated on the same footing as questions of military combat." At that time Trotsky made a distinction between militarization as a general concept and the complete and formal militarization ("freezing" workers at their enterprises, imposing penalties) to be enacted "in every case by special decrees of the Council of [Labor and] Defense." But now the distinction between the two has been obliterated. Trotsky is now posing the problem in a way [requiring] that every worker must look upon himself as a soldier. . . .

We understand the problem [41] as necessitating the introduction

[41] *Ibid.*, pp. 101–2.

of combat methods of organization and administration into the civilian apparatus and cannot, therefore, accept mechanical ways of "militarizing" the Party and the Soviets. We do not agree with the subordination of civilian institutions to military organizations. We do not need militarization, because within our civilian apparatus there is an organic gravitation toward military methods of operation. Please, do not force us to go places we do not want to go, and do not break up the existing system of administration.

When it is a question of turning the Labor Armies into regional organs in charge of economic administration, you need not tell us that the Labor Armies will act in conformity with the decisions of the Seventh Congress [of Soviets]. We are convinced that this will result not merely in the subordination of the civilian apparatus to the military but will lead to colossal confusion. This has always happened at the front, whenever military and civilian institutions came into conflict. We have absolutely nothing against the Labor Armies and we welcome them. They should be utilized for purposes of labor. But what you are doing is implanting bureaucracy under the flag of militarization and we are against it. It is possible that Comrade Trotsky will succeed in persuading a number of comrades, but I am convinced that the forthcoming Congress of Soviets, with the experience of militarization behind it, will adopt our point of view. I repeat: Do not try to break up the existing machinery [of government] under the flag of militarization. Do not propagate bureaucracy, and, please, do not pull us by a leash toward one-man management. . . .

In the unpublished part [42] of Comrade Trotsky's theses there was raised the question what to do with democratic centralism in the domain of Party work. The answer was: Replace the Party organizations with political departments, not only on the railways, but in all the basic branches of industry. Comrade Stalin, whom I highly respect, even though I disagree with him on this question, has already anticipated Trotsky's idea and has already established a political department for the Donets coal industry. . . .

Of the thirteen resolutions passed by the Ninth Party Congress, the one entitled "Current Tasks of Economic

[42] *Ibid.*, p. 106.

Reconstruction" was the most heatedly debated. It is a long, drawn-out document that contains twenty sections and deals with a miscellany of subjects. It begins with a claim of improvements in labor productivity, which allegedly have taken place, and then enumerates the measures the Party considered essential for the reconstruction of the economy on a new socialist foundation.

Only the sections that deal with the Communist policy toward labor are included in the excerpts that follow. Section II is summarized as an illustration of the system of priorities of the Communists at this incipient stage of economic planning. It shows that, even at this period of the country's utter economic exhaustion, the preferences of the planners were for producers' goods, and consumers' goods were assigned the lowest priority. Thus a precedent was set for the future economic development of the Soviet state.

"CURRENT TASKS OF ECONOMIC RECONSTRUCTION"

[Excerpts from the Resolution of the Ninth Party Congress, March 31, 1920][43]

I. On the Improvement of Labor

The Congress acknowledges with satisfaction the undisputed signs of labor improvement among the advanced strata of the toilers. However, it considers it its duty to forewarn all local and central institutions of the Soviet Republic not to exaggerate the results already achieved. Real victories in the field of labor can be achieved only if, in the first place, the Party and the trade unions, through propaganda and organizational efforts, turn their attention to the multimillion masses in the cities and the villages, and if, in the second place, the central and local economic organizations take all necessary measures to utilize adequately and

[43] *Devyatyy sezd Rossiyskoy kommunisticheskoy partii*, pp. 371–81. Trotsky claimed the authorship of this resolution, which is included in his collected works (Trotsky, *Sochineniya*, XV, 114–28).

in time the newly arriving labor and to overcome the fragmentation of effort by working within the framework of a national plan.

II. The Unified Economic Plan
[The basic prerequisite for the economic reconstruction of the country is the adoption of a unified economic plan which is to be subdivided into the following consecutive stages:
  a. Improvement of the transportation system.
  b. Machine building for transport and extracting industries.
  c. Machine building for the production of consumers' goods.
  d. Production of consumers' goods.
Electrification, which is to serve as the technological underpinning of the plan, is to be developed in a sequence corresponding to the basic stages of the general economic plan.]

III. Mobilization of Skilled Workers
Approving the theses of the Central Committee of the Russian Communist Party dealing with the mobilization of the industrial proletariat, labor conscription, the militarization of economic life, and the employment of army units for economic tasks, the Congress resolves:

The party organizations should assist in every way the trade unions and the Labor Section [of the Commissariat of Labor] in registering all skilled workers, for the purpose of drawing them into productive work, with the same orderliness with which the commanding personnel were mobilized for the needs of the army.

Every skilled worker must be returned to work at his trade. Exceptions, i.e., the retention of skilled workers for other Soviet work, are permitted only with the consent of the appropriate organs of authority either at the center or locally.

IV. Mass Mobilization for Compulsory Labor
From the very beginning, mass mobilization for compulsory labor must be placed on a proper foundation. On every such occasion a precise balance, as far as possible, must be established between the number of persons mobilized, the place of their concentration, the magnitude of their tasks, and the number of tools required. It is equally important to provide the labor units which are formed by mobilized persons with technically competent and politically reliable instructors and with Communist cells selected

through a Party mobilization. In other words, we must go along the same road as in the creation of the Red Army.[44]

V. Labor Competition

Every social order, whether based on slavery, serfdom, or capitalism, had its own methods and means of labor compulsion and labor training in the interests of the exploiters.

The Soviet regime is faced with the task of developing its own method of compulsion to attain an increase in the productivity and the efficient use of labor; this method is to be based on the socialization of the national economy in the interests of the whole people. Socialist competition, which will serve as a powerful instrument for raising the productivity of labor, is just as important as the agitation and propaganda among the toiling masses and the measures of repression taken against idlers, parasites and disorganizers.

In capitalist society competition assumed the character of rivalry and led to the exploitation of man by man. In a society in which the means of production are nationalized, labor competition is bound to increase the output of labor without infringing upon its solidarity. Competition between factories, regions, shops and individual workers must be carefully organized and studied by the trade unions and the economic organizations.

A system of premiums should become one of the powerful means of stimulating competition. The system of food supply is to be in accordance with this. As long as the Soviet Republic is short of food supplies, the industrious and conscientious worker should be better provided for than a careless worker.

[Sections VI to X deal with the organizational framework of Soviet industry as it was being developed by the Supreme Council of National Economy. Section XI, "On the Employment of Specialists in Industry," is quoted as a separate document, after this one. Section XII, entitled *Glavpolitput,* is included in Chap-

---

[44] An interesting illustration of present-day Soviet historical scholarship is to be found in the 1960 edition of *Proceedings of the Ninth Party Congress,* sponsored by the Institute of Marxism-Leninism. In the Introduction to this edition the editor makes the following observation: "Trotsky proposed to use military methods for peaceful economic construction. The Congress categorically rejected Trotsky's proposals by showing their utter inconsistency." *Devyatyy sezd RKP(b),* Moscow, 1960, p. X.

ter V, which deals with the militarization of the railway system; and Section XIII deals with problems of food supply.]

XIV. Labor Armies

The use of military units for labor tasks is important as a practical economic measure as well as for its value for socialist education. The conditions for effective use of soldiers' labor on a large scale are as follows:

a. The simple character of the work, which can easily be performed by all Red Army men.
b. Application of the method of specific assignments, with reduction of rations as the penalty for nonfulfillment.
c. Application of the bonus system.
d. Participation in the work of a given labor sector by a considerable number of Communists, capable of instilling enthusiasm among the Red Army units by their example.

When large military units are utilized for labor, it is bound to happen that a high percentage of Red Army men will not be directly engaged in production. Therefore, the use of entire labor armies, while the army commanding staff is kept intact, can be justified only insofar as it is necessary to preserve the army as a whole for military purposes. As soon as the latter need disappears, the unwieldy staffs and administrative departments must be dissolved, while the best elements from among the skilled workers should be utilized as small shock-labor detachments at the most important industrial establishments.

XV. Labor Desertion

In view of the fact that a large number of workers, in search of better food conditions and often for the purpose of speculation, are leaving their jobs without permission and moving about from place to place, thereby dealing further blows to production and debasing the general condition of the working class, the Congress considers it one of the urgent problems of the Soviet government and of the trade-union organizations to undertake a systematic, persistent, and relentless campaign against labor desertion by publishing lists of deserters who are liable to punishment, by forcing the deserters into penal work battalions, and finally by imprisoning them in concentration camps.

[The last five sections of the resolution deal with such topics as *subbotniks* (i.e., the performance of free work on Saturdays), the repair of locomotives, the organization of model plants, production of more paper for printing propaganda, and postponing the First of May celebration to Saturday and turning it into a grandiose *subbotnik*.]

ONE-MAN MANAGEMENT VERSUS COMMITTEE MANAGEMENT

In addition to endorsing labor conscription, the Ninth Party Congress resolved two other issues that had been a constant bone of contention among Bolshevik leaders throughout the early period of Soviet rule. One of the issues pertained to the employment of "bourgeois specialists" in the capacity of industrial managers; the other was concerned with industrial management generally—whether it should be in the hands of a committee or of one man.

The committee system of plant management sprang into prominence toward the end of 1918, after the collapse of workers' control. Trade unions and workers' councils favored the committee system (*kollegialnost*) because they were, to some extent, its beneficiaries. As a general rule, one-third of the management committee of a plant, trust, or Main Administration consisted of trade-union appointees; one-third represented the scientific and technical personnel; and one-third represented the Supreme Council of National Economy.[45] The Third All-Russian Congress of Councils of National Economy approved the committee system of industrial management, although—in special cases—one-man management also was recommended, provided the trade unions approved of this.[46]

There was a good deal of opposition to the committee

---

[45] Bunyan, *Intervention, Civil War and Communism in Russia*, p. 416.
[46] See p. 109 (above).

system of industrial management, and this came mainly from the disciplinarian school of labor management, which was searching for new forms of labor control and of labor's submission to authority. The typical attitude of this school of industrial management was expressed in an article by Goltsman, a follower and close collaborator of Trotsky, which appeared in *Pravda* on March 26, 1920— only three days before the Ninth Party Congress met.

"Should the working class," Goltsman asked, "build its economic system with the hands of the least able of its children, or should we call upon the most talented and gifted to do this work?" He answered: "It is quite clear that the working class must depend upon the exceptional and the more gifted of its sons. The principle of collegiality is irreconcilable with the selection of the most talented workers. Running throughout the entire economic apparatus, the principle of collegiality in management is paralyzing responsibility for whatever is being done in this field."

At the Ninth Party Congress, the Democratic Centralists—a small opposition group within the Communist Party—came out against the policy of one-man management. Their spokesman, Osinsky, attacked Lenin and Trotsky for trying to lead the Party "on a leash" to one-man management.[47] Osinsky argued that "collegiality" was a superior form of management because it provided training in industrial administration for large numbers of workers.[48]

The resolution the Congress adopted was—in form—a compromise between the two opposing standpoints; in substance, however, it was a victory for the disciplinarians. It sanctioned the adoption of the principle of committee man-

[47] See p. 123 (above).
[48] *Devyatyy sezd Rossiyskoy kommunisticheskoy partii*, p. 102.

agement for the intermediary and higher echelons of the industrial hierarchy (i.e., combines, *Glavki*, and the S.C.N.E.), but, at the lower echelons (shops, plants, and factories), there was to be one-man management.[49] This resolution permitted Trotsky to administer the transport system through appointed political commissars, and over the heads of the trade unions.[50]

The other issue, that of employing bourgeois specialists as industrial managers, resulted in a clear-cut victory for Lenin, who was greatly in favor of using these specialists in managerial positions. Although Lenin encountered a good deal of antagonism in the Congress on this issue, he succeeded in securing a favorable resolution. An excerpt from this resolution, quoted below, illustrates how far Lenin had shifted from his original theory that every worker was capable of running the state and managing the economy.

THE EMPLOYMENT OF "BOURGEOIS" SPECIALISTS IN INDUSTRY

[Resolution of the Ninth Party Congress, March 31, 1920][51]

Believing that, without a scientific organization of production, even the most extensive application of compulsory labor and the greatest labor heroism of the working class will not only fail to ensure the establishment of a powerful socialist economy but will also fall short of enabling the country to free itself from the clutches of poverty, the Congress considers it imperative to register all capable specialists in the various branches of the economy and to utilize them widely in the organization of production.

While continuing the policy of control and severe punishment of all counterrevolutionary elements striving to utilize their posi-

[49] *Ibid.*, p. 376.
[50] See Chapter V.
[51] *Devyatyy sezd Rossiyskoy kommunisticheskoy partii*, pp. 378–79.

tions for the purpose of hindering the socialist economic regime, the Congress at the same time reminds all members of the Party, in the most categorical form, of the necessity of attracting all specialists into the sphere of Soviet industrial interests by creating a proper ideological atmosphere for this group. Party workers are under obligation to create, in strict conformity with the spirit and letter of our Party program, the conditions of comradely cooperation between workers and technical specialists who were inherited by the proletarian regime from the bourgeoisie.

The Congress believes that the principal aim of production and political propaganda among the great masses of workers is to make clear to them the enormity of the economic tasks facing the country, the importance of technical training and administrative experience. Every Party member is charged with the obligation of carrying on an irreconcilable struggle against that obnoxious form of ignorance and conceit which deems the working class capable of solving all problems without utilizing, in the most responsible positions, the services of specialists of the bourgeois school. Demagogic elements who speculate on this kind of prejudice of the backward section of the working class can have no place in the ranks of the party of scientific socialism. . . .

D. The Third All-Russian Congress of Trade Unions and Labor Conscription

The question of compulsory labor was raised again at the Third All-Russian Congress of Trade Unions, which met April 6–13, 1920, just a few days after the Ninth Party Congress had adjourned. The debates were more acrimonious than those at the Party Congress. There were a few Mensheviks at the Trade-Union Congress, and—to the surprise and consternation of the Bolshevik leadership —the Menshevik attacks on the system of forced labor met with loud applause from the trade-union rank and file.

Lenin was not disturbed by the hostile demonstrations; he gave full support to the policy of labor compulsion and

argued that "labor must be organized in a new way, that
new forms of incentives to work, of submission to labor
discipline, must be found." [52] But Trotsky emerged as the
principal defender of labor militarization. Trotsky ridiculed the idea of free labor and tried to provide a forensic
justification of the position of the Party Central Committee.

Obviously irritated by the opposition to his schemes,
Trotsky gave full play to his grotesque fancy when he
touched upon the origins of free industrial enterprise.
"The bourgeoisie," he said, "first drove the peasant to the
high road and robbed him of his land. When he refused to
work in the factories they branded him with red-hot irons,
hanged him and shot him, and in this way trained him to
work in factories."

TROTSKY'S DEFENSE OF LABOR CONSCRIPTION

[Excerpts from Trotsky's speech at the Third All-Russian
Congress of Trade Unions, April 9, 1920] [53]

. . . Our idea of the militarization of labor differs from the
militarization of the bourgeois world in the same way in which
the organized proletariat differs from the organized bourgeoisie.
The main source of error and prejudice in this question lies in the
identification of the concept of the proletarian and communist
militarization with the bourgeois concept of militarization. And
I should like to say at the very outset that Menshevik criticism of
militarization at this congress and other congresses is based entirely on this confusion. When we talk about militarization of
labor, they tell us that militarization is a bourgeois concept which
leads to anti-proletarian action. The Menshevik resolution states
that militarization of labor leads to low productivity of labor and
the destruction of the labor force because, so the resolution says,
compulsory labor is always unproductive. In saying this they

[52] *Tretiy Vserossiyskiy sezd professionalnykh soyuzov, Gosizdat,* Moscow,
1921, Part 1, p. 25.
[53] *Ibid.,* pp. 87–90.

merely show that they are captives of bourgeois ideology and fail to recognize the very foundations of a socialist economy. . . .

They have formulated the concept of free labor, labor that is freely bought on the market. But what is the free, non-compulsory labor which the Mensheviks advocate? Let the spokesmen of this party explain what is meant by free, non-compulsory labor. We know slave-labor, we know serf-labor, we know the compulsory, regimented labor of the medieval guilds, we have known the hired labor which the bourgeoisie calls free. We are now advancing toward socially regulated labor, on the basis of an economic plan which is compulsory for the whole country, i.e., compulsory for every worker. This is the foundation of socialism. . . .

Compulsory labor means that every worker takes a definite place, assigned to him by the *oblast* or *guberniya* or *uezd* economic institutions. It is regulated labor, governed not by the elemental forces of supply and demand, but based instead on an economic plan which covers the whole country and embraces the whole working class. This is the meaning of compulsory labor which has always been a part of the socialist program. Every worker in the new social order must be a soldier in the labor army and he must obey the orders of the government which he himself has established.

They [the Mensheviks] say that compulsory labor is unproductive. If this is so, then a socialist economy is doomed to failure, because there are no other ways to socialism except by controlled distribution, from one economic center, of the entire labor force of the country in accordance with a national economic plan. Once we have recognized this, we thereby recognize fundamentally—not formally, but fundamentally—the right of the workers' state to send each working man and woman to the place where they are needed for the fulfillment of economic tasks. We thereby recognize the right of the state, the workers' state, to punish the working men or women who refuse to carry out the order of the state, who do not subordinate their will to the will of the working class and to its economic tasks. . . .

If the worker should retain the freedom of selecting the factory, freedom of movement, freedom of leaving a factory in search of better conditions, if he does these things under present conditions of utter disruption of the entire production mechanism and of the transportation system, this is bound to lead to complete economic anarchy, to the complete ruin and pulverization of the working class, to the utter impossibility of anticipating the future of our industry. Militarization of labor in this fundamental sense in which I have used it is the inevitable and basic method of organizing our labor force, [of bringing about] its compulsory grouping in accordance with the requirements of socialism during the period of transition from the reign of capitalism to the communist state. If this new form of compulsory organization and distribution of labor is unproductive, then you might just as well put a cross over socialism.

The evolution of society may be looked upon as the organization of labor in ever new forms for the purpose of raising its productivity. If our new form of labor organization must lead to a decline in productivity, then we are condemned to perdition and defeat, no matter how we maneuver or what effort we make to organize the working class.

Is it true that compulsory labor is always unproductive? My answer to this is that this is the most pitiful and the most vulgar superstition of liberalism. Serf-labor was productive; it was superior to slave-labor. To the extent that serf-labor and the domination of the feudal lords made the cities secure against other feudal plunderers and gave protection to peasant labor, to this extent this was a progressive form of labor. Compulsory serf-labor did not grow out of the evil will of the feudal lords. It was a progressive phenomenon and was supplanted by hired labor. . . . At the outset, hired and free labor were not productive, and he who thinks otherwise is full of liberal superstitions. Free and hired labor became productive only gradually. Social discipline was necessary and all sorts of methods were used to bring this discipline about. The bourgeoisie first drove the peasant on to the high road and robbed him of his land. When he refused to work in the factories they branded him with red-hot irons, hanged him and shot him, and in this way trained him to work in the factories. . . . The bourgeoisie were forced to advertise their system of labor as free and were deceiving simpletons about the productivity of that labor. But we know that all labor is socially compulsory labor. Man must work in order not to die. He does not want to work. But the social organization compels and whips him in that direction. . . .

MENSHEVIKS OPPOSE THE MILITARIZATION OF LABOR

[Excerpts from speeches delivered at the Third
All-Russian Congress of Trade Unions]

DAN: . . . To represent the socialist revolution as a military campaign in which the masses of workers are not the active creators of new forms of social life and social relationships, but are used as a blind army of soldiers under the command of revolutionary specialists, is a monstrous perversion of Marxism.[54] [*Applause from the right.*]

ABRAMOVICH: . . . Trotsky says that compulsory labor is the foundation of a socialist society, that he who opposes compulsory labor is against socialism.[55] This is the first time that I hear it asserted that compulsory labor is the principle on which socialist construction is based. It is not true that labor on which a genuine socialist order can be built is socially compulsory labor. Rather is it labor which results from the consciousness of inner obligation. Trotsky maintains that we must first place an individual under compulsion and use violence, and that in the course of time this violence will become transformed into a feeling of inner obligation to perform socially necessary labor. This is the way Comrade Trotsky advocates. There is an altogether different way, however, which we advocate when we fight against compulsion. Trotsky says: "There is no labor without compulsion. Every labor is compulsory labor." But this is a play of ideas in which the very concept of compulsory labor disappears. When we talk about compulsory labor, we have in mind juridically compulsory labor. When we talk about free labor, we have in mind juridically free labor. Free labor in bourgeois society does not mean that man is free not to work. Juridically he has a right not to work, but hunger compels him to work. When we talk about free labor, there is no concealment of the fact that economically it is compulsory labor. . . .

We are now confronted with the problem of how to organize industry, of deciding what is more rational to do from the point of view of reestablishing industry; whether we should create con-

[54] *Ibid.*, p. 72.
[55] *Ibid.*, pp. 96–97.

ditions that would enable the proletariat to base their work on economic advantage, assisted by a flexible wage system, and self-rule, or whether the proletariat should be forced to work by juridical compulsion, forced to carry out the orders of the state.

Trotsky takes his point of departure from a deep pessimism. He says that people are lazy and would not work unless they are driven by a knout. But we deny the rationality of this method and believe that Socialists should remain in their old position, according to which the construction of socialism should be left to the free initiative of the working masses. This is not a liberalistic superstition but is the essence of human experience, which teaches us that it is impossible to build a planned socialist economy by methods which the Egyptian Pharaohs used in building the pyramids. . . .

The fine distinction that Abramovich made between juridical and economic compulsion apparently had little influence on the Trade-Union Congress, where the preponderant majority was Communist. The resolution adopted by the Congress generally approved Communist policies toward labor and pledged assistance in carrying them out. To make sure that the outside world did not put a wrong interpretation on labor militarization, the Third All-Russian Congress of Trade Unions, on Trotsky's initiative, adopted a resolution that was issued in the form of an appeal to the proletarians of the world. The main objective of the resolution was to create the impression that Soviet militarization of labor was a clear manifestation of the democratic ideal and was initiated by the laboring masses themselves. "We, the workers of Russia," the resolution asserted, "are our own lawgivers, and, having decided on labor militarization, we enforce it ourselves through the medium of our own proletarian organizations."

THE THIRD ALL-RUSSIAN CONGRESS OF TRADE UNIONS
APPEALS TO THE WORKERS OF THE WORLD

[Resolution of the Third Congress of Trade Unions, April 9, 1920][56]

The telegraph, the radio, and the press—these powerful instruments of capitalist lies—have told you many times during the past few weeks about the militarization of labor in Soviet Russia. The lackeys of imperialism are playing for a double stake: they want to slander Socialist Russia and they want to justify their own exploitation of the workers.

The more than fifteen hundred delegates assembled at the Third All-Russian Congress of Trade Unions, who represent over three million industrially organized workers, consider it their duty to warn you in a fraternal manner against both the praises and the abuses of bourgeois public opinion relating to Soviet methods of labor organization.

Our economy is ruined and exhausted by the imperialist slaughter, by the inhuman blockade, and by the ceaseless attacks upon us by the mercenary bands of Churchill and Clemenceau. We now need a supreme effort to free the country from these conditions of misery and privation. This task requires from every toiler of Soviet Russia the maximum of effort and the highest sacrifice. Just as a conscientious Red Army soldier is ready to sacrifice his life at any moment for the workers' cause, so every honest worker, man and woman, must be ready to strain himself to the utmost in the cause of the economic salvation of the socialist republic. We have not, nor can we have, any other aim but that of working energetically for the common good. Firm labor discipline, unshaken solidarity in the fulfillment of economic plans— these are the things we call militarization of labor.

We have no kings, no high-ranking officials, no bourgeois deputies with their ministers, no landlords and capitalists with their agents, no bourgeois generals and judges with their executioners. The methods of militarization of labor are not prescribed to us from above, as before by rapacious exploiters and their

---

[56] *Rezolyutsii III Vserossiyskogo sezda professionalnykh soyuzov*, Moscow, 1921, pp. 55–56. The resolution was written by Trotsky and is reprinted in his *Sochineniya* (XV, 205–6).

plundering state. We, the toilers, of our own free will, undertake this heavy labor which our duty to the revolution and to the generations to come demands from us. The fruits of our heavy toil will not be turned into profits for the parasites but will make life decidedly easier for the working masses who are tired of poverty. We, the workers of Russia, are our own lawgivers, and, having decided on labor militarization, we enforce it ourselves through the medium of our own proletarian organizations.

Proletarians of all countries! In the midst of the intensive struggle and toil we send you our fraternal greetings. We confidently await the hour—and it will not be long in coming—when the workers of the whole capitalist world will overthrow their oppressors, will uproot the inheritance of age-long oppression, insolence, and torture, and will transform this earth into a blossoming land of liberated humanity.

Long live the world union of labor!

THE THIRD ALL-RUSSIAN CONGRESS
OF TRADE UNIONS

CHAPTER IV

APPLICATION OF MILITARIZED FORMS
TO CIVILIAN LABOR

The five main sources from which additional labor could be drawn for the revival of industry were (1) the section of the population that was classified as "the bourgeoisie," (2) skilled workers who fled from the cities into the villages to escape starvation, (3) Red Army units that were due for demobilization but, instead, could be converted into labor armies, (4) penal labor from forced-labor and concentration camps, and (5) the rural population, which could be drafted to perform various kinds of unskilled work.

The first and the fourth sources of labor were somewhat intermingled. Many members of the formerly well-to-do groups of the population found themselves in forced-labor or concentration camps for no other reason than that they were looked upon as the "parasitic" elements of society. Concentration camps also included many political opponents of the regime. The majority of the "bourgeois" population was free, however, but subject to compulsory labor. Figures on the use of these two sources of labor are not available, but, because of the close attention the Central Committee on Compulsory Labor gave these two groups, the figures must have been rather large.[1]

For the second category, about twenty professional mobilizations were promulgated during 1920, affecting every

[1] Frequent references to these groups are found in the publication of the *Glavkomtrud*, entitled *Izvestiya glavnogo komiteta po vseobshchey trudovoy povinnosti* (Nos. 1–7, 1920).

trade and profession. These mobilizations, however, failed to bring about an improvement in industrial employment. On the contrary, the flight of workers from the large industrial centers continued through 1920, despite the Draconian laws enacted against labor desertion. By 1921 the Soviet industrial labor force had decreased by more than 200,000 workers, as compared to the total for the previous year.[2]

Labor armies, although they involved large numbers, made only modest contributions to production, and mainly those of an unskilled nature. The largest group in the forced-labor category came from the rural population.

A. The Labor Armies

Perhaps the most spectacular innovation the Bolsheviks introduced in the Marxist system of economics in 1920 was the creation of labor armies from Red Army formations, which, with the close of the civil war, were no longer needed for combat duty. These armies were given the high-sounding name of Revolutionary Armies of Labor and were assigned, as units, to specific tasks, mostly of an unskilled nature. This innovation was Trotsky's favorite idea, and was associated with his grandiose concept of a unique politico-economic experiment. These labor armies would function as the nuclei of economic-administrative systems that would be in charge of the organization and administration of the entire life of the territories in which they were located, and the communist society of the future would be built around these nuclei.

According to Soviet historiography, the origin of the

[2] See p. 172 (below).

labor armies was due to a spontaneous movement by the Third Red Army.[3] On January 10, 1920—so the story goes—a telegram was received from the commander of the Third Army, which was stationed in the Urals, by the chairman of the Council of Workers' and Peasants' Defense (Lenin) and the chairman of the Revolutionary War Council of the Republic (Trotsky). The telegram suggested transforming the Third Army into a labor army, under the name of the First Revolutionary Army of Labor.

The timing of the telegram and the fact that the employment of army formations for civilian labor tasks was one of Trotsky's cherished ideas justify a strong presumption that Trotsky, the People's Commissar of War, had a hand in the "spontaneous" suggestion of the commander of the Third Red Army. Whatever the facts may have been, Lenin telegraphed his approval on January 12, and three days later Trotsky drafted a decree on the organization of the First Labor Army. The decree was approved by the *Sovnarkom* and issued by the Council of Defense the same day.[4]

This decree was followed by a number of similar decrees that transformed other Red armies into labor armies. On January 21, 1920, the Ukrainian Labor Army was formed, with Stalin at its head. Two days later the Reserve Army was given the assignment of improving the railway line between Moscow–Kazan–Ekaterinburg, which was one of the principal arteries that connected the eastern food-supply districts with Moscow.[5]

In the case of the Ukrainian Labor Army, its mission was defined not only in terms of labor but also in terms of

---

[3] See Editor's Note No. 7 in Trotsky, *Sochineniya*, XV, 524.
[4] Trotsky, *Sochineniya*, XV, 524.
[5] *S.U.R.*, 1920, No. 6, Art. 31.

introducing discipline into industrial establishments and of serving as "an instrument of compulsion."

ESTABLISHMENT OF THE FIRST LABOR ARMY

[Decree of the Council of Workers' and Peasants' Defense, January 15, 1920][6]

1. The Third Workers' and Peasants' Red Army is to be utilized for labor purposes, on a regional scale and as an intact organization, without disrupting· its apparatus. It is to be known under the name of the First Revolutionary Labor Army.

2. The utilization of the Third Red Army for labor purposes is a temporary measure. The periods of its utilization are to be determined by a special decree of the Council of Defense, depending on the military situation as well as the character of the work which the army will be able to perform, especially the demonstrated productivity of the Labor Army.

3. The following are the principal types of work to which the forces and resources of the Third Army are to be applied:

First:
a. Procurement of food and forage, in accordance with the allotments imposed by tħe People's Commissariat for Food, and the concentration of the procured items at certain points;
b. Procurement of firewood and its delivery to factories and railway stations;
c. Organization for this purpose of wagon transport within the framework of cartage duty;[7]
d. Mobilization of necessary additional labor power for work involving the application of mass labor;
e. Construction work needed in carrying out the above tasks, as well as construction projects on a larger scale to serve the needs of future permanent work.

Second:
f. Repairing agricultural machinery;
g. Agricultural work.

[6] *S.U.R.*, 1920, No. 3, Art. 15.
[7] See the Decree on Compulsory Labor and Cartage Duty (p. 154, below).

4. The first duty of the Labor Army is to secure provisions, not below the Red Army ration, for the local workers in those regions where the army is stationed, using the army supply organization in those cases when, in the judgment of the representative of the Commissariat of Food attached to the Labor Army Council, there are no other ways of supplying the local workers with requisite quantities of food.

5. The area where the Third Army is to perform its work should coincide with the area where the basic units of the army are stationed. This [matter] is subject to special and precise determination by the leading organ of the Army (par. 6), with subsequent confirmation by the Council of Defense.

6. The organization in charge of the above-mentioned work is the Revolutionary Council of the Labor Army, whose area of competence within the economic sphere coincides with the area where the Army is operating.

7. The Revolutionary Council of the Labor Army is to be composed of members of the Revolutionary War Council and of authorized representatives of the People's Commissariat of Food, the People's Commissariat for Agriculture, the People's Commissariat of Railways, the People's Commissariat of Labor, and the Supreme Council of National Economy.

At the head of the Council is a specially appointed representative of the Council of Defense, who serves in the capacity of chairman of the Council of the Labor Army.

8. Final decision in all questions relating to internal military organization, as defined by the regulations of internal military service and other military regulations, is to be made by the Revolutionary War Council, which is authorized to introduce into the internal life of the Army all the necessary changes consequential upon the use of the Army for economic activity.

9. In every sphere of work (food, fuel, railway, etc.) the final decision in matters of carrying out the work is to be left to the representative of the corresponding member institution of the Council of the Labor Army.

10. In the event of radical disagreement, the case is to be referred to the Council of Defense.

11. All local institutions (Councils of National Economy, Food Committees, Land Departments, etc.) are subordinate to

the Council of the Labor Army, either entirely or in that sphere of work which requires the application of mass labor power.

12. All local institutions (Councils of National Economy, Food Committees, etc.) continue in their work and carry out, through their regular apparatus, the work which is assigned to them in the execution of the economic plans of the Council of the Labor Army. Local institutions cannot be changed, in their structure or functions, without the consent of the appropriate departmental representatives who are members of the Council of the Labor Army. In case of radical changes the consent of the corresponding central departments must be obtained.

13. In the case of work for which Army units can be utilized only casually, or in the case of units located outside the principal area of the Army, the Council of the Labor Army has the authority to consign that work to local institutions and to place Army units temporarily at their disposal, provided there are no obstacles to the transfer [of these units].

14. Skilled workers, insofar as they are not indispensable for the support of the life of the Army itself, may be transferred by the Army to local factories and to economic institutions generally, at the request of the corresponding representatives of the Labor Army Council.

Note: Skilled labor can be sent to factories only with the consent of those economic organs to which the factory in question is subordinated. Members of trade unions may be withdrawn from local enterprises for economic needs connected with the work of the Labor Army, provided that the local organs give their consent.

15. The Council of the Labor Army, acting through its departmental representatives, must take all necessary measures to make sure that local institutions of a given department see to it that the Army units, in discharging their share of work, do not violate the laws, regulations, and instructions of the Soviet Republic.

Note: It is particularly necessary to take care that the national pay rates in remunerating the peasants for the delivery of food or for work in procuring timber or other fuel are not violated.

16. The Council of the Labor Army is under obligation to keep correct records of the work performed by the Labor Army, how workers were fed, and the productivity of labor.

The Central Statistical Administration, in agreement with the Supreme Council of National Economy and the military establishment, is to prepare instructions setting forth the forms and periods of reporting labor performance.

17. This regulation goes into effect by telegraph.

V. Ulyanov (Lenin)
*Chairman of the Council
of Labor and Defense*

THE UKRAINIAN LABOR ARMY COUNCIL

[Decree of the *Sovnarkom*, January 21, 1920][8]

1. A Ukrainian Labor Army Council is herewith established in the region of the Southwestern Front.

2. The purpose of the Ukrainian Labor Army Council is to increase as much as possible the procurement of food supplies, fuel, and raw materials; to introduce labor discipline in enterprises; and to supply industrial establishments wth a labor force.

3. At the disposal of the Ukrainian Labor Army Council are military and reserve units, as well as reservists of not less than army strength.[9] Depending on circumstances, these units are to be used either for purposes of labor or as an instrument of compulsion.

4. The Ukrainian Labor Army Council consists of representatives, one each, of the People's Commissariat of Food, the Supreme Council of National Economy, the People's Commissariat of Agriculture, the People's Commissariat of Railways, the People's Commissariat of Labor, and of the Southwestern Front.

5. Comrade Stalin, plenipotentiary member of the Counci! of Defense, is placed at the head of the Ukrainian Labor Army Council in the capacity of chairman.

Note: All questions arising within the Ukrainian Labor Army

[8] Trotsky, *Sochineniya*, XV, 527; *S.U.R.*, 1920, No. 45, Art. 26.

[9] According to *Bolshaya Sovetskaya entsiklopediya*, the numerical strength of a Soviet army during the civil war was smaller than that of Russian armies during World War I, when the latter averaged about 250,000 men (1st ed., III, 398–99). According to Trotsky, the Ural Army had "no less than 150,000 men" (*Sochineniya*, XV, 71).

Council are decided by simple majority. In case of basic disagreements, the matter is referred to the Council of Defense.

6. The area of jurisdiction of the Ukrainian Labor Army Council is to coincide with the area of the Southwestern Front, plus the Aeksandrovo-Grushevsky coal mines of the former Don *oblast.*

7. All local institutions of the above-mentioned agencies (Councils of National Economy, Food Committees, Land Committees, local departments of the People's Commissariat of Labor and of the People's Commissariat of Railways), while preserving their connection with their respective central institutions, as defined by the general legislation of the two Soviet Republics,[10] must carry out the orders and instructions of the Ukrainian Labor Army Council.

V. Ulyanov (Lenin)
Chairman of the Sovnarkom
G. Petrovsky
*Chairman of the All-Ukrainian
Revolutionary Committee*

With the passage of time, the labor armies increased in number and changed the character of their mission. The decree of January 15, 1920, which transformed the Third Red Army into the First Labor Army, described the diversion to labor duties as a "temporary measure."[11] Three months later the decree was revoked and a new statute was issued for the First Labor Army that made no reference to the temporary character of its work but turned it into a regional economic unit with the responsibility of restoring normal economic and military life in the Urals. Later, similar decrees were issued for the other labor armies. In some of these decrees, references to military functions were completely omitted, and the labor armies

[10] Legally, the Ukraine was an independent Soviet republic, distinct from the R.S.F.S.R.
[11] See p. 142 (above).

assumed all of the administrative functions of local governments. Leadership in these armies was organized around a core of Red Army veterans, mostly Communists, thus ensuring a reliable instrument of control by the Soviet government.

THE REVOLUTIONARY COUNCIL OF THE URAL LABOR ARMY

[Decree of the *Sovnarkom*, April 15, 1920][12]

Taking into consideration the need for greater energy and unity in the economic and military work of a region as remote from the center as the Urals and the Ural region, which still carries all the vestiges of the destructive economic policy of the Whites, the *Sovnarkom* herewith resolves:

To entrust the Revolutionary Council of the First Labor Army with the general direction of the work relating to the restoration and consolidation of normal economic and military conditions in the Urals. . . .

1. The Council of the First Labor Army is designated by the Council of Labor and Defense of the R.S.F.S.R. as the economic and military organ which unifies all economic and military institutions in the Ural region and coordinates the work of all other institutions concerned with economic and military problems within that region.

Note: Pending the precise delimitation of the region's borders, the Council of the Labor Army assumes jurisdiction over the following *guberniyas:* Yekaterinburgskaya, Permskaya, Tyumenskaya, Chelyabinskaya and Ufimskaya.

2. The Council of the Labor Army acts as the regional representative of the Council of Labor and Defense of the R.S.F.S.R. and is the direct executor of the orders [of the Council of Labor and Defense] within the aforementioned *oblasts.*

3. The Council of the Labor Army has a right to issue, independently, orders and instructions relating to economic and military problems affecting the Ural region, provided these orders are

[12] *S.U.R.*, 1920, No. 30, Art. 151.

within the limits of decrees and ordinances of the central Soviet
organs and institutions.

4. The Council of the Labor Army is to observe all decrees
and orders issued by individual commissariats and other central
institutions affecting the work of these institutons.

5. The decrees and orders of the Central institutions affecting
the aforementioned five *guberniyas* are issued through the corresponding plenipotentiary members of the Council of the Labor
Army.

6. All decrees, orders, and regulations of the Council of the
Labor Army are binding upon all local Soviet institutions of the
above-mentioned *guberniyas*.

7. Representatives of central institutions, as well as individual
commissions whose economic and military prerogatives lie within
the Urals and the Ural region, are subordinate to the Council of
Labor Army either directly or through the corresponding members of the Council.

8. The Council of the Labor Army is composed of (1) a chairman appointed by the Council of Labor and Defense, (2) the Regional Military Commissar of the Urals, (3) a representative of
the Supreme Council of National Economy, (4) a representative
of the People's Commissariat of Food, (5) a representative of the
People's Commissariat of Railways, (6) a representative of the
People's Commissariat of Agriculture, (7) a representative of
the All-Russian Central Council of Trade Unions.

Note: All representatives must be approved by the Council of
Labor and Defense. Such approval does not terminate the subordination of the representatives to the corresponding central
agencies, nor does it prevent these agencies from recalling their
representatives.

9. The staffs of the executive organs of the Council of the
Labor Army have to be approved by the Council of Labor and
Defense. The executive staffs of the representatives composing
the Council of the Labor Army are subject to the approval of the
corresponding central agencies.

10. All questions arising in the Council of the Labor Army are
decided by a simple majority.

V. Ulyanov (Lenin)
Chairman of the Sovnarkom

THE REVOLUTIONARY COUNCIL OF THE SOUTHEASTERN
LABOR ARMY

[Decree of the *Sovnarkom*, August 17, 1920][13]

Taking into consideration the need for energetic and coordinated work in the sphere of economic and military administration, in a region as remote from the center as Southeastern Russia, which includes the Don *oblast*, Stavropol *Guberniya*, Kuban *oblast*, Terek *oblast*, and Dagestan, the *Sovnarkom* herewith resolves:

To entrust the Revolutionary Council of the Southeastern Labor Army, which is the representative of the government in the Southeast, with the general direction of the work relating to the restoration and consolidation of normal economic-administrative life and the administrative organization of the Southeast.

The basic work of the Revolutionary Council of the Southeastern Labor Army, which is to proceed within the framework of the state economic plans and objectives, will consist in giving every possible assistance to local organs [of administration], in strengthening and improving their apparatus, and in establishing firm connections with the central government.

1. The Council of the Southeastern Labor Army, which is appointed by the Soviet of People's Commissars, is an organ which represents the central government in Southeastern Russia and which coordinates the work of all economic and administrative institutions in the above-mentioned Southeastern *oblasts*.

2. The Revolutionary Council of the Southeastern Labor Army acts as the regional organ of the Council of Labor and Defense of the R.S.F.S.R. and is the direct executor of its orders relating to the designated region. All administrative and economic decrees affecting this region are issued by the various commissariats through their representatives attached to the Council of the Labor Army. . . .

3. The Revolutionary Council of the Southeastern Labor Army has a right to issue, independently, orders and instructions, provided they are within the limits of the decrees and ordinances of the central Soviet organs and institutions.

[13] *Ibid.*, No. 74, Art. 344.

4. The Council of the Labor Army is to observe all decrees and orders issued by individual commissariats and other central institutions affecting the work of these institutions.

5. All decrees, orders, and regulations of the Revolutionary Council of the Southeastern Labor Army are binding upon all local Soviet institutions of the above-mentioned region.

[The remainder of the decree deals with the composition of the council and accounting procedures, and closely follows the decree pertaining to the establishment of the Ural Labor Army on April 15, 1920.]

V. Ulyanov (Lenin)
Chairman of the Sovnarkom

The performance reports that the commanders of the labor armies sent to their supervisors usually were written in typical military style, and every effort was made in the Bolshevik press to give the work of these armies an attractive appeal. But the accomplishments of the labor armies did not justify the hopes Trotsky had placed in them. As the following documents indicate, the army organization proved to be a rather unproductive and wasteful way of utilizing human labor.

PERFORMANCE OF THE LABOR ARMY IN THE URALS
AS VIEWED BY A LEADING MENSHEVIK

[From an account by F. Dan][14]

. . . The supreme power in Ekaterinburg was the Council of the Labor Army. After the Third Army operating in the Urals was converted into a labor army, it was intended to reconstruct the entire administration of the region on the basis of that army. These were Trotsky's plans, who thought that in the "labor armies" he had found a sure instrument of Russia's salvation.

The transformation of the regular armies into "labor armies"

[14] F. Dan, *Dva goda skitaniy*, Berlin, 1922, pp. 45–46.

was usually accompanied by much pomp. The newspapers were full of solemn resolutions; they carried daily reports of accomplishments. But this enthusiasm soon burst like a bubble. The exaggerated accounts of officials who wished to please their superiors with fanciful successes could not alter the fact that from the very beginning the productivity of the labor armies was negligible and the cost of their maintenance enormous. Peasants from remote provinces, driven as members of the labor armies to the Urals, could not understand why, when the war with Kolchak was over, they had to cut timber, mow grass, etc., here in a foreign district, under military command, and could not do this freely in their own homes. They therefore ran away in large numbers. At the same time the local peasants, resentful that outsiders should have been ruling in their home districts, burned up the stacks of hay and timber which the soldiers of the labor army had piled up. The whole plan of the labor armies proved an empty bureaucratic fantasy. . . .

TROTSKY IS DISSATISFIED WITH THE FIRST LABOR ARMY

[Telegraph communication to Com. Mulin, March (?), 1920][15]

The Labor communiques give a picture of the most disgraceful failure of the Labor Army. In spite of the enormous apparatus at work, the results are altogether insignificant. The existence of a Political Department, with a large personnel and a daily paper, is, under present conditions, a glaring contradiction. I suggest that the whole apparatus of the Political Administration should be reduced to a minimum. The maximum number of workers should be sent to the labor front in the capacity of Commissars and Assistant Commissars. The *Krasnyy Nabat*[16] should write about work, i.e., about the actual failures of the Labor Army. It is necessary to brand and expose the Commanders and Commissars who failed to place the Army on a labor footing.

This should be done with full precision and frankness, naming the units, the Commanders and Commissars whose records are exceptionally bad. As it is, *Krasnyy Nabat* is engaged in general

[15] Trotsky, *Sochineniya*, XV, 322.
[16] *Krasyy Nabat* (*The Red Clarion*) was the official organ of the Political Administration of the First Labor Army.

theorizing and in making appeals for the militarization of industry while the Army itself is being demilitarized at a rapid pace. It [*Krasnyy Nabat*] is full of accusations against various *Guberniya* and city institutions, while the institutions of the Army itself are absolutely unsuitable for the new task.

L. TROTSKY
*Chairman of the Council
of the Labor Army*

THE LOW PRODUCTIVITY OF THE LABOR ARMIES

[Statement by Trotsky at the Ninth Party Congress,
March 30, 1920][17]

. . . There is no doubt that labor productivity of the labor armies is for the present still rather low. During the first period it was even lower. Reading the reports for the first days and weeks during which the former Third Army applied itself on the labor front, we noticed that as many as thirteen to fifteen and sometimes twenty to thirty Red Army soldiers were needed to cut one cubic *sazhen* of firewood. This is a stupendous figure.

As far as I know, before the war three or four men were needed for this work. They say that a *Zyryanin* [ancient name of an inhabitant of the Komi A.S.S.R.] can do this work singlehanded, but here they needed thirty men. The most recent reports, however, show that only 5.5 workers are needed to cut a cubic *sazhen* of firewood. . . . The mobilized peasants who work side-by-side with the labor army show a lower productivity. They require seven workers per one cubic *sazhen*, which means that the productivity of the Red Army soldiers is higher than that of the peasants.

B. COMPULSORY LABOR IN THE RURAL AREAS

The system of compulsory labor was designed primarily to serve the needs of Soviet industry, but the heaviest burden of this system fell upon the rural population. In-

---

[17] *Devyatyy sezd Rossiyskoy kommunisticheskoy partii*, p. 87.

dustrial workers, skilled and unskilled, were conscripted, and in the majority of cases merely "tied down" to their current places of employment. The rural population, on the other hand, was uprooted and torn away from its normal ways of life and work and was forced to carry out tasks of a particularly onerous character. During the period in which labor conscription was applied to the rural population, the peasant—and his horse—were called upon to perform all sorts of "socially necessary" work: cutting timber, sawing firewood and bringing it to town, hauling requisitioned grain to railroads and other shipping points, driving state and Party officials from place to place, clearing roads and railroads of snow, repairing roads, loading and unloading freight cars, cultivating the fields and harvesting the crops of the families of Red Army soldiers, sweeping streets, doing janitor service in railroad stations, and similar work.[18] Much of this work, even when it involved the use of the peasant's work animals, was frequently without compensation.[19] According to the information supplied by the People's Commissariat of Labor, the Timber Trust alone owed the workers 23.5 billion rubles and large quantities of supplies that were part of the workers' wages.[20]

Labor conscription of the rural population went into effect about two months earlier than the conscription of industrial workers. The basic decree for the compulsory labor and cartage duty that was imposed on the rural population was enacted on November 19, 1919.

[18] *Dopolneniya k obzoru deyatelnosti narodnogo komissariata truda za 1921 god*, Moscow, 1921, p. 22, and the decree on compulsory labor and cartage duty quoted below.

[19] *Sbornik deystvuyushchikh postanovleniy, instruktsiy i telegrafnykh rasporyazheniy po provedeniyu trudovykh i guzhevykh povinnostey*, Moscow, 1921, p. 5.

[20] *Dopolneniya k obzoru deyatelnosti narodnogo komissariata truda za 1921 god*, p. 24. A more detailed listing of the indebtedness of the Timber Trust is given on p. 175 (below).

COMPULSORY LABOR AND CARTAGE DUTY IMPOSED ON THE RURAL POPULATION

[Decree of the Council of Workers' and Peasants' Defense, November 19, 1919][21]

In view of the necessity of straining every effort of the country to overcome the present fuel crisis, the Council of Workers' and Peasants' Defense decrees:

1. Immediate introduction in certain areas of the Soviet Republic, and in accordance with the rules given below, of the following state duties:

    a. Firewood procurement duty;

    b. Compulsory labor for storing, loading and unloading all forms of fuel;

    c. Cartage duty for the delivery of fuel, army supplies, food provisions, and other state goods to the cities, railways, docks, and other shipping points.

2. The call upon the population to fulfill labor and cartage duties will be issued by the People's Commissariat of the Interior and carried out locally by the Chiefs of the *Guberniya* and *Uezd* Administrative Departments of the Executive Committees, through the *volost* Executive Committees, and the village Soviets with the participation of the militia.

[Paragraph 3 places the responsibility for this work on the Commissariat of Internal Affairs. Paragraph 4 authorizes the Main Timber Committee to take charge of all firewood procurement.]

5. Compulsory labor in connection with the storing, loading and unloading of fuel is imposed upon all citizens between the ages of thirty-five and fifty, who have not as yet been called for military service, as well as those exempted from military duty, with the exception of those obviously unfit for work. Compulsory labor is likewise imposed upon all women between the ages of eighteen and forty.

6. Cartage duty is imposed on all citizens having carts and horses or other animals capable of being harnessed.

[21] *S.U.R.*, 1919, No. 57, Art. 543.

7. Persons called to perform compulsory labor are required to continue working until such time as is indicated in their summons while those mobilized for cartage duty cannot leave their work prior to fulfilling their norm. Those guilty of unauthorized departure from work, resistance to, or evasion of compulsory labor will be treated as deserters, while those guilty of evading cartage duty will suffer, in addition, confiscation of their horses and carts.

8. If necessary, Internal Security Troops, as well as local Extraordinary Commissions [*Chekas*], will be called upon to give energetic assistance to the representatives of the People's Commissariat of Internal Affairs in enforcing compulsory labor regulations.

11. Those called upon to perform compulsory labor will be paid in accordance with the wage scales established by the trade unions, while those engaged in cartage duty will be paid in accordance with the rates approved by the Presidium of the *Guberniya* Executive Committee.

V. ULYANOV (LENIN)
*Chairman of the Council
of Workers' and Peasants' Defense*

After the proclamation of universal compulsory labor—on January 29, 1920—and the subsequent establishment of the Central Committee on Compulsory Labor, conscription of the rural population was placed under the jurisdiction of this new committee. The committee then proceeded to create a special agency to take charge of the rural sector of the forced-labor front. The agency was called the Central Extraordinary Commission on Firewood and Cartage Duty, and abbreviated as *Tsechrezkomtopguzh*.[22] For emphasis on the importance of the agency, Dzerzhinsky was appointed chairman. There also were local Commissions on Firewood and Cartage Duty that paralleled the structure of the Committees on Compulsory Labor.

[22] For *Tsentralnaya chrezvychaynaya komissiya po toplivo-guzhevoy povinnosti.*

ESTABLISHMENT OF THE CENTRAL EXTRAORDINARY
COMMISSION ON FIREWOOD AND CARTAGE DUTY

[Decree of the *Glavkomtrud*, April, 1920][23]

1.   Central and local Extraordinary Commissions on Firewood
and Cartage Duty are hereby established to take direct charge of
the mobilization of the population for work connected with the
procurement of firewood and other large-scale work for the procurement of fuel. The commissions are also to take charge of the
mobilization and the distribution of carts and horses for the
hauling of firewood, military supplies, food products, and other
loads. These commissions are subordinate to *Glavkomtrud,* and
the *Guberniya* and *Uezd* Committees on Compulsory Labor.

2.   The Central Extraordinary Commission on Firewood and
Cartage Duty (*Tsechrezkomtopguzh*) directs the *Guberniya* and
Uezd Extraordinary Commissions on Firewood and Cartage
Duty in the following matters:

   a.   Mobilization of the population for firewood procurement
        and other fuel procurement.
   b.   Mobilization of carts and horses belonging to the popula-
        tion and their assignment to the hauling of firewood, mili-
        tary and food supplies, and other loads.

3.   The Central Commission on Firewood and Cartage Duty is
to consist of Comrade Dzerzhinsky (Chairman), Comrade Vasilev of the N.K.V.D. (Deputy Chairman), and the following
members: Safonov (representing all fuel *Glavki*), Eyduk (a
special plenipotentiary representative of all fuel *Glavki*), Smirnov
(representing the People's Commissariat of Food), Semenov
(representing the People's Commissariat of War), Ikhnovsky
(representing the Interdepartmental Commission attached to the
All-Russian Extraordinary Commission to Fight Counterrevolution), Fafanova (representing the People's Commissariat of
Agriculture).[24]

F. Dzerzhinsky
Chairman of Glavkomtrud

[23] *Izvestiya glavnogo komiteta po vseobshchey trudovoy povinnosti*, No. 2, p. 17.
[24] An appendix to the decree deals with the organization of the local Extraordinary Commissions on Firewood and Cartage Duty.

In the rural areas, compulsory labor operated on military principles and had the following table of organization. The basic unit was the *druzhina* (a brigade), consisting of 300 workers, headed by a *Nachalnik* (chief) and his deputy. The *druzhina* was broken down into three parts, with 100 workers in each; these were called *sotnya*. A *sotyna*, in turn, was broken down into ten groups, each called *desyatka*. Care had to be taken that members of the same family were not included in the same *druzhina*, *sotnya*, or *desyatka*. Every *sotnya*, as well as every *desyatka*, had its own chief.[25]

Complete data on the number of rural workers who were mobilized for compulsory labor are not available. A glimpse of the magnitude of the numbers involved only in the field of firewood procurement, however, is provided in the figures released by *Glavkomtrud* for the first six months of 1920 and pertaining to thirty-six *guberniyas* (out of a total of fifty-five) in which rural labor conscription was in force. These figures show that 5,824,182 rural workers and 4,161,859 horses were mobilized for firewood and cartage duty.[26] Another set of incomplete data, for the three months of August, September, and October, 1920, and relating to only seventeen *guberniyas*, shows that 1,727,016 laborers and 1,032,409 horses were conscripted for the same kind of work.[27]

The right to use mobilized labor was granted to a great variety of "extraordinary" committees and commissions of the central government, as well as to local Soviet authorities,[28] and the basic decrees on the subject of compulsory

[25] *Izvestiya glavnogo komiteta po vseobshchey trudovoy povinnosti*, No. 6, pp. 15–16; *Krestyanstvo i trudovaya povinnost*, Gosizdat, Moscow, 1920, pp. 6–7.
[26] *Izvestiya glavnogo komiteta po vseobshchey trudovoy povinnosti*, No. 3, p. 61.
[27] A. Anikst, *Organizatsiya rabochey sily v 1920 godu*, Moscow, 1920, p. 62.
[28] *Krestyanstvo i trudovaya povinnost*, p. 6.

labor contained few provisions for safeguarding the rights of the mobilized population. That this led to an outrageous exploitation of the peasant masses was publicly admitted by the People's Commissariat of Labor in 1921; i.e., after the New Economic Policy was introduced. This admission is given in the following document.

HOW THE SYSTEM OF COMPULSORY LABOR OPERATED
IN RURAL AREAS

[Excerpt from an Introduction to a collection of laws
issued by the Commissariat of Labor in 1921][29]

. . . In reviewing our previous policies in the field of compulsory labor and cartage duty, it is important to observe that these policies frequently assumed monstrous and wholly negative forms. In the first place, the labor and cartage duties were not conditioned by any standards, but were determined in relation to existing state needs which were almost limitless. In the second place, the very process of mobilization for compulsory labor had the mark of irresponsibility on the part of the user agencies who, because there were no definitive standards of enlistment, failed to recognize any sense of responsibility in relation to the masses mobilized for work. This gave rise to a heavily charged political atmosphere.

The negligent attitude on the part of employer agencies expressed itself frequently either in abuse or in failure to make actual use of the mobilized labor force. The employer agencies also showed a criminal absentmindedness toward workers' conditions of work and life, as well as toward payment for the work performed.

It is, furthermore, necessary to point out that the compulsory methods used in the enrollment of labor by resorting to military force created open hostility of the population to the government.

[29] *Sbornik deystvuyushchikh postanovleniy, instruktsiy i telegrafnykh rasporayzheniy po provedeniyu trudovykh i guzhevykh povinnostey*, p. 5.

C. Militarization of the Industrial Labor Force

The decision to militarize the Soviet economy was intended primarily to remedy the alarming conditions that had developed in the operation of Russian industry as a result of the catastrophic shrinkage of the industrial labor force. By 1920, Russian industrial manpower had dwindled to less than one half of its 1917 numerical strength.[30] Particularly threatening was the supply of skilled labor, which relatively had declined even more than the industrial labor force. As has already been noted, some of these skilled workers fled into the country to engage in agriculture or in rural industries and co-operatives; others became black-market operators; and others joined the state bureaucracy, which grew by leaps and bounds. Reassembling these widely scattered, industrially trained workers was no small undertaking, and the activity of the central and local institutions in charge of compulsory labor was devoted to this task.

The success of the undertaking, clearly, depended upon the degree to which industrial labor could be mobilized. The materials of this section indicate that the militarization strategy, as applied to the industrial labor force, was not a success, even in a numerical sense. The flight of Russian workers from the big industrial centers continued through 1920 despite the stern measures against labor desertion; and labor productivity showed no signs of improvement.

Twenty-some mobilizations were decreed in 1920 and affected the most important trades and professions. Some of the mobilized workers were "militarized"; that is, they were forced to remain in their places of employment and

[30] Ya. S. Rozenfeld, *Promyshlennaya politika SSSR, Gospolitizdat,* 1926, p. 317.

could not leave without the permission of their superiors. Others were sent under military convoy, on orders of *Glavkomtrud*, to distant plants that were short of labor power.

The industrial mobilization decrees are fairly uniform in style, and the two examples quoted below are typical of the others. A chronological list of the recorded mobilization decrees is included.

MOBILIZATION OF MINE WORKERS

[Decree of the Council of Labor and Defense, April 16, 1920][31]

In connection with the liberation of the mining regions of the Republic and because of the acute shortage of skilled miners, the Council of Labor and Defense, by way of supplementing the *Sovnarkom* decree of 13 October 1919, relating to the mobilization of the mining-technical forces, herewith resolves:

1. Persons between the ages of eighteen and fifty who have worked in the mining industry are declared mobilized.

   Note: The registration of those subject to mobilization, as defined in the present paragraph, is in charge of the Subsections of Registration and Distribution of the Labor Force of the Department of Labor. The procedures to be followed are those provided in the *Sovnarkom* decree of 26 February 1920, relating to specialists in the petroleum industry.

2. Assignment of the mobilized workers to their places of work is the responsibility of the Section of Registration and Distribution of the Labor Force of the People's Commissariat of Labor, of the Commissariat of Social Insurance, in consultation with the Mining Council of the Supreme Council of National Economy, acting through the corresponding subsections of Accounting and Distribution of the Labor Force.

[31] *S.U.R.*, 1920, No. 27, Art. 132.

3. [Paragraph 3 states that petitions on the part of those mobilized to remain in their present place of work, not within their specialty, are to be declined.]

4. Mobilized individuals who are subject to assignments by the Department of Registration and Distribution of the Labor Force of the Commissariat of Labor and the Commissariat of Social Insurance are sent with transportation documents by the Subsection of Registration and Distribution of the Labor Force to the War Commissariat to provide them with food, while on route to their destination, on the same general basis as Red Army commanders.

5. Responsible managers of enterprises, institutions, and establishments guilty of concealing or failing to report individuals in their service who were mentioned in Paragraph 1 of this decree are to be handed over to the court on charges of concealing deserters.

6. Individuals indicated in Paragraph 1 of this decree, who are in active military service in the Red Army or in rear institutions of the military establishment, are to be placed immediately at the disposal of the Mining Council of the Supreme Council of National Economy.

7. This decree goes into effect by telegraph.

V. Ulyanov (Lenin)
*Chairman of the Council
of Labor and Defense*

MOBILIZATION OF METALLURGICAL WORKERS

[Decree of the Council of Labor and Defense, August 20, 1920][32]

To satisfy the requirements for skilled and trained workers in the shock-group plants and in especially important plants of the Division of Metals, attached to the Supreme Council of National Economy, the Council of Labor and Defense hereby decrees:

1. Mobilization of workers who were formerly employed in plants listed below.[33]

[32] *S.U.R.*, 1920, No. 75, Art. 347.

[33] A list of eighty-six plants are given in the appendix to this decree. These plants were designated as belonging to the "shock group" of metallurgical plants, which had first priority in manpower and supplies. See *Narodnoe khozyaystvo*, 1920, Nos. 9–10, pp. 2–6, where the idea of "shock-group" plants is elaborated.

2. Subject to mobilization are males between the ages of eighteen and fifty irrespective of whether they are presently employed or not, except those who are in active service or work in agencies of the military establishment.

3. Subject to mobilization are all workers of Soviet institutions and of nationalized enterprises.

   Note: Those working in *kustar* [handicraft] enterprises, irrespective of whether their work is for the government or the private market, are not exempt from mobilization.

4. Those subject to mobilization must register within a week's time following the publication of this decree locally by the Commissariat of War.

[Paragraphs 5 to 8 deal with registration procedures.]

9. Summoning the mobilized to perform labor duty is within the jurisdiction of the local representatives of the Subsection of Registration and Distribution of the Labor Force, attached to the Commissariat of Labor, acting in conjunction with the corresponding *Glavki*, and, in the absence of these, with the plant administrations of the Division of Metals [of the S.C.N.E.] and using the machinery of the military establishment.

10. Wages of those mobilized for labor service, as well as travel and per diem allowances, will be in accordance with existing rates.

    Note: Relevant instructions are to be worked out by the People's Commissariat of Labor, together with the Supreme Council of National Economy.

11. Individuals who conceal their [past] connection with a [metallurgical] plant, or their specialty, as well as those evading registration or failing to appear when summoned, are considered deserters and are liable to the same penalties as are applicable to deserters from military service.

12. Responsible managers of enterprises, institutions, and establishments who are guilty of concealing or failing to

report individuals in their service who were mentioned in Paragraph 1 and in the Appendix to this decree are to be handed over to the court on charges of concealing deserters.

V. Ulyanov (Lenin)
*Chairman of the Council
of Labor and Defense*

LIST OF OFFICIAL MOBILIZATION DECREES
ISSUED DURING 1920

1. Former Railway Workers, January 30, 1920 (*S.U.R.*, 1920, No. 8, Art. 52)
2. Skilled Railway Personnel, March 15, 1920 (*S.U.R.*, 1920, No. 17, Art. 98)
3. Workers in the Sugar Industries, March 24, 1920 (*S.U.R.*, 1920, No. 28, Art. 136)
4. Water Transport Workers, April 7, 1920 (*S.U.R.*, 1920, No. 29, Art. 146)
5. Mining Workers, April 16, 1920 (*S.U.R.*, 1920, No. 27, Art. 132)
6. Skilled Personnel of Water Transport, April 27, 1920 (*S.U.R.*, 1920, No. 33, Art. 158)
7. Construction Workers, May 5, 1920 (*Izvestiya Glavkomtrud,** 1920, No. 3, p. 12)
8. Statistical Workers, June 25, 1920 (*Izvestiya Glavkomtrud,** 1920, No. 3, pp. 14–15)
9. Medical Personnel, July 14, 1920 (*Izvestiya Glavkomtrud,** 1920, Nos. 4–5, p. 14)
10. Workers Formerly Employed in Fishing Industries, August 6, 1920 (*S.U.R.*, No. 72, Art. 332)
11. Workers in Shipbuilding, August 8, 1920 (*Izvestiya Glavkomtrud,** 1920, No. 6, p. 16)
12. Workers in Wool Industries, August 13, 1920 (*S.U.R.*, 1920, No. 75, Art. 350)
13. Former Metal Workers, August 20, 1920 (*S.U.R.*, 1920, No. 75, Art. 347)
14. Domestic Servants, August 31, 1920 (*S.U.R.*, 1920, No. 75, Art. 356)

15. Call-up of Three Age Groups, 1886–1888, September 13, 1920 (*S.U.R.*, 1920, No. 79, Art. 372)
16. Workers in the Tanning Industries, September 15, 1920 (*Izvestiya Glavkomtrud,** 1920, No. 6, p. 17)
17. Electro-Technical Workers, October 8, 1920 (*S.U.R.*, 1920, No. 91, Art. 476)
18. Workers Formerly Employed in Aviation Industry Either in Russia or Abroad, October 20, 1920 (*Izvestiya Glavkomtrud,** 1920, No. 7, pp. 58–59)
19. Women for Sewing Underwear for Red Army Men, October 30, 1920 (*S.U.R.*, 1920, No. 90, Art. 468)
20. Mobilization of Tailors and Shoemakers Who Worked in Great Britain and the United States, October 1920 (*Izvestiya Glavkomtrud,** 1920, No. 7, p. 55)

Every mobilization decree provided penalties for those who failed to comply with the provisions of the decree, and such persons were called "deserters from the labor front." The gravity of labor desertion was emphasized by the Ninth Party Congress, which met toward the end of March, 1920, and adopted a resolution that urged "a systematic, persistent, and relentless campaign against labor desertion."[34] This resolution was codified in the form of an official decree of the *Sovnarkom*, on May 4, 1920, that provided stern punishment for labor desertion. Milder forms of punishment, for absenteeism, had been provided for in an earlier decree, made public on April 27, 1920. To enforce the provisions of these decrees, a special agency, *Dezertirkomissiya*,[35] was established and was attached to *Glavkomtrud*. Every local Committee on Compulsory Labor had its own commission on deserters. Trade unions also were enlisted in the campaign against labor deserters.

* *Izvestiya glavnogo komiteta po vseobshchey trudovoy povinnosti.*
[34] See p. 127 (above).
[35] "Commission on Deserters."

LABOR DESERTION AND HOW TO COMBAT IT

[Decree of the *Sovnarkom*, May 4, 1920][36]

Supplementing the decree on Universal Compulsory Labor (*S.U.R.*, 1920, No. 8, Art. 49),[37] the Soviet of People's Commissars herewith resolves:

1. Labor desertion is defined as follows:
   a. Noncompliance with the registration orders issued by agencies empowered to proclaim or to enforce compulsory labor;
   b. Concealment of their special skills by workers, employees and technical personnel who are subject to registration, even if at the time of registration they were employed in some other work;
   c. Noncompliance with call-up orders by persons summoned in accordance with the decree on labor mobilization, as well as persons assigned to work by the organs of the People's Commissariat of Labor;
   d. Unauthorized leaving of one's work or official duties;
   e. Being absent from work without valid reason;
   f. Any form of evasion of compulsory labor, such as falsification of documents, fictitious employment, simulation of sickness, etc.;
   g. Failure to appear before the organs of registration and distribution of the labor force, after one has been discharged from work or employment.

2. Combating labor desertion, as well as its various forms of concealment, complicity, and incitement to desertion, is placed in the charge of the Central Committee of Compulsory Labor and its local organs with the participation of the trade unions. These [agencies] are to act through the All-Russian Extraordinary Commission [to Fight Counterrevolution], the Central Commission to Fight against Desertion, and their local organs. These agencies are subordinate to the Central Committee of Compulsory Labor and are under obligation to carry out its orders.

V. Ulyanov (Lenin)
Chairman of the Sovnarkom

[36] *S.U.R.*, 1920, No. 35, Art. 168.
[37] The reference is to the decree that legalized compulsory labor (cited above, pp. 110–12).

MEASURES TO COMBAT ABSENTEEISM

[Decree of the *Sovnarkom*, April 27, 1920][38]

In order to bring an end to absenteeism, the Soviet of People's Commissars hereby decrees:

1. To make deductions over and above the non-payment of wages, from bonuses in money or kind for absenteeism (failure to appear for work without legitimate reasons), in accordance with the following rules:

For the first day of absenteeism—15 percent of the monthly bonuses; for the second day—25 percent; and for the third day— 60 percent. In addition to these deductions, absenteeism carries with it the obligation to make up the time lost in compulsory labor, either after work or during holidays. [In performing this compulsory labor] workers and employees may be assigned to work not in their specialty, in which case their remuneration is to be in accordance with wage scales established for the particular work. No bonuses or payment for over-time may be added to their remuneration.

2. Absenteeism of more than three days a month is considered sabotage and is dealt with by the Disciplinary Courts.

3. Persons declining to make up the time lost, as provided in Paragraph 1, are subject to confinement in concentration camps.

4. Responsible managers of enterprises and institutions have the obligation to institute strict supervision over the registration tables showing attendance by workers at their place of work.

5. Commissions on Compulsory Labor have the responsibility of making, from time to time, unexpected inspections to uncover violations in work attendance.

6. Responsibility for compliance with this decree rests upon the Commissions on Compulsory Labor and the Plant Committees, which are liable to court action in the event of negligence.

7. Exemption from work on grounds of sickness may be granted only upon presentation of a hospital certificate.

[Paragraphs 8 to 17 contain detailed provisions for ensuring that exemption from work on grounds of sickness is not violated.

[38] *S.U.R.*, 1920, No. 36, Art. 172.

An appendix to the decree lists thirty-two kinds of illness on the basis of which leave may be granted.]

V. ULYANOV (LENIN)
Chairman of the Sovnarkom

COMMISSIONS COMBATING LABOR DESERTION

[Order of *Glavkomtrud*, May 28, 1920][39]

In compliance with the decrees of the Council of Labor and Defense of 27 April and 4 May, the Central Committee on Compulsory Labor herewith decrees:

1. All militarized and non-militarized institutions, establishments and businesses have the following obligations:

   a. Preparing lists of all workers and employees, containing information about their place of birth, the permanent residence of their families, and their status in respect to military duty.

   b. Reporting immediately every unauthorized departure from work or absenteeism without valid reason, not only to the Section of Registration and Distribution of the Labor Force [of the Commissariat of Labor] but also to the Commission on Deserters.

2. Upon receipt of such information, the Commission on Deserters is to take measures to apprehend the deserter. If he is not found the Commission is to question his family as to the deserter's whereabouts. The information thus obtained is to be forwarded to the Commission on Deserters of the locality where the deserter is presumed to be.

3. Agencies in charge of labor mobilizations are under obligation to forward lists of those who failed to appear to the corresponding Commission on Deserters.

4. In making raids or checking documents [of citizens], the Commission on Deserters must at the same time learn what kind of work the person is doing and whether he is a labor deserter.

5. The Commission on Deserters is authorized to arrest individuals who by virtue of their qualifications should be listed in a

[39] *Izvestiya glavnogo komiteta po vseobshchey trudovoy povinnosti*, No. 3, pp. 24–25.

special register but have failed to register or declined to accept work in their specialty.

6. The Commission on Deserters, acting in the name of the Committee on Compulsory Labor, is authorized to take the following measures in relation to those guilty of labor desertion:

    a. Those guilty of leaving their work for the first time, and for not more than three days preceding their arrest, are to be brought back to their place of work and handed over to the Disciplinary Court on charge of sabotage.

    b. Those guilty of leaving their work for a longer period, or for the second time, are subject to arrest for not more than two weeks or to be sent to a penal labor battalion for a period up to six months.

    c. Those failing to appear for work after they have been mobilized are subject to penalties ranging from [monetary] fines up to prison terms not exceeding three weeks.

    d. Those concealing their specialty or failing to appear to work in their specialty are subject to loss of property or to arrest up to two weeks in cases when there are mitigating circumstances. In the absence of such mitigating circumstances, the guilty are to be sent to penal labor battalions for a period up to six months or to be handed over to the Revolutionary Tribunal.

7. Connivers and helpers in harboring labor deserters are liable to fines ranging from partial to full confiscation of their property, as well as to arrest for periods of not more than two weeks. In cases of a more serious nature they are to be handed over to the *Guberniya* Revolutionary Tribunal.

[Paragraphs 8 to 10 pertain to the duties of the *Uezd* and *Guberniya* Commissions on Deserters and to the formation of *Guberniya* Revolutionary Tribunals to try labor deserters.]

11. The Central Commission on Deserters, when engaged in mass operations, is to act in conjunction with the organs of the Extraordinary Commission to Fight Counterrevolution.

Antonov–Ovseenko
Acting Chairman of Glavkomtrud

THE ROLE OF TRADE UNIONS IN THE FIGHT
AGAINST LABOR DESERTION

[Order of *Glavkomtrud*, May 28, 1920][40]

In compliance with the decrees of the Council of Labor and Defense, of April 27 and May 4, 1920, *Glavkomtrud*, with the concurrence of the All-Russian Council of Trade Unions, has resolved:

Trade Unions are to take part in the fight against labor desertion if such desertion takes place in factories, plants, institutions, and enterprises comprising trade-union organizations. The trade unions are to carry out the following tasks:

1. To ensure, by using the machinery of plant administration and the Commissions on Compulsory Labor, that those mobilized in accordance with the provisions for compulsory labor actually appear for work and carry out the task assigned to them. Those who fail to appear or refuse to work should be reported to the Committee on Deserters.

2. To ensure, by using the machinery of factory-shop committees, that those who leave their job illegally, as well as managers who hire workers without proper authorization, are handed over to the courts.

3. [Paragraph 3 calls upon trade unions to ensure that workers and employees comply with the regulations for leave. Those failing to comply with these regulations are to be handed over to the Disciplinary Courts. Workers and employees who fail to return from leave are to be counted as labor deserters and should be reported to the Central Committee on Labor Deserters, or, in case of necessity, to the *Cheka*.]

4. To be on the watch for those who fail to appear for work without legitimate reasons and to apply, through the medium of the plant administration, such disciplinary measures as are provided in the statute relating to the struggle against absenteeism (reduction of wages and food rations, making up for the time lost, and turning them over to the Disciplinary Courts).

5. To ensure that the output norms established in the wage agreements and special decisions on bonuses are fulfilled, and to

[40] *Ibid.*, pp. 25–26.

bring those failing to fulfill their norms before the Disciplinary Courts. In cases of malicious sabotage, the guilty, whether he be worker, employee, or member of the administration, is to be turned over to the All-Russian *Cheka*.

6. [Paragraph 6 calls upon trade unions to ensure that sick leave is properly granted and to turn over violators to the All-Russian *Cheka*.]

7. To ensure that official business trips are properly assigned.

8. To ensure that regulations relating to labor discipline and working hours are enforced.

9. To ensure that the plant administration reports promptly to the Committee on Labor Desertion and to the All-Russian *Cheka* all persons who deserted from the labor front or were found guilty in violating the decrees relating to the struggle against absenteeism and labor desertion.

10. To carry on extensive propaganda, both oral and in the press, in favor of compulsory labor and against labor desertion in all its forms, utilizing for this purpose the entire trade-union machinery.

ANTONOV–OVSEENKO
Acting Chairman of Glavkomtrud

FAILURE TO ARREST THE DECLINE OF THE SKILLED INDUSTRIAL LABOR FORCE

The avalanche of restraining orders issued for the purpose of combating labor desertion and absenteeism proved rather unsuccessful. A writer in the *Ekonomicheskay zhizn*, the official organ of the Supreme Council of National Economy, complained that "the reestablishment of control over the labor force was accomplished only to a limited extent. The requirements of economic commissariats, which were estimated at 2–3 million workers, could not be satisfied. Actually the *Komtruds* had at their disposal only thousands or, at best, tens of thousands of industrial workers." [41]

[41] *Ekonomicheskaya zhizn*, No. 132, June 19, 1920.

This was written about the middle of June, but conditions did not improve very much in subsequent months, and labor shortages continued to plague Soviet industry throughout 1920. According to the official estimate of the labor difficulties, two principal factors contributed to these shortages: one was employment "desertion" by workers who were dissatisfied with the conditions of labor; the other was absenteeism (which the Russians called *proguly*).

In a study on the organization of the Russian industrial labor force in 1920, prepared by A. Anikst, a deputy chairman of *Glavkomtrud*, there are many interesting data on the troublesome problems of desertion and absenteeism. The data relate only to high-priority branches of industry, viz., armaments, transport machinery, and locomotive repair plants. All of these establishments were within the category of "shock plants," [42] and the workers employed in them were entitled to an "armor-clad" food ration (*bronirovannyy paek*) that was far superior to the average ration of other Russian workers. During the first nine months of 1920, according to Anikst, 38,574 workers were mobilized and delivered to thirty-five armaments plants. During the same period, 34,939 workers deserted from these plants. The net increment in this sector of industry thus amounted to only 3,635 workers.[43] In the transport machinery and locomotive repair plants, conditions were even worse. The data for the first six months of 1920 show that, of the 16,223 workers mobilized, 15,201 deserted.[44]

The data for the high-priority sectors of industry show that, with the enormous efforts of the various extraordinary committees and commissions on labor mobilization

[42] The meaning of "shock plants" is given on p. 161, n 33 (above).

[43] See Anikst, *Organizatsiya rabochey sily v 1920 godu*, p. 50, Table 25.

[44] *Izvestiya glavnogo komiteta po vseobshchey trudovoy povinnosti*, No. 7, p. 7.

and the imposition of severe penalties for labor desertion, Soviet authorities were scarcely able to maintain the existing level of employment—a level far short of what these industries required.[45] In the industrial labor force as a whole, there was a sharp drop in total employment in the years 1920 and 1921. The decline continued in 1922.

A study of industrial policy during the early years of the Communist experiment in Russia gives the following figures for the movement of the industrial labor force. In 1917 there were 3,024,000 workers; in 1918 the number fell to 2,486,000; by 1920 and 1921, the industrial labor force had declined to 1,480,000; and it reached the lowest point—1,243,000—in 1922.[46]

The downward trend in industrial employment was not due entirely to labor desertion. The high rate of civilian mortality that prevailed during the period under consideration also had much to do with the decline of the industrial labor force.[47] To the officials engaged in labor mobiliza-

[45] According to the Central Committee on Compulsory Labor, the armaments plants were short 39,000 workers, mostly skilled; the transport machinery plants lacked 36,000 workers; and railway and water transport were short 140,000 workers, mostly unskilled (*ibid.*, p. 6).

[46] Ya. S. Rozenfeld, *Promyshlennaya politika* SSSR, p. 37.

[47] A statistical analysis of the excess civilian mortality in Russia during the early years of the revolution was published by S. Strumilin in *Narodnoe kho-zyaystvo* (December, 1920). According to Strumilin, excess mortality among the civilian population between January 1, 1918, and June 1, 1920, reached a figure of over 7 million, or 7 percent of the 100-million population he took as the basis for his estimate. Strumilin did not compute the peripheral areas of Russia, such as Siberia and the Southeast—in order to simplify his estimate. If his percentage of excess civilian mortality is applied to the entire Russian population, which in 1918 numbered about 136 million, the total of premature deaths must have been in excess of 9 million. Strumilin's analysis also shows that famine and epidemics wreaked a much greater toll in human life than the fighting during the Russian civil war. The number of deaths resulting from combat operations are estimated by Strumilin at about 350,000. Famine and epidemics, on the other hand, accounted for a large percentage of the excess mortality of the period.

Strumilin's analysis of excess civilian mortality during the early period of the Soviet regime is generally supported in Frank Lorimer's study of population trends during the period 1918–20, based on the official Soviet population census taken in 1926 (Frank Lorimer, *The Population of the Soviet Union: History*

tion, however, the manpower difficulties appeared to be due almost exclusively to desertion, absenteeism, and the lack of labor discipline. The document that follows is typical of this point of view. The official of *Glavkomtrud* who wrote the article is not always clear of the difference between production and productivity, but he leaves no doubt as to the point he was trying to make. He was quite certain that, if stern labor discipline was not enforced, the entire labor mobilization effort was bound to fail.

REASONS FOR THE DECLINE IN INDUSTRIAL PRODUCTIVITY

[Resumé of a statement by *Glavkomtrud*, October, 1920][48]

Provisioning our industry with the requisite labor force will not solve the problem of labor productivity. The productivity of our plants deteriorated not only on account of the labor shortage but also because of the decline in labor discipline. Labor desertion on a wide scale is taking place even in the militarized war-production plants and the transport machinery establishments. During the first half of 1920, 8,014 workers arrived at four war-production plants. At the same time, 8,324 workers took flight. Conditions had not improved during the month of July, when 1,806 workers were added, but 1,444 fled. In the eight transport-machinery plants, 16,223 new workers arrived during the first half of 1920, but, during the same period, 15,201 workers departed from these same plants.

At the same time, the percentage of absenteeism from work has greatly increased. The average rate of absenteeism from plants before the war amounted to about 10 percent. In 1920 the percentage of absenteeism in shock plants increased threefold. In

---

and Prospects, Geneva, League of Nations, 1948, p. 41). Since Lorimer deals with a longer period, his estimate of excess mortality reaches a figure of 12 million for the years 1918–22. Lorimer also makes it clear that famine and epidemics were the major causes for this catastrophy. The most serious epidemics reached a peak in 1918–20. Death from typhus alone, in these two years, numbered 1.6 million, and typhoid, dysentery, and cholera added another 700,000 deaths.

[48] *Izvestiya glavnogo komiteta po vseobshchey trudovoy povinnosti*, No. 7, p. 7.

the Sormovsky plant it reached 36 percent in July; in August it dropped to 32 percent. At the Bryansk plant it was 40 percent during the winter months and it has risen to 48.5 percent in June and to 50 percent in August. At the Tver plant it was 44 percent during July and August.

Systematic absenteeism (*proguly*) is among the principal reasons for the sharp decline of labor productivity. The same decline in labor productivity was taking place in the railroad repair shops and transport machinery plants. However, since March of this year a radical change has taken place in our transport. Absenteeism declined to its normal proportions and does not exceed 10 to 12 percent. In some places it is even lower. By introducing piece work and the premium system, and by taking energetic action against absentees, an increase in labor productivity was achieved on the railways. This example shows that under present conditions an increase in labor productivity can be achieved by introducing stern labor discipline. Without enforcing such discipline in the plants, the entire labor mobilization effort of the *Komtruds* must fail to produce desirable results.

AN EVALUATION OF COMPULSORY LABOR IN INDUSTRY

[Excerpts from an official review by the People's
Commissariat of Labor, 1921][49]

Previous practice [in matters of labor conscription] has made it necessary to review the whole question of compulsory mobilization of workers and employees in state institutions and enterprises.

The mobilization of these categories of toilers has resulted in no appreciable gain. There was the difficulty of rational utilization of large masses for temporary work, and there were defects in the operation of economic organizations. These factors sharply reduced labor productivity in the basic professions and disturbed the general course of work. . . .

A painful inheritance of the past year is the heavy indebtedness incurred by various economic organizations to the population for work performed in line of compulsory labor. This indebtedness

[49] *Dopolneniya k obzoru deyatelnosti narodnogo komissariata truda za 1921 god*, p. 24.

was due to the shortage of money tokens and material resources. The general figures of this indebtedness have reached colossal dimensions. Thus the Main Committee of Timber Industry alone owes the workers 23.5 billion rubles in money, 180 *puds* of fats, 13,293 *puds* of meat, 63 *puds* of tea, 841,286 boxes of matches, 1,790,916 *puds* of oats, 48,869 *puds* of salt, 20,847 *puds* of kerosene, 314,407 *arshins*[50] of textiles, 214,966 *puds* of bread, 1,281 *puds* of *makhorka* (tobacco), 489 *puds* of sugar, 387,244 *puds* of herring, and 232 *puds* of millet.

THE USE OF INCENTIVES TO STIMULATE LABOR PRODUCTIVITY

During the period under consideration, sporadic efforts were made to stimulate labor productivity by incentives rather than merely by compulsion. One incentive was the payment of money bonuses for greater output, but this measure could not be made effective because of the catastrophic depreciation of the Russian currency. By 1920 the purchasing power of the ruble was practically nil, and a decree was issued in June, 1920, that authorized the payment of bonuses in kind.[51] This measure also proved ineffective, because of the shortage of food and other consumers' goods.

Another attempt to adjust wages to the status and skill of the worker was made in a decree of the *Sovnarkom* of October 23, 1920, which announced that a special reserve of 500,000 *puds* of bread, quantities of other food products, and industrial consumers' goods had been set aside to be used as bonuses for increased productivity. Whether deliberately or by oversight, the bread reserve was not used exclusively as an incentive to factory workers but also for raising the meager bread rations of the Moscow

---

[50] An *arshin* is 28 inches.
[51] *S.U.R.*, 1920, No. 55, Art. 239.

population. Toward the end of January, 1921, Lenin complained that the special reserve of 500,000 *puds* of bread was being improperly used—that the 170,000 *puds* of bread that had already been used had not been spent for the purpose for which they were intended—and said that he was setting up a commission to look into this irregularity. Lenin thought that equality in food distribution was not the proper guiding principle; it was better, he said, to take bread and meat away from slow workers and give them to "shock" workers.[52]

WAGE DIFFERENTIALS IN KIND

[Decree of the *Sovnarkom*, October 23, 1920][53]

1. Wage bonuses in kind are introduced for the purpose of increasing labor productivity in enterprises. Bonuses are to be awarded on the basis of a worker's labor intensity in fulfilling his work program.

2. The total number of articles to be distributed to workers and employees (bonus fund) is to be fixed monthly by the Department of Labor Standards of the *Guberniya* Trade-Union Council or the *Uezd* Trade-Union Bureau on the basis of fulfillment of the work program. A 200 percent fulfillment entitles the plant to receive the full bonus fund.

Fulfillment of 175 percent entitles the plant to 85 percent of full bonus;

Fulfillment of 150 percent entitles the plant to 70 percent of full bonus;

Fulfillment of 125 percent entitles the plant to 55 percent of full bonus;

Fulfillment of 100 percent entitles the plant to 40 percent of full bonus.

No premiums in kind are to be issued if the work program is fulfilled by less than 100 percent. In the case of model plants, the

52 Lenin, *Sochineniya*, XXVI, 73.
53 *S.U.R.*, 1920, No. 92, Art. 497.

base for computing bonuses is higher; i.e., no bonuses are awarded if the production program is fulfilled less than 125 percent.

The distribution of wage bonuses, which is effective until January 1, 1921, comes from a special fund established by the *Sovnarkom.*

Note: The production programs of enterprises must be approved by the Supreme Council of National Economy. Output norms cannot be below those during any time in 1920.

3. If the percentage of plan fulfillment has been set incorrectly and an erroneous bonus allowance was made, the bonus award during the next month is made with the view of correcting the previous error.

4. The staff of an enterprise is divided into two groups. In the first group are included all workers and the technical and administrative personnel. Bookkeepers and clerical and servicing personnel are included in the second group. Employees of Main Administrations are included in the second group. The total premium fund is to be distributed between the two groups in the ratio 1.5 to 1.

Note: Depending on the character of the production process, the formation of a third group is permissible, if this is found necessary.

5. Bonuses are allotted to individual workers in accordance with their overfulfillment of established production norms:

For 1.5 output norms, 25 percent of the full premium;
For 2.0 output norms, 50 percent of the full premium;
For 2.5 output norms, 75 percent of the full premium;
For 3.0 output norms, 100 percent of the full premium.

6. Premiums for administrative and technical personnel of the first group and those included in the second group are computed on the basis of the average productivity of the factory or workshop; i.e., if the output is increased threefold, the administrative-technical personnel and those of group 2 receive 50 percent of the maximum premium for their group.

7. Items of the bonus fund, in case of substitution, are compared on the basis of a special table of equivalents.

8. Bonuses are awarded for working days only. Individuals who violated labor discipline may be deprived of their bonuses either in part or as a whole.

V. ULYANOV (LENIN)
Chairman of the Sovnarkom

FUND OF BONUSES IN KIND

[Appendix to Art. 497 (n 53)]

Bread .... 500,000 *puds* [a]
Fish .... 200,000 *puds* [b]
Salt .... 30,000 *puds* (allocated until Jan. 1, 1921)
Sugar .... 50,000 *puds* [b]
Fats .... 10,000 *puds* [b]
Tea .... 30,000 *funts*
China .... 65 car loads (for one year)
Pots and pans ...... 10 car loads (issued only once)
Textiles .... 5.5 million *arshins* (for one year)
Kerosene .... 575,000 *puds* (for one year)

Haberdashery valued
at 100 million rubles [b]

[a] A *pud* is 36 pounds; a *funt* is nine-tenths of a pound; an *arshin* is 28 inches.
[b] Period of time not specified.

INEFFICACY OF SOCIAL-BENEFITS LEGISLATION

Social-benefits legislation, of which there was no lack during the period under consideration, had but little relationship to the realities of the time. Numerous decrees dealt with the protection of labor, health insurance, and unemployment benefits, but, because of the confusion and the catastrophes of the period, these decrees had almost no effect on the welfare of the masses and represented little more than the well-meaning intentions of the Bolshevik leaders. This, in so many words, was admitted by Schmidt, People's Commissar of Labor, in a speech before the Third All-Russian Congress of Trade Unions in April, 1920.

Reviewing the previous social-benefits legislation of the Soviet government, he observed: "Experience and practice have demonstrated that it is one thing to say that we shall adopt a policy of labor protection, but another thing to carry it into practice in the face of the unfavorable economic conditions of the country. . . . In practically every problem relating to labor protection we were forced to retreat from our general declarations and general principles by the economic conditions of the country." [54]

In addition, the Central Council of Trade Unions had been busily engaged in formulating elaborate wage agreements, but these agreements had no direct bearing on the workers' standard of living—as was pointed out by Ye. Preobrazhensky, a Bolshevik expert in public finance, in a statement he made at the Tenth Party Congress on March 15, 1921. Viewing Soviet wage policies in retrospect, Preobrazhensky called attention to the utter lack of co-ordination between wages and prices during the first three years of Soviet rule in Russia. Also, he attributed the deterioration of the workers' standard of living to the unlimited printing of paper money, which was one of the pillars of Bolshevik financial policy.

CURRENCY DEPRECIATION AND ITS IMPACT ON THE WORKERS' STANDARD OF LIVING

[Excerpt from a statement by Ye. Preobrazhensky at the Tenth Party Congress, March 15, 1921][55]

. . . During the French Revolution of 1789, the value of the French Assignats depreciated 500 times, but the value of our ruble dropped 20,000 times. We are thus 40 times "ahead" of

[54] *Tretiy Vserossiyskiy sezd professionalnykh soyuzov*, pp. 51–52; see also the speech by Devyatkin, a Menshevik, at the same Congress. Devyatkin charged the Soviet government with having destroyed the well-organized and well-run hospital-insurance system that had been established by the trade unions for the benefit of their members (*ibid.*, pp. 54–55).

[55] *Desyatyy sezd RKP(b)*, pp. 429–30.

the French Revolution. We are still alive and manage to get along with the paper [money] which the People's Commissariat of Finance is printing. But a limit must be reached sometime. . . .

The workers receive part of their wages in money and spend it in the market. Should the value of the paper ruble reach the zero point, the position of the masses of workers and employees would be adversely affected, and the present dissatisfaction among the non-party masses is bound to increase progressively. This dissatisfaction is due, among other things, to the catastrophic depreciation of our ruble and the utter lack of correspondence between our wage rates and the price level. No one seems to know the basis of the economic laws on which the All-Russian Central Council of Trade Unions develops the wage rates. There is a complete lack of coordination between the wage rates and the requirements of a minimum standard of living. We are now facing the necessity of reexamining our financial and wage policies in their entirety. Until now we thought that the best policy of currency *emission* was to print as much paper money as possible. There was no scientific foundation for this policy, except one idea which was basically correct; namely, that the more paper [money] we print, the more commodities we can snatch. The financial idea [behind this policy] was a sound one, but there was no scientific correlation between the wage rates and the amount of paper money in circulation. During the past three years no one in the Soviet Republic paid any attention to these problems. . . .

CHAPTER V

MILITARIZATION OF THE TRANSPORT SYSTEM AND THE REVOLT AGAINST TROTSKY'S POLICIES

The policy of labor militarization was applied with special severity to the Russian transport system after the system had been placed under Trotsky's control, in the early part of March, 1920. It was in the transport system, moreover, that the validity of the institutions of labor militarization was most sharply questioned. A revolt by a group of leaders of the railway and the water-transport trade unions was so serious that for several months the Communist Party leadership was gripped by indecision and grave internal conflicts.

Sharp differences on labor policies emerged toward the end of 1920 and were aggravated by the eruption of tensions and conflicts among the leaders who were competing for influence. Rivalries at the center, which made it increasingly difficult to maintain a consistent policy toward labor, created a situation that led to a relaxation of the severity of the labor militarization regime.

A. Establishment of "Glavpolitput" and the Merger of the Railway and Water-Transport Unions

Upon assuming the duties of Commissar of Railways, Trotsky proceeded to apply to the railway system the methods he had used in the organization and operation of the Red Army. The principal agency he employed for the enforcement of strict military discipline on the railways was the Central Political Administration of the Railways, more generally known by its abbreviated name, *Glavpolitput* [*Glavnoe politicheskoe upravlenie putey soobshcheniya*].

The political administration of the Commissariat of Railways was first established in March, 1919,[1] and this agency was reorganized on February 17, 1920—after the mobilization of the entire railway service was decreed on January 30, 1920. The reorganization decree, over L. Krasin's[2] signature, defined the mission of *Glavpolitput* mainly in the field of production propaganda and political indoctrination of the railway personnel.[3] A mobilization of 5,000 Communists was also ordered to help in restoring the transport system.[4]

When Trotsky took over the administration of the railway system he brought with him a good many Red Army political commissars, and with their aid he proceeded to redirect the activities of *Glavpolitput* along lines that were analogous to the operations of the Central Political Administration of the Red Army. This agency served as a watchdog over the Red Army military commanders and, at the same time, enforced strict military discipline among the rank and file.

The new agency proceeded to reorganize the entire railway administration by appointing its own local railway executives and political commissars. It did this over the heads of the All-Russian Central Council of Trade Unions, the Central Committee of the Railwaymen's Union, and local party organizations, thereby creating much resent-

---

[1] *Vestnik putey soobshcheniya*, 1919, No. 11, pp. 26–27; *Bolshaya Sovetskaya entsiklopediya*, 1st ed., XVII, 144.

[2] Krasin was Trotsky's predecessor as People's Commissar of Railways and he was shifted to Soviet diplomacy.

[3] *Izvestiya tsentralnogo komiteta Rossiyskoy kommunisticheskoy partii*, No. 13, March 2, 1920.

[4] *Ibid.*

ment among trade-union men as well as among local party politicians.

The "problem" of *Glavpolitput* came up at the Ninth Party Congress, when Trotsky introduced a resolution that sought to justify the methods the new agency was using. Trotsky alleged that the principal difficulties of the transportation system were due to the weakness of the railwaymen's trade union, that the primary mission of *Glavpolitput* was to assist the railwaymen's unions in raising the efficiency of the railway system, and that this mission could be achieved only by appointing trusted Party members to take charge of the railroads for the period of the emergency.

Trotsky's resolution was criticized by a number of speakers, and several amendments were introduced. After a protracted debate, on March 31, 1920, the resolution was referred to a special committee, where it was approved in exactly the same form in which it had originally been introduced.[5]

THE MOBILIZATION OF FORMER RAILWAY WORKERS

[Decree of the Council of Workers' and Peasants' Defense, January 30, 1920][6]

The Council of Workers' and Peasants' Defense herewith resolves:

1. To proclaim a general labor mobilization of all persons between eighteen and fifty years of age who during the past ten years have been employed on the railways in the capacity of locomotive engineers, assistant engineers, firemen, stokers of all classes and grades, as well as boilermen, technicians and assemblymen in depots and main repair shops, and train crews of every kind.

[5] The debates are printed in *Devyatyy sezd Rossiyskoy kommunisticheskoy partii*, pp. 178–81; the draft resolution is on pp. 189–90; and the final resolution is on pp. 379–80.

[6] *Izvestiya glavnogo komiteta po vseobshchey trudovoy povinnosti*, No. 1, March, 1920, pp. 45–47; see also *S.U.R.*, 1920, No. 8, Art. 52.

2. Subject to mobilization are all individuals of the above-enumerated trades, irrespective of whether they are employed in some other enterprise or institution, engaged in some other occupation, or are presently not engaged in any work.

[Paragraphs 3 to 12 describe the procedures of registration and of distribution of the mobilized workers to their new assignments.]

13. Individuals who are subject to mobilization in accordance with this decree and who fail to register in due time (three days following the promulgation of the decree) are to be turned over to the Revolutionary Tribunal, or are liable to be sentenced to confinement in concentration camps for five years. The same sentence is to be imposed on responsible managers and administrators of institutions and enterprises [who are found] guilty of concealing the fact that individuals enumerated in paragraph 1 of this decree are in their employment.

14. The present decree is promulgated by telegraph. The present decree is also applicable to individuals whose trades are enumerated in paragraph 1 of this decree and who have previously registered with the People's Commissariat of Railways in accordance with the decree of the Council of Defense and published in the *Izvestiya VTsIK*, No. 281, 14 December 1919.

V. Ulyanov (Lenin)
*Chairman of the Council
of Workers' and Peasants' Defense*

WHY "GLAVPOLITPUT" WAS ESTABLISHED

[Resolution of the Ninth Party Congress, April 4, 1920][7]

For the near future, railway transport is bound to remain the center of attention and effort of the Party and the Soviet government. Improvement in this field is the indispensable prerequisite even for the most modest achievements in all other sectors of the economy, particularly in the food-supply problem.

The basic difficulty in the matter of improving the transportation system is due to the weakness of the railway trade union, a

---

[7] *Devyatyy sezd Rossiyskoy kommunisticheskoy partii*, pp. 379–80.

result of the heterogeneous character of railway personnel, among whom there are large numbers who worked during the Rukhlov [8] period, and of the mobilization for military service of the Communists, who were the most class-conscious and self-sacrificing members of the railway proletariat.

Believing that one of the most important tasks of the Party is to assist in every possible way the railway trade union, whose participation in raising the efficiency of the railway system is essential, the Congress recognizes at the same time the absolute urgency of taking exceptional and extraordinary measures (such as martial law), necessitated by the frightful disintegration of the transport system, in order to prevent its complete paralysis and the ruin of the Soviet Republic.

The Congress considers the Central Political Administration of the Railways (*Glavpolitput*) as a provisional organ of the Communist Party and the Soviet government that will require further strengthening, and that will pursue simultaneously two interconnected tasks: to improve immediately the transport system by the organized efforts of experienced Communists—the best representatives of the working class; and to strengthen the railwaymen's trade union by including the best workers whom the Central Political Administration of the Railways is sending to the railroads, and by helping the [railway] trade union introduce iron discipline in its organization in order to make the railwaymen's trade union an indispensable instrument for the further improvement of the railway system.

Upon the accomplishment of this work, *Glavpolitput* and its local organs should, in as short a time as possible, be made a part of the railwaymen's trade unions, on the one hand, and of the regular institutions of the People's Commissariat of Railways, on the other.

FRICTION AMONG "GLAVPOLITPUT," THE RAILWAY TRADE UNIONS, AND THE WATER-TRANSPORT UNIONS

Glavpolitput soon found itself in open warfare with the Central Committee of the Railwaymen's Trade Unions—

---

[8] Sergey Vasilevich Rukhlov was a Tsarist Minister of Railways (1909–15) and one of the founders of the Russian National Union, a political organization of the extreme right.

which was known as *Tsekprofsozh*[9]—on the one hand and with the Central Committee of the Water-Transport Trade Unions—known as *Tsekvod*[10]—on the other. In the first encounters with *Glavpolitput*, the two unions suffered a smashing defeat; their central committees were abolished by order of the Party Central Committee on August 28, 1920, and were replaced by a new Central Committee combining the two transport unions, known as *Tsektran*.[11] But the bitterness of the struggle that accompanied these organizational changes, as well as the high-handed methods used in the administration of the transport system, aroused such fierce opposition among the transport workers that it led to an open revolt within *Tsektran*—just at the time that Trotsky's position in the Communist hierarchy was seriously challenged by his rivals for political power.

Although the story of how Trotsky applied his military model to the administration of the transport system is rather complicated, and there is little official material to assist in relating it in detail, the general course of developments can be reconstructed on the basis of the various charges and countercharges that were made at the Tenth Party Congress in March, 1921. Some of the editorial notes in Trotsky's *Collected Works* (Vol. XV) and the editorial notes in the 1933 edition of the stenographic records of the Tenth Congress of the Russian Communist Party also are of help. These sources reveal the following sequence of events.

Apparently, when Trotsky took charge of the railway system in March, 1920, he demanded that the water-transport union be consolidated with the railwaymen's trade union and that their central committees (*Tsekvod*

---

[9] From *Tsentralnyy komitet profsoyuzov zheleznodorozhnogo transporta*.

[10] From *Tsentralnyy komitet profsoyuzov vodnogo transporta*.

[11] From *Tsentralnyy komitet profsoyuzov rabotnikov transporta*.

and *Tsekprofsozh*) be merged into one committee.[12] He urged this merger in order to ensure complete control over the entire transport system. This demand was granted, and on March 13, 1920, the Party Central Committee passed a resolution that authorized the All-Russian Central Council of Trade Unions to make the necessary arrangements for the unification. To facilitate matters, Ishchenko, the chairman of *Tsekvod*—who was known to be against the merger—was removed from his position and a committee that represented the two trade unions was appointed to work out the details of the merger.[13]

The committee took its time in developing the arrangements for the forthcoming unification of the two transport unions, for it was generally known that the central committees of the unions were opposed to the amalgamation. So, too, was Tomsky, the chairman of the All-Russian Central Council of Trade Unions, who was consistently among the opponents of Trotsky's labor militarization policies.[14] Trotsky then decided to force the issue by a flanking movement. Without waiting for the formal merger of the two trade unions, on April 19, 1920, he established a central political administration for the water-transport union, called *Glavpolitvod*, which he placed under the jurisdiction of *Glavpolitput*. *Glavpolitvod* proceeded to introduce the same measures that *Glavpolitput* had employed in the railway system into the administration of the water-transport system: political commissars were appointed to ships, ports, and other installations of the water-transport system.[15] In this way were the two transport

[12] The railway and water-transport unions were among the largest in Russia. In 1919 the railwaymen's union included 400,000 workers and employees; the water-transport union during the same year numbered 200,000 members (*Vestnik putey soobshcheniya*, 1919, No. 12, p. 18). No data are available for 1920, but the membership of these unions must have risen considerably.

[13] Trotsky, *Sochineniya*, XV, 589.

[14] *Desyatyy sezd RKP(b)*, p. 372.

[15] Trotsky, *Sochineniya*, XV, p. 589.

systems merged, before the trade-union leaders of these services knew what was happening.

Trotsky, in his next step, removed the most serious obstacle to his methods for enforcing strict military discipline in the operation of the railways—the Central Committee of the Railwaymen's Union, or *Tsekprofsozh*. This was accomplished by calling a congress of the railway unions, which met in July, 1920, and created a central committee. Only one member of the old central committee survived, a man named Amosov, and Trotsky headed the list of the new central committee members.

Meanwhile, the committee that had been set up to work out the procedures for the merger of the two transport unions had proceeded slowly, and only toward the end of August, 1920, did it issue its report. In a last effort to forestall the merger, Tomsky appealed to the Party Central Committee—at its meeting on August 26—to reconsider the decision to merge the central committees of *Tsekprofsozh* and *Tsekvod*. The Party Central Committee, however, rejected Tomsky's request[16] and adopted the following resolution.

MERGER OF THE CENTRAL COMMITTEES OF THE
RAILWAY AND WATER-TRANSPORT TRADE UNIONS

[Resolution of the Party Central Committee, August 26, 1920][17]

A provisional central committee of the amalgamated trade unions of the water-transport workers and the railway workers is to be organized by the All-Russian Central Council of Trade Unions. Preference is to be given to members of the two [existing] central committees, provided that a majority is secured for the comrades who follow the line approved by the Central Com-

---

[16] *Desyatyy sezd RKP(b)*, p. 872.
[17] *Ibid.*

mittee of the RKP(b). In the event that the Presidium of the All-Russian Central Council of Trade Unions requires the presence of Party Central Committee members to assist in carrying through this resolution in the [Communist] faction of the All-Russian Central Council of Trade Unions, Comrades Stalin, Bukharin, and Krestinsky are appointed to attend the meeting as representatives of the Central Committee of the RKP(b).

B. Creation of "Tsektran" and the First Open Revolt Against Trotsky's Policies

Whether with or without the assistance of the members of the Party Central Committee who had been delegated so as to bolster the merger resolution, the Communist faction of the All-Russian Central Council of Trade Unions, as well as the Plenum of this organization, accepted the merger on September 3, 1920. A new central committee of the union of transport workers, known as *Tsektran*, came into existence.[18]

The formal establishment of *Tsektran* did not immediately settle the question of amalgamating the trade unions. Many influential members of the water-transport union continued their opposition to the merger, and unification procedures did not actually start until October, 1920.[19] By this time the resentment against the high-handed methods of *Glavpolitput* and *Glavpolitvod*—as well as resentment against the newly established *Tsektran*, which soon became the symbol of oppression of the working class—reached a high-fever point. Resentment, furthermore, spread to other trade unions, which feared that Trotsky harbored designs to extend his unrestrained disciplinary policies to other organizations. The discontent became too widespread to be concealed, and it burst out at the Fifth All-

---

[18] Trotsky, *Sochineniya*, XV, 589; *Desyatyy sezd RKP(b)*, p. 872.
[19] Trotsky, *Sochineniya*, XV, 586.

Russian Conference of Trade Unions, which was held November 3–7, 1920.[20]

As was customary on such occasions, the Bolshevik members of the conference met in advance to decide their stand on the issues to be considered at the conference, and a sharp clash of points of view developed at this meeting. Trotsky, who continued to look upon labor conscription as an essential feature of a socialist economy, advocated a policy of gradually transforming the trade unions into instruments of Soviet economic policy. He launched a general attack on the trade unions, which, in his view, needed a good deal of shaking up (*peretryakhivanie*) before they could become suitable instruments for the administration of industry.

One of Trotsky's principal lieutenants, Goltsman, was even more violent in his outbursts. Goltsman urged the necessity of using "merciless black-jack discipline in relation to the working masses who are pulling us back to the old order of things." Speaking for *Tsektran*, Goltsman made it clear that this organization "will not hesitate in using jails, exile, and hard labor on people who are incapable of understanding what we are aiming at." [21]

Trotsky and his followers were vigorously attacked by Tomsky,[22] Chairman of the All-Russian Council of Trade Unions, and by A. S. Lozovsky, Alexander Shlyapnikov, and others who felt that the time had come to relax the methods of labor militarization. Because of the sharp differences that developed among the leading Communists on the question of trade-union policy, it was decided, at Tomsky's suggestion, that the problem be taken up by the Plenum of the Party Central Committee.

[20] A conference is a much smaller assembly than a congress.
[21] *Desyatyy sezd RKP(b)*, p. 871.
[22] See the extracts from Tomsky's speech at the Tenth Party Congress, quoted below (pp. 256–58); also see Lenin, *Sochineniya*, XXVI, 623, 632.

At the first meeting of the Plenum, on November 8, 1920, two sets of "theses" were presented—one by Trotsky, the other by Lenin—and excerpts from Trotsky's theses are quoted below. Although Lenin's theses have not been preserved, the resolution the Plenum adopted on the following day was based largely on Lenin's arguments. The main burden of these arguments seems to have been that a line of demarcation should be drawn between "healthy forms of labor militarization," which presumably were to remain in force, and "the degeneration of centralized and militarized forms of work into bureaucracy, bullying, red-tapism, and petty tutelage over the trade unions," which were to be repudiated. The resolution also suggested that *Tsektran* should adopt the "normal methods of proletarian democracy." [23]

THE TRADE-UNION CRISIS AND HOW TO SOLVE IT

[Trotsky's theses, presented before the Plenum of the
Party Central Committee, November 8, 1920] [24]

1. Our trade unions are passing through a most severe crisis which is being felt, recognized and corroborated by nearly all trade-union workers, both local and central. This crisis has been brought about by numerous causes and is assuming different forms in different trade unions. The crisis is aggravated by the unhealthy phenomena which have arisen in consequence of the separation of the "tops" and the "bottoms" [in the administrative hierarchy]. It will help us to understand the special and *peculiar character of the crisis which the trade unions are going through*, if we abstract from the general conditions and difficulties which characterize the life of all organizations and institutions in Soviet Russia.

2. The basic reason for the crisis is the *indefiniteness and the dual position and role of the trade unions in production*. During

---

[23] *Ibid.*, p. 624; also *Desyatyy sezd RKP(b)*, p. 798.
[24] *Desyatyy sezd RKP(b)*, pp. 785–89; italics as in the original text.

the first period of Soviet rule the trade unions tried to take over the machinery of production, but they were not adapted to the task. Concurrently with this attempt, the Soviet machinery of industrial administration, as well as the administration of other branches of the economy, began to take shape. Leaning to some extent on the trade unions, the Soviet administrative machinery became completely independent of the unions and concentrated economic leadership in its own hands. In this way the trade-union machinery exists side by side with the machinery which has effective charge of the administration of industry. As time goes on, the independence and separateness of the economic administrative machinery develops increasingly, and that means isolation from the trade unions which are being pushed out from actual participation in economic life. They are given dubious and rather limited missions, such as recommending candidates for positions in the administrative departments or engaging in production propaganda. There are no future prospects for the trade unions. Some of the more active trade-union workers are dissatisfied with existing conditions and are trying to leave trade-union work. If the crisis in its present form continues, the trade unions are in danger of complete collapse.

3. In a workers' state a trade union is an organization which comprises the workers of a given branch of the economy and which aims to serve adequately the interests of production and at the same time to improve the material and spiritual life of the workers. A union of producers does not mean a union which is connected with production but means a union for production; i.e., a union which fully participates in its work, including the management of production. If this is true, it becomes clear that in a workers' state the parallel existence of economic organizations and of trade-union organizations can be tolerated only as a temporary phenomenon. The thoughts and energies of the Communist Party, of the trade unions', and of the workers' state must be directed toward fusing, in the more or less near future, the economic organizations with the trade unions. . . .

4. In this way the working class, which is at the helm of the state, is confronted with a double task in relation to the trade unions. On the one hand, it is necessary that the trade unions take over production, but on the other hand it is essential to ensure that the unions are capable of taking over production. It

is this task that should be presented to the trade unions with precision and clarity. The production role of trade unions in a workers' state is radically different from the role of "trade unions" in a capitalist state. But as the independence of the state-economic institutions increases, the trade unions continue to look upon the state as one side of the [collective] *bargaining process.* This [traditional] trade-union attitude, which is penetrating the psychology of a good many trade-union leaders, is fraught with great danger, both to the trade unions and to the economic organizations; in other words, to the working class as a whole.

5. After presenting to the trade unions the clear and distinct goal of placing them in a dominant position in the economic life [of the country], the Party must raise the problem of reorganizing, reconstructing, and re-educating the unions *with the above objective in mind.*

Insofar as the state-economic institutions [25] are concerned, we build, rebuild, break them up, and build again, selecting and checking on many workers in various positions. The trade unions stand completely aside from this work. And yet it is so patently clear that, if the trade unions are given the task of mastering the production processes, it is necessary right now to start reorganizing the unions by selecting, first of all, its leading personnel.

6. It is absolutely clear that only the Party, the All-Russian Central Council of Trade Unions, and the Soviet state as a whole are capable of taking charge of transforming the trade unions into production unions and of providing personnel and material resources needed for this transformation. In the case of *Tsektran,* the organizational changes needed to transform the union into a productional type of organization were achieved by extremely rough and violent measures which were dictated by exceptional circumstances. If, on the other hand, the role of the trade unions in the Soviet state is clearly and distinctly defined and is made acceptable to all trade-union workers, the organizational measures needed for the reconstruction of the trade unions are very likely to assume a moderate character and involve a minimum of friction. For it is absolutely clear that in this critical question, on which the future of the trade unions depends, the unions cannot

[25] By "state-economic institutions" Trotsky meant the administrative framework that had been established by the Supreme Council of National Economy. The same is true of "economic organizations."

be left to themselves. They should receive clear and explicit directives from the Party, as well as material help from the workers' state. In one case, the guiding role was played by *Glavpolitput*; in another, by the provisional commission attached to the All-Russian Central Council of Trade Unions with the participation of representatives of the Party Central Committee.*

7. [This section repudiates the charge that the program leans toward syndicalism].

8. The reorganization of the trade unions should proceed in the following manner:

    a. The unions should be given a broad production task (mastering industrial production), which is to serve as the basis for propaganda, agitation, organization, and the selection of personnel.

    b. The unions should be strengthened through the addition of a substantial number of employees whose economic and administrative abilities have been proven by their work in other fields.

    c. The unions should be provided with the necessary apparatus that is technically able to take care of all the problems which the unions are facing.

9. The present conditions of the country exclude the possibility of a simultaneous improvement in every economic field and therefore prevent the concurrent strengthening of all trade unions. For this we have neither the people nor the resources. The shock principle [26] [therefore] becomes inevitable under present conditions. Its necessity is fully understood by the wide masses of workers, including trade-union workers. Leaders of industrial branches that have no claim to exclusive attention are

---

* It is not clear what Trotsky means by the "provisional committee attached to the All-Russian Central Council of Trade Unions with the participation of representatives of the Party Central Committee." He may be making reference to the role played by the All-Russian Central Council of Trade Unions during the negotiations for the merger of *Tsekprofsozh* and *Tsekvod* and the three members of the Party Central Committee who were designated to assist in the merger negotiations. See pp. 188–89 (above).

[26] Toward the end of 1920 a movement developed of designating specific plants and industries as "shock plants" and "shock industries." Most of these plants were in the metallurgical industry, and especially armaments and transport-construction plants. The designated plants were given first priority in manpower and other resources. This practice became the principal feature of Soviet industrial policy throughout the entire period of the so-called "planned economy" and is still widely used even at the present time.

taking the initiative in applying the shock principle, in the sense that they select a few enterprises and devote every resource to their reorganization.

10. At the present time, first priority should be given to strengthening the Metal Workers' Trade Union.[27] There should be established at once a commission consisting of representatives of the All-Russian Central Council of Trade Unions, [representatives] of the Central Committee of Metal Workers, [representatives] of the Party Central Committee, and [representatives] of the Section of Metals [of the S.C.N.E.] to make a detailed study of conditions in the Metal Workers' Union and to take the most energetic measures to strengthen the central and local organizations of the union by the addition of energetic workers and organizers.

11. The production union should include all workers employed in a given branch of the economy, beginning with the unskilled laborer and [continuing] up to the highly trained engineers. The union should keep a record of all its members from the point of view of production and should have a complete and precise characterization of the productional capabilities of every member.

The union should impose certain union obligations on all workers occupying administrative or administrative-technical positions. *Work for the union should constitute an essential and prescribed addition to work for production.*

It is essential that the rank and file of the workers should realize that their interests are best defended by those administrators who raise the productivity of labor, restore the economy, and increase the amount of material goods. It is essential that this type of organizer and administrator be selected for the leading positions in the trade unions, whether they be workers from the bench or specialists in the field of trade-union work.

12. [In this section Trotsky proposes that in those unions where a shift toward improvement has already taken place, the methods of workers' democracy should be applied gradually, encouraging such practices as discussion at mass meetings of production problems and election of economic administrators to a number of positions.]

13. The problem of employing specialists in industry presents

[27] Shlyapnikov, Chairman of the Metal Workers' Union, probably did not cherish Trotsky's attention to his union.

some difficulties, especially [those of] fitting the specialists into the trade-union pattern. However, with sufficient persistency and consistency this problem can be solved.

14. All specialists, without exception, should be investigated by the trade unions. By virtue of past conditions and the fact that the civil war is not yet over, the specialists should be divided into three categories: (1) probational (recent adherents of Kolchak and Wrangel), (2) candidates [for trade-union membership], and (3) full members of trade unions. Only specialists in the third category may be appointed to responsible positions, with no commissars watching over them. Specialists of the second category may occupy responsible positions only when they are attached to commissars of production unions. Specialists in the first category can serve only as assistants or consultants of administrators who are members of the union. In this way the title of a union member will become an important symbol in the consciousness of the workers as well as of the specialists.

There is no contradiction between the principle of labor militarization (in the spirit of the resolution of the Ninth Party Congress) and the principle of labor democracy and the initiative of the masses. Militarization of labor is the unavoidable and essential method for the transition from the system of the labor market, which has been destroyed, to a system of planned and universal labor conscription which was adopted during the critical economic conditions of the country. This militarization, as the Ninth Party Congress has made clear, can be made effective only under the leadership of class-conscious workers and revolutionary peasants. During the transitional period, the unavoidable measures of compulsion must find their justification in developing the initiative, and raising the cultural and productivity levels of tens of millions of workers and peasants.

Drawing a sharp contrast between "military" methods (command, punishment) and trade-union methods (persuasion, propaganda, initiative) is nothing but the expression of the Kautskyite–Menshevik–Socialist Revolutionists' prejudices. Militarization of labor in a workers' state cannot be realized without the initiative of hundreds of thousands of workers and peasants, which is then transformed into the initiative of millions and millions and gradually absorbs and dissolves the harsher features of compulsion. The mere antithesis between labor organization and military organization in a workers' state represents a shameful capitulation to Kautskyite ideas. The Red Army is the fruition of the initiative of the proletariat and the revolutionary peasantry. It is on this initiative and the uninterrupted agitation and propaganda among backward layers of the peasantry that the foundation was laid for the "militarization" of the Red Army; i.e., bringing up [that Army] in the spirit of obedience to orders and of self-sacrifice in the defense of the Soviet republic.

15. By developing this system still further, by gradually increasing the application of the principle of election, and by binding closer and closer the responsibilities within the union with those of production, we shall arrive, in the more or less near future, to a point at which the union will gain complete control over a given branch of production and, using the methods of selection and election, will form the apparatus of economic management from its own midst and under the general control and guidance of the workers' state which coordinates the operation of every branch of the economy.

THE PARTY CENTRAL COMMITTEE CONDEMNS "UNHEALTHY" FORMS OF LABOR MILITARIZATION

[Resolution of the Plenum of the Party Central Committee, November 9, 1920][28]

1. The resolution of the Ninth Party Congress concerning the necessity of directing every effort to the economic reconstruction of the country is now acquiring a new significance on account of the expected victory over Wrangel and the possibility that the Party, the Soviet organizations, and the trade unions may now be in a position to concentrate on the struggle against destruction.

The Central Committee calls the attention of all workers' organizations to the resolution of the Ninth Party Congress, which emphasized the absolute necessity of adopting military forms of work at a time when the government of workers and peasants was trying to liquidate the unprecedented ruin of the economy.

2. On the other hand, [the Central Committee recognizes that] the successful achievement of this work requires the maximum initiative of workers' organizations, especially of the trade unions. This makes it necessary to wage a relentless and systematic campaign against the degeneration of centralized and mili-

[28] *Desyatyy sezd RKP(b)*, pp. 798–99.

tarized forms of work into bureaucracy, bullying, red-tapism, and petty tutelage over the trade unions. Healthy forms of labor militarization will be crowned with success only to the extent that the Party, the Soviets and the trade unions succeed in explaining the necessity of these methods, if the country is to be saved, to the widest masses of the workers and in attracting to this work the most advanced groups.

3. The role of trade unions in [industrial] production and management has been set forth in sufficient detail in the resolution of the Ninth Party Congress. The Ninth Congress of our Party characterized the current tasks of the trade unions in the following terms:

"In conformity with this, the methods and tempos of trade-union work have to be changed radically. If the proletariat as a class faces the problem of transition to military methods of work, i.e., extreme punctuality, obedience to orders, responsibility, rapid and energetic work, and supreme self-sacrifice, then the above relates, first of all, to the organs of industrial administration generally and, consequently, to the trade unions."

The present task before us is to reconstruct and strengthen the trade-union apparatus in order to make it possible for the unions to enlarge their role in production and to influence the wide masses of the proletariat (by means of production propaganda) [to work for] the most rational reconstruction of the national economy.

4. Recognizing the necessity of retaining the shock principle [29] in carrying out economic plans, the Central Committee, in full solidarity with the last Party Conference, finds it necessary to bring about a gradual but undeviating transition to equality in the position of the various groups of workers and their trade unions, and to strengthen, at the same time, the all-union organization [of trade unions].

5. In view of the production successes already achieved, the Party Central Committee believes that the time for using exceptional methods of administration (for which *Glavpolitput* was created) is approaching an end and, therefore, recommends that *Tsektran* should increase and develop the normal methods of proletarian democracy within the union, a task which *Tsektran* has already placed on the agenda of the day. At the same time

[29] See footnote 26 of this chapter.

the Central Committee believes that *Tsektran* should take a more active part in the general work of the All-Russian Central Council of Trade Unions on equal terms with other trade-union organizations.

6. The Central Committee has resolved to create a commission, with the participation of trade-union members, to formulate detailed instructions for the benefit of trade unions, dealing with the following problems:

   a. Formulation of a detailed program of strengthening the All-Russian Central Council of Trade Unions by means of additional workers, newspapers, and finances;

   b. Development and wider application of the methods of workers' democracy, i.e., democracy within the trade unions;

   c. Increasing the participation of the trade unions in production management, in relation to such points as procedures, methods and means;

   d. The same applies to specialists: their classification into three categories or more, their proper employment, systematic utilization, etc.;

   e. Changing the working methods of trade-union centers by virtue of the new responsibilities conferred upon the trade unions.

The commission which the Plenum of the Central Committee has appointed consists of the following comrades: Zinoviev, Tomsky, Rudzutak, and Trotsky. The chairman of the commission is Comrade Zinoviev. The commission also includes Comrades Anreev, Shlyapnikov, Lozovsky, and Lutovinov, representing the [Communist] faction of the Fifth All-Russian Conference of Trade Unions.

C. The All-Russian Conference of "Tsektran" Leaders Debates the Issue

The resolution of the Party Central Committee of November 9, which enjoined *Tsektran* leadership to adopt "the methods of proletarian democracy," apparently had little influence on the day-to-day conduct of the administration of the transport system. Nor did it affect Trotsky's outlook on the place of the working class in the proletarian state and on the role of the trade unions as the spokesmen for the working class.

In a speech delivered at the All-Russian Conference of *Tsektran* leaders in the early part of December, 1920, Trotsky defended his record as People's Commissar of Railways. He argued that militarization of labor and the appointment of union officials from above rather than election from below in no way contradicted the methods of proletarian democracy. He admitted that cruel methods were needed to teach the masses new ways of work, but he felt that the need for compulsion was in inverse proportion to the powers of the administrative machinery. "The stronger we are," he said, "the less frequent are the instances of hostility to our orders." He finally expressed the hope that other trade unions would learn something from the experience of *Tsektran*.

The majority at this conference were Trotsky's followers, and the resolution that was adopted on December 8 fully approved his policies. The resolution stressed the fact that conditions on the transport system continued to be critical and, therefore, that the decrees on militarization of the railways and water transport continued to be in force. The resolution further asserted that there was no opposition between the methods of workers' democracy and the militarization of labor: "In a proletarian state, militarization is the self-organization of the working class."

TROTSKY DEFENDS HIS RECORD AS COMMISSAR OF RAILWAYS

[Excerpts from Trotsky's speech at the Plenary Conference of *Tsektran*, December 2, 1920][30]

. . . The place which the trade unions should occupy in the general structure of Soviet institutions is far from being clear as

[30] Trotsky, *Sochineniya*, XV, 412.

a practical issue. [On the other hand,] as a theoretical question it has been fully clarified in our program. I have in mind the program of the Communist Party, the leading party of the Soviet government. In the economic section of that Program you can read the following: "The organizational apparatus of the socialized industry must be based first and foremost on a trade-union foundation. The trade unions must gradually free themselves of their narrow guild outlook and transform themselves into large-scale production associations embracing the majority, and in the course of time, every worker of a given branch of production. . . . [Ellipses in the text.] The trade unions must achieve a de facto concentration in their own hands of the entire administration of the whole national economy, considered as a single economic unit. By ensuring the closest possible tie between the central state apparatus, the national economy, and the large masses of the toilers, the trade unions will facilitate the widest possible participation of the toiling masses in the management of the economy. At the same time the participation of the trade unions in the management of the economy will serve as an instrument in the fight against the bureaucratization of the Soviet economic apparatus. . . . [Ellipses in the text.]

Although the program was written one and one half years ago, i.e., prior to the experience and the internal struggle,[31] it fully describes the problem which occupies us at this time. The trade unions must concentrate in their hands the entire management of economic life. They do not merely assist in production; they must organize production and must become fully empowered leaders in the organization of production. . . .

To reject the principle [32] of working through appointees, as a practical method of strengthening the transport system and the trade-union movement itself, is tantamount to locking up the transport system within the confines of a narrow guild of workers which we inherited from the past. It is an absolutely false idea, which will impede the transformation of the trade unions into production unions. . . .

The trade unions,[33] in their present position in the workers' state which is engaged in the building of a communist economic

[31] Trotsky had the labor militarization policy and the opposition it created in mind.
[32] Trotsky, *Sochineniya*, XV, 414.
[33] *Ibid.*, pp. 418–19.

order can either become the vehicle of all the superstitions and the prejudices of the most backward masses, or they can become the most important instruments for organizing these masses into production organizations. There is no third way available: an intermediate position reduces the trade unions to a nonentity. I consider it to be the great merit of *Tsektran* that it adopted the right course, not the course of [traditional] trade-union psychology, but the course of the emerging trade unions.

The success in the water-transport union has been less pronounced because it is a more backward sector and administratively not as centralized as railway transport. My basic conclusion is that we cannot permit the more revolutionary and advanced wing of our transport system to be held back by the more backward wing. Our aim is to transfer a large number of railway workers to the waterways in order to rectify this retarded and unprogressive sector and bring it to the general level of our production front. . . .

At the same time [34] I am bound to acknowledge that the methods which *Tsektran* was using are not the only possible methods which other trade unions must adopt. The methods [of *Tsektran*] originated at a certain time and in a certain union to meet a necessity. You know that we had to carry on a fight against the old *Tsekprofsozh*. It was an internal struggle in which the Party became involved, supporting one side against another. Was this interference justified? Was it correct that a certain tendency within the trade-union movement was given encouragement? Was it proper for the state to say that the union's head should be cut off? The [old] union did not meet the revolutionary needs of the working class and one faction within that union was engaged in a fierce struggle against those who were backward, who acted in ways that were contrary to the processes of history. What else was there to do [but to disperse the old union]? . . .

The interference of the state [35] and of the leading Party organs in the internal affairs of the Railway and Water-Transport Unions was not only justified historically but was also dictated by practical necessity. Other trade unions will learn something from our experience, but it is not at all necessary that the reconstruction of these unions should necessitate an internal struggle or brutal

[34] *Ibid.*, p. 420.
[35] *Ibid.*, pp. 421–22.

state interference. The unions can reconstruct themselves by their own efforts and we already have examples of this.

The methods of *Tsektran* were dictated by the most critical conditions of transport, the destruction of which threatened the destruction of the country. [Trotsky cited statistics on disabled locomotives.] Resolute measures were needed and we had to show the masses new methods of work, by the help of which we could carry on the struggle for the reconstruction of the country's transport. These painful and provoking methods were employed by *Tsektran*, and they called forth a certain amount of opposition and resentment which in some cases have not subsided even now. We treated some of the comrades roughly, but now we work with them in full solidarity. . . .

. . . When we talk [36] about the militarization of the transport system, we mean that every worker must give his devotion to the work on the success of which depends the life and death of the country. . . . Does it mean that militarization contradicts workers' democracy? Not at all! . . . We are not liberals, we are a class engaged in a struggle. Democracy, in the sense of political democracy, is an empty frame which has to be given economic content. I believe that this is the most important task of *Tsektran*. By means of cruel methods it has already created an administrative machinery. It secured the sympathy and the support of an overwhelming majority of the best trade-union workers. This is not as yet true in the case of the water-transport workers, but tomorrow or the day after tomorrow this is bound to happen. . . .

TROTSKY'S POLICIES ARE ENDORSED

[Excerpts from the Resolution adopted by the Plenary Conference of *Tsektran*, December 8, 1920] [37]

1. The trade union of transport workers aims to become a real production union and not merely an organization of workers of a certain trade. In a workers' state a trade union can become a meaningful organization only insofar as it takes possession of the process of production, attracts into its ranks every worker, improves the organization of labor, increases its productivity, advances the material conditions of the workers, and raises their spiritual level.

[36] *Ibid.*, pp. 423–24.
[37] *Ibid.*, pp. 438–40.

3. The Conference believes that the assignment to responsible positions in the transport system of officials who have been investigated by the workers' state is in no way objectionable but is, on the contrary, made necessary by existing conditions and is contributing to the improvement of the transport system and of the trade union.

The task of the union is to give to the working masses a business-like explanation of the nature of the so-called "appointments from above," to initiate the officials appointed by the Soviet state into the general trade-union atmosphere, to establish a close and correct collaboration between the officials appointed from above and the elected representatives of the union. [The union should also] fight against the harmful trade-union prejudices which find their expression in the propaganda against "appointments from above" and in creating animosities between the old trade-union officials and those recently appointed and placed there for the express purpose of strengthening the transport system and of helping the union to switch completely to new production methods.

4. Notwithstanding certain improvements achieved with the participation of the union, conditions of the transport system continue to be critical and require exceptional efforts. As of now, the decrees on the militarization of railway and water transport remain fully in force. They bear witness to the fact that work on the transport system requires from the railwaymen and water-transport workers the same exertion and self-sacrifice in the cause of the country's salvation as is required from Red Army soldiers on the battlefield.

5. The persistent and untiring inculcation of this idea into the minds of the masses of transport workers is one of the most important tasks of the union because the success of the so-called military methods of work (precision, submission to orders, strict responsibility, and supreme self-sacrifice) fully depends on agitation, education, organization and the punitive work of the trade union—the organization that manages production in the Soviet state.

[Paragraph 6 makes the point that the trade union should rely on the worker who has the interests of production close to his heart. Paragraph 7 urges the introduction of output quotas and the adoption of the Taylor System.]

8. The conference is fully aware of the fact that so far only the first steps have been taken in the [union's] problems. Among the workers of the railway transport, and especially of the water transport, there are large numbers of backward and semi-proletarian people. In spite of the large number of [new] officials which the union received, it is proving utterly impossible to attend to even the basic problems of the transport system, especially the water transport. The Conference considers it its duty to appeal to the central organs of the trade-union movement, the Party, and the Soviet state to help in the improvement of the work of the transport union by assigning a large number of officials capable of overcoming the widespread backwardness and inertia which prevail among the water-transport workers.

13. The Conference [38] is radically opposed to the erroneous attempts to represent the methods of workers' democracy and the militarization of labor as contradictory ideas. The militarization of labor in a proletarian state is the self-organization of the working class.[39] Proletarian discipline does not contradict proletarian democracy, they supplement each other; and this means that the introduction of workers' democracy should not be looked upon as the abandonment of militarization methods which the Ninth Party Congress and the Third All-Russian Congress of Trade Unions adopted as the basis for the reconstruction of the entire railway system.

D. The Party Central Committee is Deadlocked on the Issue of "Tsektran"

Because Trotsky's speech at the *Tsektran* conference did not satisfy many members of the transport trade unions, they formed an opposition group, led by a "committee of

[38] *Ibid.*, p. 442.

[39] The resolution was written by Trotsky and is included in his collected works. The sentence "The militarization of labor in a proletarian state is the self-organization of the working class" closely resembles a passage in Bukharin's *Ekonomika perekhodnogo perioda* (Moscow, 1920, p. 109) in which the latter argued that "universal compulsory labor under capitalism is the enslavement of the working class; but the same thing under the dictatorship of the proletariat is nothing but the self-organization of the working class." Both statements appeared about the same time, and it is not known who was the originator of this sophistry.

ten," most of whom were members of the deposed central committees of *Tsekvod* and *Tsekprofsozh*. The opposition charged that *Tsektran* had failed to carry out the provisions of the resolution that had been passed by the Party Central Committee on November 9, 1920, which prescribed that methods of proletarian democracy be adopted in the administration of the transport system.[40] They demanded, therefore, that *Glavpolitput* and *Glavpolitvod* be abolished and that the membership of *Tsektran* be changed so as to give a better representation of the real attitude of the rank and file workers. When their demands were rejected by the majority of the conference, the opposition group left the conference and appealed to the trade-union section of the Party Central Committee, which was headed by Zinoviev.[41] The oppositionists were sure to receive a sympathetic hearing from Zinoviev, who at this time was the leading figure of a powerful group within the Party Central Committee that was trying to undermine Trotsky's influence.

Zinoviev was very obliging. In his recommendations to the Party Central Committee for settling the conflict that had developed at the *Tsektran* conference, Zinoviev went even further than the oppositionists had demanded. He proposed to abolish *Glavpolitput* and *Glavpolitvod*, to dissolve *Tsektran* as it was then constituted, and to speed up the calling of a new congress of railway and water-transport unions for the election of a new *Tsektran*. Zinoviev also proposed that the new *Tsektran* be incorporated within the general trade-union structure.[42]

When Zinoviev's recommendations came up before the Party Central Committee, on December 7, 1920, they were

---

[40] *Izvestiya tsentralnogo komiteta Rossiyskoy kommunisticheskoy partii*, No. 26, December 20, 1920, p. 3.
[41] *Desyatyy sezd RKP(b)*, p. 873.
[42] Lenin, *Sochineniya*, XXVI, 624–25.

rejected by a majority vote. Bukharin then advanced a compromise solution, which is cited below. This solution, which attempted to steer a middle course in the trade-union controversy, came to be known as the Buffer Resolution and was adopted by a majority of one vote, 8 to 7.

BUKHARIN'S "BUFFER RESOLUTION"

[Adopted by the Party Central Committee, December 7, 1920][43]

[The first five paragraphs of this resolution are expressed in highly confused terms, and their rendering into precise English, without departing substantially from the text, is rather difficult. They make the following points: (1) The trade-union controversy should be given as wide a forum as possible; (2) the methods of workers' democracy should be greatly extended; (3) no forced trade-union reorganization should be attempted; (4) workers should be drawn into the problems of production organization, not only in the sense of control but also in respect to management; (5) the selection of leaders should be guided not only by considerations of political reliability but also with regard to economic competence and administrative experience.]

6. The Party is under obligation to support and educate a *new* type of trade-union leader—an energetic manager with initiative—a leader who looks upon economic life not from the point of view of distribution and consumption, but from the point of view of production, a leader who does not bargain with the Soviet government, but is [a good] organizer and manager.

7. The forthcoming Party Congress is to set forth concretely the ways in which the production role of the trade unions can be augmented. The Central Committee invites the workers of trade unions and of other economic organizations of the Republic to prepare relevant proposals and to submit them to the Central Committee.

As regards the conflict between *Tsektran* and the Water-Transport Union, the Central Committee resolved:

[43] *Desyatyy sezd RKP(b)*, p. 800.

1) To create within the consolidated *Tsektran* a water-transport section;

2) To call in February [1921] a Congress of the Railwaymen's Union and Water-Transport Union for the purpose of electing in a normal way a new *Tsektran*;

3) Meanwhile the old *Tsektran* should continue in operation;

4) To abolish *Glavpolitvod* and *Glavpolitput* immediately and to transfer their personnel and resources to the trade-union organization on the basis of normal democratic principles.

DISSENSION WITHIN THE PARTY CENTRAL COMMITTEE ON THE TRADE-UNION ISSUE

The Buffer Resolution satisfied none of the parties to the dispute.[44] Trotsky's supporters resented the abolition of *Glavpolitput* and *Glavpolitvod*, which were the principal agencies for the enforcement of discipline in the transport system. The opponents of *Tsektran*—especially the representatives of the water-transport union—were embittered by the retention of the organization in which Trotsky's followers constituted a majority. On December 10, 1920, the delegates of the water-transport union issued a statement declaring that *Tsektran*, as then constituted, was incompetent to administer water transport. The delegates submitted their resignations from *Tsektran* and withdrew from the organization.[45] They were supported in their open defiance by the knowledge that a large and influential group in the Party Central Committee, including Lenin, also was opposed to *Tsektran*.

The revolt within *Tsektran* was a turning point in the policy of labor militarization that had been introduced by the Bolsheviks early in 1920. It did not put an end to this

[44] In a pamphlet published on January 19, 1921 (in which he gave a brief outline of the principal stages of the trade-union conflict), Lenin characterized the Buffer Resolution as a "scrap of paper" (Lenin, *Sochineniya*, XXVI, 89).

[45] *Desyatyy sezd RKP(b)*, p. 873.

policy but it led to a protracted and acrimonious debate among the top-ranking party leaders—a debate that nearly split the Party Central Committee on the interconnected problems of the place of labor under communism and the role of the trade unions in the Soviet state.

At first the dissension was kept within the small group of the Party's top policy makers, but by the end of December the fight had been thrown open to everyone who wished to take part. It continued for more than two months, until the Tenth Party Congress met (March 8–16, 1921) and resolved—among other things—to put an end to the formation of groups that opposed the general Party line.[46]

STALIN'S ROLE

There was more to the acrimonious debates of these months than the disputed place of the trade unions in Soviet society. It was widely known that powerful forces within the Party Central Committee—forces led by Zinoviev, with Stalin operating behind the scenes—were trying to undermine Trotsky's position and influence. Reviewing the debates that took place during January and February, 1921, Rafail—a speaker at the Tenth Party Congress and a member of the so-called Democratic Centralists, who were basically opposed to Trotsky's program—charged that Zinoviev was circulating letters throughout the country and alleging that Trotsky's followers had seized the government and that Lenin and his followers had to go into hiding.[47] Rafail also made some caustic observations on Stalin's role in the controversy. "Not only in Petersburg under comrade Zinoviev," he said, "but also here in Moscow, in place of communiques from the military

[46] *Ibid.* ("Resolution on Party Unity"), pp. 585–87.
[47] *Ibid.*, p. 101.

fronts, our party organs are issuing communiques from the party front under the supervision and editorship of that military strategist and archdemocrat, Stalin. Every day we read dispatches telling us that victories were attained on this or that front, that Lenin's point of view has received so many votes while Trotsky had only six votes, of which one was cast by one political commissar and another by his deputy." [48]

RIFT BETWEEN LENIN AND TROTSKY

Lenin's position in the controversy seemed somewhat enigmatic. He did not object to the high-handed methods employed by *Tsektran*; on the contrary, he thought that its use of force in maintaining labor discipline worked to its credit. [49] Lenin and Trotsky were in full agreement on the need for establishing a form of military discipline, if the Communist economic experiment was to succeed, that would enable them to shift the industrial and agricultural labor force in accordance with a centrally elaborated plan. The Central Committee for Compulsory Labor had been created for this purpose and had spread its tentacles all over the country in an effort to secure labor for industry. In all this work, *Glavkomtrud* was in close contact with the Party Central Committee, headed by Lenin. Lenin knew very well that cruelty and violence were being used in carrying out labor mobilization and in enforcing harsh disciplinary measures on workers who were exposed only to the miseries of hunger and cold. At the same time there is no doubt that Lenin stood behind Zinoviev's attacks on Trotsky and pushed a few assaults of his own.

[48] *Ibid.*
[49] Lenin, *Sochineniya*, XXVI, 80.

It is a plausible assumption that the rift between Lenin and Trotsky must have been rather deep at that time and that at least some of the members of the Party Central Committee thought that the fissure could not be closed. This can be seen from a letter Stalin sent Lenin—probably early in January, 1921—in which he congratulated Lenin on the Eighth Congress of Soviets' acceptance of the electrification plan (known as *Goelro*). Lenin was supposed to have been the principal advocate of the plan, which early in 1921 he looked upon as the essence of socialism. In contrast, Stalin characterized Trotsky's theses of the previous year in the following words: "You remember Trotsky's 'plan' of last year (his theses) for the economic rebirth of Russia on the basis of mass application to the fragments of pre-war industry of the labor of unskilled peasant-worker masses (labor armies). What mediocrity, what backwardness . . . ! A medieval craftsman, fancying himself an Ibsen hero, with a calling to 'save' Russia by an ancient saga." [50]

On the whole, Lenin took only a perfunctory part in the public discussions of Soviet labor policies during January and February of 1921.[51] In a pamphlet written on January 19, 1921, and devoted to the trade-union debate, then at its apogee, Lenin said: "The party is sick, the party is shaking with fever." [52]

In many party notables, this fever seems to have taken strange forms. The great majority of the contending Communists (including Lenin), who only a few months previously had hailed forced labor as the true expression

[50] Stalin, *Sochineniya*, V, 50.
[51] A good account of the numerous proposals, as well as various moves by the contending groups, is given in L. Schapiro, *The Origin of the Communist Autocracy*, pp. 282–93.
[52] Lenin, *Sochineniya*, XXVI, 87.

of socialism in action, suddenly turned into ardent advocates of workers' democracy, trade-union democracy, etc., which they had so often ridiculed in speech and in writing.

The cult of labor democracy that swept so suddenly over the various factions of the Communist Party was shortly followed by a number of measures that were aimed at improving the workers' living conditions. In December, 1920, a number of decrees were issued that authorized the free distribution of food, fuel,[53] and industrial consumers' goods[54] to workers and employees in state enterprises and institutions. In January, 1921, another decree abolished rents and payments for water, gas, and electricity for workers and employees who lived in state-owned and municipal houses.[55] These measures, however, came too late to have any impact on the course of events. They did not prevent the outbreak of food riots by industrial workers in February, 1921,[56] nor were they effective in moderating the heated polemics within the Party over the role of labor in the socialist state.

In the course of this polemic, eleven points of view—or platforms—were formulated; but these were greatly reduced by various mergers and combinations. When the Tenth Party Congress met, in March, 1921, only three platforms came up for consideration: the Workers' Opposition platform, the Trotsky and Bukharin platform, and the platform of the Ten, which was sponsored by Lenin and Zinoviev.[57]

[53] *S.U.R.*, 1920, No. 100, Art. 539.
[54] *Ibid.*, No. 99, Art. 531.
[55] *Ibid.*, 1921, No. 6, Art. 47.
[56] See Chapter VI, p. 217.
[57] A list of all the platforms is given in *Desyatyy sezd RKP(b)*, pp. 827–28.

CHAPTER VI

THE REVOLUTION IN CRISIS

The grave, internal conflicts over the place of labor in the Soviet state and over the role of trade unions under socialism—the conflicts that agitated the Party leadership during December, 1920, and January, 1921—received comprehensive reviews at the Tenth Party Congress. This congress had been scheduled to meet early in February, 1921, but the meetings were postponed to March 8, 1921. No explanation for the postponement was given at the time, but developments during the first two months of 1921 provide the reasons for the delay. There were clear signs of a crisis, and danger of an all-out conflict with the urban workers and with the peasantry. Time was needed to evolve a strategy that would enable the Party to face the perils that were thought to be imminent.

After the Tenth Party Congress assembled it had to deal not only with the trade-union crisis but with the general crisis of the revolution as well. The Congress sanctioned a retreat from Communist positions in agriculture but it made no changes in the policy of labor compulsion. The resolution that was adopted on the labor problems was replete with ambiguities, which may have served the purpose of obtaining a majority for the proposals sponsored by Lenin, but which also helped to conceal Lenin's real purpose, which was to maintain the existing relationships with labor. The resolution, moreover, failed to reconcile the differences within the Party leadership on the role of trade unions in the Soviet state.

To prevent these differences from causing a split, and at Lenin's urging, two other resolutions were adopted.

One of these resolutions condemned the Workers' Opposition as an anarchist deviation, and the other prohibited the formation of groups within the Party that challenged the validity of the general Party line.

A. Retreat from Communist Policies in Agriculture

In the early part of 1921, Lenin began to realize that he had failed to achieve most of the grandiose political and economic objectives he had so confidently dramatized in the early stages of the revolution. Applied to Soviet labor relations, this realization must have been especially disconcerting because it was here that the contrast between what was aimed at and what was realized was most strikingly clear. In a speech on the role of the trade unions that Lenin delivered January 23, 1921, at the Second All-Russian Congress of Mine Workers, he gave frank expression to his disillusionment by asking: "Does every worker know how to administer the state?" And he answered: "Practical men know that this is a fairy tale."[1]

In making this admission, Lenin nullified years of Bolshevik propaganda, including his own, that had fostered self-generated delusions about the ease of transition from capitalism to socialism and the historic mission of the working class to usher in the classless society.

Another disillusionment must have been the realization that the gigantic, nation-wide mobilization that had been intended to bring about a speedy transformation of backward Russia into a highly organized society, working under a unified industrial and agricultural plan, also had

[1] Lenin, *Sochineniya*, XXVI, 108. In the early part of 1918, Lenin had said it was an old bourgeois prejudice "to assume that the plain worker and peasant are incapable of managing the affairs of the state" (see p. 16 and the introduction to Chapter I, above).

ended in failure. By the end of 1920, Soviet agriculture had been reduced to a congeries of small, self-contained farms that produced only what was required for the consumption of the peasant and his family. Dairy farming was on the verge of ruin. In industry, there was an almost complete breakdown of production, which by the end of 1920 yielded only about 17 percent of its pre-war output. In some of the basic branches of production the decline was even more catastrophic. Textiles had declined to 6.6 percent of the pre-war output; manufacturing of food products, widely used in the rural districts, declined to 12.3 percent; and the production of agricultural machinery stopped altogether.[2]

In his report to the Eighth All-Russian Congress of Soviets, toward the end of December, 1920, Rykov, the Chairman of the Supreme Council of National Economy, sounded a warning that the stocks of goods inherited from the bourgeoisie were now depleted and that "the next few years . . . will show whether the workers and peasants are able merely to spend what they have inherited or to produce themselves what they need."[3]

The next few years showed that the Russian workers and peasants were able to produce what they needed and to set the economy on the road to rapid recovery. They were able to do this, however, only after some of the more oppressive features of the socialist economy, which the Bolsheviks had tried to impose between 1918 and 1920, had been revoked and a new set of regulations introduced, which in some degree legalized private initiative and commercial relations. This took place at the Tenth Party Con-

---

[2] V. Sarabyanov, *Ekonomika i ekonomicheskaya politika SSSR, Gosizdat,* Moscow, 1926, pp. 204–5. This source provides extensive data on the decline of the Russian economy between 1918 and 1921 (see esp. pp. 204–47).

[3] *Vosmoy sezd sovetov rabochikh, krestyanskikh i soldatskikh deputatov,* Gosizdat, Moscow, 1921, p. 94.

gress, in March, 1921, and Lenin played the leading role in bringing about this important change. The decision to abandon the plan for the immediate socialization of Russia's entire national economy was not an easy decision for Lenin to make. He resisted it as long as he could, but the turbulent events of the first two months of 1921 convinced him that a compromise was essential if the Communists were to retain power. The sequence of major developments was somewhat as follows.

1. During the winter months of 1920/21, rebellions occurred in many rural areas in Russia as spontaneous protests against food requisitions and the imposition of compulsory labor. These, the peasantry felt, were inimical to their interests. In January, 1921, an official of the Commissariat of Food returned from the Ukraine and reported that 1,700 food-requisition officers had been killed by enraged peasants, that conditions in Siberia and the Northern Caucasus were getting out of hand, and that the wave of peasant reprisals threatened to turn into a calamity that would be difficult to control.[4]

2. On February 2–4, 1921, a conference of metal workers took place in Moscow, attended by 850 representatives of the Metal Workers Union. The principal problems under consideration were the severe food shortage in the capital and Bolshevik policy toward the peasants. According to a report by A. Vyshinsky, who at that time was with the Commissariat of Food, the conference was in an aggressive mood and defiant of anyone who defended government policy. Only opponents of government policy were allowed to express their views. The opposition demanded the abolition of all food privileges, including those enjoyed by the People's Commissars, and passed a resolu-

---

[4] *Desyatyy sezd RKP(b)*, pp. 425–26. This information was made available by Tsyurupa, the Commissar of Food, at the Tenth Party Congress.

tion demanding the replacement of food requisitioning by a food tax.[5]

3. On February 8, 1921, the *Politburo* of the Party Central Committee discussed the question of replacing crop requisitioning by a tax.[6] Its decision was not made public, but on February 16 the Party Central Committee decided to sound out party opinion on this question and allowed *Pravda* to publish articles dealing with it—one by Sorokin (February 17) and another by Rogov (February 26).[7]

4. On February 22, 1921, Petrograd workers went on strike in protest against food and fuel shortages. In some districts of the city the strike took on a political aspect because of the demand for a constituent assembly. The strike was broken by early March, partly by force and partly by rushing food and fuel to the city.[8]

5. On February 28 a revolt of the Kronstadt sailors broke out. This revolt was directed not against the Soviets but against the Communists who controlled the policies of the Soviets. The battle cry of the insurgents was "Soviets without Communists." Their program included the immediate re-election of the Soviets on the basis of free propaganda; freedom of the press, assembly, and trade; free trade unions; equality in rations; freedom for the peasants to dispose of the fruits of their labor; and freedom to engage in small-scale industry provided no hired labor was used.[9]

The Tenth Party Congress met on March 8, the day that

[5] *Pravda*, No. 27, February 8, 1921; *Desyatyy sezd RKP(b)*, pp. 861–62.

[6] *Desyatyy sezd RKP(b)*, p. 943. The *Politburo* was the small but dominant group within the Party Central Committee that handled the most important problems that confronted the Party.

[7] *Ibid.*, p. 841.

[8] *Ibid.*, p. 851; see also *Pravda o Kronstadte*, Prague, 1921, pp. 5–7.

[9] *Pravda o Kronstadte*, pp. 46–47. A concise account of the Kronstadt revolt is given in L. Schapiro, *The Origin of the Communist Autocracy*, pp. 296–313.

government troops began storming the Kronstadt naval fortress. On the very first day a change was made in the original agenda of the Congress. Item 5, entitled "Current Tasks of Economic Construction," was deleted and its place was taken by a new topic: "The Problem of Food Requisitioning and the Food Tax." [10] Lenin was the *rapporteur* on this subject, which came up for consideration on March 15.

Lenin began his argument for the repeal of the food levy by saying that it was basically a political problem of the relation between social classes, and that the proletariat could stay in power only by compromising with the peasants.

We know that, pending the outbreak of revolution in other countries, only agreement with the peasantry can save the socialist revolution in Russia. . . . We must not try to hide anything, but state plainly that the peasantry are not satisfied with the form of relationship which we have established with them, that they do not want this form of relationship, and that they will not go on living like this. This is indisputable. This will of the peasantry has been expressed conclusively. This is the will of the immense masses of the working people. We must reckon with it, and we are sufficiently sober politicians to say plainly: "Let us reconsider our policy in relation to the peasantry." [11]

Lenin did not go into the details of the new relationships that were to be established between the Soviet state and the peasantry, which he believed could be worked out later. He pointed to a more urgent problem, whose solution brooked no delay: the fight against the Kronstadt rebels. He concluded with the following words.

I urge you to bear in mind the fundamental thing. . . . This very evening there should be broadcast by radio to every corner

[10] *Desyatyy sezd RKP(b)*, p. 8.
[11] *Ibid.*, p. 407.

of the globe that the congress of the governing party replaces the levy by a tax, thereby creating for the small farmer a number of incentives to enlarge his farm and to increase the area under cultivation . . . ; that the congress in taking this step improves the relationship between the proletariat and the peasantry and expresses its conviction that in this way a durable relationship between the proletariat and the peasantry will be established.[12]

On Lenin's motion, the Tenth Party Congress passed a resolution to replace the food levy by a tax. It thereby transformed the peasant from the status of a mere worker on state land to that of a small farmer carrying on business for himself, making his own plans, and assuming his own risks.[13]

B. THE STRATEGY OF AMBIGUITY TOWARD LABOR

The decision to retreat toward a new economic policy in agriculture was made on the assumption that relationships in other areas of Communist economic activity would remain unaffected. Consequently, the trade-union controversy, which had been dragging on for more than three months and which threatened to split the Party, lost none of its urgency. The Tenth Party Congress devoted the entire session of March 14 to debating the issue. The debates were full of animation and excitement, of charges and countercharges. However, all this did little to alleviate the tensions and animosities that had been generated by the earlier debates on the function of trade unions under socialism and the place of labor in the Soviet state.

The three trade-union platforms that survived for consideration by the Tenth Party Congress[14] had been made public about the middle of January, 1921. Used as points

---

[12] *Ibid.*, p. 407.
[13] The resolution is in *ibid.*, pp. 564–66.
[14] See p. 212 (above).

of departure by the various speakers, they represented three sharply divergent points of view.

At one extreme was the Trotsky and Bukharin platform, which advocated the continuation of the methods of compulsion and administrative injunction in dealing with labor problems. It also urged that the trade unions be made part of the machinery of the Soviet state and perform such functions as stimulating labor productivity, maintaining labor discipline, and propagating Communist ideas among the laboring masses.

At the other extreme was the group of trade-union leaders who came to be known as the Workers' Opposition. This group was led by Alexander Shlyapnikov, who had been the first People's Commissar of Labor.[15] The Workers' Opposition stood for retracting the Party's policies toward labor that had been taken during 1919 and 1920 and returning to the pristine ideas of labor democracy that had been practiced during the short period of workers' control. It demanded that a National Producers' Congress take charge of the entire economy of Russia, with factory-shop committees and trade unions acting as local executors of the policies developed by the Producers' Congress.

Between these two extremes were the proposals that were known as the Platform of the Ten, sponsored by Lenin and Zinoviev, which stressed the pedagogical role of the trade unions as a school of communism, made extensive promises to enlarge workers' democracy, and opposed the rapid fusion of the trade unions with the state apparatus.

The three documents that follow are excerpts from the three platforms.

---

[15] As Commissar of Labor in the first Bolshevik government, Shlyapnikov was sharply critical of the practices of workers' control. In March, 1918, he delivered a highly condemnatory speech about the role of the shop committees in the disorganization of the railway system. See pp. 20–21 (above).

TROTSKY'S THESES ON THE ROLE OF THE TRADE UNIONS

[Excerpts from the platform of Trotsky and Bukharin,
submitted to the Tenth Party Congress]

Introduction [16]

The comprehensive Party discussion on the role of the trade union has already accomplished a positive result in that it helped to clarify the basic issues at stake and to remove imaginary differences and plain misunderstandings. As a result of this discussion, it is possible now to affirm that there exist within the party three points of view on the trade-union question.

The position of the "Ten" is essentially an endorsement of the old practice of the All-Russian Central Council of Trade Unions, which repudiates the need of a *radical change in the methods and the tempo of work* of the trade unions, sanctioned by the Ninth Party Congress. The position of the "Ten" completely ignores the deep crisis which the trade unions are passing through, a crisis which expresses itself in the utter aloofness in which the trade unions stand in relation to the economy and the lack of co-ordination between the methods and procedures of trade-union work and the production problems which the unions are facing.

While justly emphasizing the need for a resolute transition to methods of workers' democracy, the position of the "Ten" shuts its eyes to the fact that in and by themselves the methods of democracy within the unions—*without changing the position and the role of the unions in the workers' state*—will fail to solve the problem and bring the crisis to an end.

In some of its practical conclusions, the platform of the "Ten" is making a number of concessions to our point of view, but by and large it retains and sanctifies the condition of aloofness existing between the trade unions and the economic organizations. At times the two sides enter into temporary agreements, at others they are in conflict.

The platform of the "Workers' Opposition," while expressing a legitimate aim of concentrating the administration of industry in the hands of the trade unions, gives to this aim an utterly erroneous expression, both from a theoretical and practical point

[16] *Desyatyy sezd RKP(b)*, Moscow, 1933, p. 701. Italics as in the original text.

of view, and is shifting more and more in the direction of syn-
dicalism.

Completely ignoring the fact that our economic organizations
came into existence with the help of the trade unions and that,
with all their bureaucratic traits, these economic organizations
incorporate the accumulated organizational and economic experience of the workers' state, the "Workers' Opposition" proposes
to consider dead and buried what has been done in the past in the
field of economic construction and, rather than reorganize the
existing economic organizations by the inclusion of larger numbers of workers in them, they propose to replace them mechani-
cally by an elective representation of workers, starting with the
plant and the mine and ending with the higher economic institutions of the Republic. Such a solution must inevitably lead, no
matter what the intentions of the authors of these proposals may
have been, to a disruption in the relations among factories and
plants, to the destruction of the centralized economic machinery,
and to the loss of the Party's leading influence over the trade
unions, as well as over the economy. . . .

The Nature of the Trade-Union Crisis [17]

1. Concerning the question of the role and aims of the trade-
union organizations during the epoch of the dictatorship of the
proletariat, our Party program says: "The organizational apparatus of socialized industry must be based, first and foremost, on
a trade-union foundation. Since, according to the laws of the
Soviet Republic and existing practice, they are already participating in all local and central organs of industrial administration,
*the trade unions must achieve a de facto concentration of the
whole national economy* considered as a single economic unit.
This will ensure the closest possible tie between the central machinery of state administration, the national economy, and the
large masses of the toilers. In this way the trade unions will
facilitate the widest possible participation of the toiling masses
in the conduct of economic affairs. *The participation of the trade
unions in the administration of the economy is at the same time
the most important factor in the fight against the bureaucratiza-*

[17] *Ibid.*, pp. 703–10.

tion of the Soviet economic apparatus and will make possible a genuine people's control over the results of production."

2. This self-evident and undisputable idea, expressed in the Party program, points to the fact that the taking over of production [management] by the trade unions, under the leadership of the Party and the general supervision of the workers' state, is something which cannot be achieved by a single act, but requires a long process of training, organization and grouping of the working class, necessitated by the economics of socialism. This process has already gone through a number of stages corresponding to the forms in which the trade unions participated in the organization of the economy. Thus, soon after the November Revolution the working class, mainly through the medium of the trade unions, created elementary organs to take over the nationalized enterprises. With the further development of economic institutions, an inevitable segregation between these economic institutions and the trade unions has taken place. The parallelism is leading to jurisdictional disputes, organizational friction, and conflicts. The efforts of the economic organizations during this period of specialization and segregation were directed toward limiting trade-union interference in economic life. . . .

3. What is most urgently needed at this time is an earnest effort on the part of the trade-union leaders, as well as of the Party as a whole, to revitalize and strengthen the trade unions as soon as possible, to create a more intimate connection between the unions and the economic organizations, to correlate trade-union methods of work with the tasks in the economic field, and to ensure a greater influence of the trade unions in the organization of production. These are the objectives of the Party during the new epoch of economic construction.

The Trade Unions as the Prop of the Party

4. In presently undertaking their basic work directed toward the organization of the economy, the trade unions must not only preserve but also expand and intensify their role as mass organizations of the working class and draw systematically the millions of toilers, no matter how backward they may be, into participation in the life of the Soviet state. Real, i.e., living and conscious, as

opposed to formal, consolidation of millions of workers into trade
unions can be achieved only on the basis of active and creative
participation of the trade unions in the economic life of the country. At the same time the conscious participation of millions of
workers in economic construction will secure for the Party a firm
class foundation and will enable the Soviet government to meet
the difficulties arising from the economic fragmentation and the
political backwardness of the multimillion masses of the peasantry.

Educational Work of the Trade Union ("The School of Communism")

5. The greatest problem of our epoch is the transformation of
the trade unions into production unions, not in name only but in
content as well. Under present-day conditions, the educational
work of the trade unions can unfold itself only on condition that
greater and greater masses of workers are drawn into the work
of organizing production.

[Paragraphs 6 and 7 repeat points that were stressed by Trotsky again and again: trade unions must shift their work to problems of industrial production rather than concentrate on workers'
welfare.]

8. It is important to implant into the minds of working masses
the idea that their interests are best defended by those who try to
raise the productivity of labor, who are trying to improve the
operation of the economy and to increase the amount of material
goods. It is this type of organizer and administrator, if he satis-
fies the necessary political prerequisites, who should be elected to
the leading positions in the trade unions on the same bases as
workers from the bench [are elected]. The trade unions should
train and support a new type of trade-union leader, [a leader]
full of energy, economic initiative, looking upon economic activity
not from the point of view of distribution and consumption, but
from the viewpoint of expanded production, looking not with
the eyes of a man bargaining with the Soviet government, but
with the eyes of an economic organizer.

9. Production propaganda, which is a component part of production education, has as its basic aim the establishment of new relationships between the workers and what they are producing. Under capitalism the worker's ideas [about production] were determined by the fact that he was trying to liberate himself from the clutches of hired labor. But under present conditions the thoughts, the initiative, and the will of the workers must be centered first and foremost on improving the organization of production and on the more efficient use of machines and mechanisms. . . .

The Fusion of the Trade Unions with the State

10. The fusion of the trade unions with the state has already gone a long way insofar as the claims of the state upon the workers are concerned. It is through the medium of the trade union that the state registers the worker, puts him on a specific job, sets norms for his output and wages for his work, and punishes him for infraction of labor discipline.

The other side of the fusion process, viz., the influence of the workers' trade unions on the organization of the economy, is lagging behind to a considerable extent. And yet, it is only the development of this second aspect of the fusion process that is capable of securing a proper place for the trade unions in the workers' state, and making it possible for the great masses of workers to understand the socialist character of compulsory labor which the trade unions are called upon to enforce and without which no solid economic improvement is possible.

11. The gradual concentration of production management in the hands of the trade unions, as is required by our [party] program, means the transformation, according to plan, of the trade unions into agencies of the workers' state, i.e., the gradual fusion of the trade union with the Soviet apparatus. . . .

12. Fortifying the trade-union positions in the economic sphere is the most effective method of fighting against bureaucracy. On this point our party program states: "Participation of trade unions in economic management and the drawing of large masses of workers into this work are the principal methods of fighting against the bureaucratization of the economic apparatus." It follows that the fight against bureaucracy is not an independent problem that can be solved by means of special organizational

measures. It is a component part of trade-union work directed toward training the masses in the processes of production and in the management of production. It follows that the fight against bureaucracy requires not so much the creation of new control organs as the improvement of existing economic organizations.

Methods of Persuasion and Methods of Compulsion in the Trade Unions

13. The principal method of trade-union work is not the method of compulsion but the method of persuasion, which does not in the least exclude the possibility that in case of necessity the trade unions should also apply the methods of proletarian compulsion (mobilization of thousands of trade-union members for service, disciplinary courts, etc.). Reorganizing the trade unions by orders from above is certain to defeat its own end. The methods of workers' democracy, which were sharply curtailed in the three years of the most cruel civil war,[18] should be re-established on a wide scale and first of all in the trade-union movement. It is necessary first of all to re-establish the system of electing officials for the various trade-union organs and to reduce to an unavoidable minimum the practice of appointments from above.[19] The trade unions should be built on the principle of democratic centralism. At the same time care should be taken to ensure that centralization and militarized forms of work do not degenerate into bureaucracy and "standpatism." The recourse to labor militarization made necessary by events will be crowned with success only to the extent that the Party, the Soviets, and the trade unions succeed in explaining to the masses of toilers the necessity of these measures for the salvation of the country.

[18] The documents included in this study do not sustain the allegation that the methods of trade-union democracy were curtailed in consequence of the civil war. On the contrary, these documents show that, from the outset, the Bolsheviks followed a consistent policy of depriving the trade unions of their independence and converting them into auxiliary organs of the Soviet state. The sharpest curtailment of trade-union democracy occurred in 1920, when the civil war was over.

[19] Section 13 of Trotsky's platform is a verbatim repetition of Section 6 of the Platform of the Ten. There is a difference, however, in one point. Trotsky recommended the reduction of appointments from above "to an unavoidable minimum" but the Platform of the Ten wanted "to put a stop to all appointments from above." See the Resolution of the Tenth Party Congress, p. 243 (below).

The Party and the Trade Unions

14. In view of the exceptional importance which the trade-union movement is bound to acquire in the near future the Party should pay greater attention to the unions than it has done in the past. Party leadership within the trade-union movement should be greatly increased. But this leadership should involve, mainly, steering the ideological work of the trade unions and should not turn into petty tutelage over them or excessive interference in their daily work. The Communist factions within the trade unions are under control of the party organizations. The selection *(podbor)* of the leading trade-union personnel should be under the supervisory control of the Party, which uses the party factions of the trade unions to ensure that the leading positions in the trade unions are occupied by men recommended by the Party. But the party organizations must strictly adhere to the normal methods of proletarian democracy, especially in the trade unions, where the selection *(otbor)* of leaders must be made by the organized masses themselves.[20]

15. [In this paragraph Trotsky maintains that only under the above conditions will the Party be in a position to exercise complete control over trade unions and at the same time to leave a certain amount of local independence to trade union leaders.]

The Trade Unions and the Political Departments

16. In the past, when the attention and the energies of the Party were directed predominantly to the [civil war] fronts, the Party was forced, under pressure of economic necessity, to create special organs, known as political administrations, for the purpose of carrying out special tasks which the trade unions were unable to perform. It was for this reason that the temporary organ—*Glavpolitput*—came into existence. The Ninth Party Congress has authorized that body "to adopt extraordinary measures necessitated by the terrific collapse of the transport system, so as to prevent its complete paralysis and the ruin of the Soviet Republic."

The Tenth Congress recognizes that the economic objective for which *Glavpolitput* was created has been accomplished (as indi-

[20] See n 32 (below) for an explanation of the *podbor* and *otbor*.

cated in the resolution of the Eighth Congress of Soviets) and endorses the liquidation of that organization.

17. The All-Russian Central Council of Trade Unions, the organization which unites several million trade-union members, should be transformed by the Party into a powerful organization, capable of carrying out the gigantic tasks which the Russian trade-union movement is facing.

It would have been impossible to build the Red Army without abolishing the elected committees of the old type. On the other hand, the national economy cannot be raised to the necessary level without, at the same time, raising the level of trade-union organization by using the methods of workers' democracy.

18. The transition to the methods of workers' democracy should be made effective in all trade unions. At the same time, the Tenth Congress recognizes that, *without changing the position and the role of the unions within the workers' state*, the transition to workers' democracy within the trade unions will not solve the basic question of socialist economic construction.

Practical Steps to Be Taken

19. The present position of the All-Russian Central Council of Trade Unions and the central committees of individual industrial unions is such that they stand outside the basic economic activity [of the country]. This cannot be recognized as normal. It is necessary to remedy a situation under which nearly every trade-union worker who demonstrates high qualities as an organizer and economic administrator is torn away from the union, as well as from the masses of workers, and is swallowed up by the machinery of production.

20. To establish better relationships [between trade unions and economic organizations], it is necessary that the trade unions themselves participate directly in the elaboration of economic plans, as well as in the methods of plan implementation.

In the workers' state there can be no organizational separation between specialists in production management and specialists in the trade-union movement. As a general principle, it should be recognized that anyone needed for work as a production specialist is, by the same token, needed by the trade unions and vice versa. Every valuable trade-union worker should also be a participant in the organization of production. With this in view, the Tenth Party Congress considers it essential to establish a central committee (consisting of [representatives of] the Central Council of Trade Unions, the Supreme Council of National Economy, the People's Commissariat of Agriculture, the People's Commissariat of Railways, and others) to coordinate the relationships between the trade unions and the economic organizations in a manner that would correspond to the facts of production experience.

The rest of the Trotsky and Bukharin platform contains a number of suggestions for bringing about better coordination between the trade unions and the economic organizations. Some of these suggestions restate points Trotsky had made in his theses of November 8, 1920;[21] others repeat positions that were taken in previous sections of the platform. The platform was signed by L. Trotsky, N. Bukharin, A. Andreev, F. Dzerzhinsky, N. Krestinsky, E. Preobrazhensky, X. Rakovsky, and L. Serebryakov— all members of the Party Central Committee.

Five other high-ranking Party members who signed this platform were members of the Ukrainian Central Committee of the Communist Party; two signers were members of the Presidium of the Central Council of Trade Unions; twenty-one signers were members of the central committees of the various trade unions; and eighteen signers were prominent Moscow Communists. There were fifty-four signers in all.

The sponsors of the Workers' Opposition platform cited the official resolutions of the first three trade-union congresses as well as the resolution of the Eighth Party Congress, in which the trade unions were given assurances that they would be placed in charge of the administration

[21] See p. 194 (above).

of industry. The Workers' Opposition group, headed by Shlyapnikov, argued that it was high time that these promises be made good, and they proceeded to outline their concept of the communist society they would like to see established in Russia.

THE PLATFORM OF THE WORKERS' OPPOSITION

[Excerpts from Shlyapnikov's theses, presented to the Tenth Party Congress][22]

General Statement

1. The role and the aims of the trade unions in the present transitional period were clearly defined in the resolutions of the All-Russian Congresses of Trade Unions. The First All-Russian Congress of Trade Unions, in January, 1918, thus defined the aims of the trade unions: "The center of gravity in the work of the trade unions at the present moment must be shifted to the field of economic organization. Trade unions, being class organizations of the proletariat organized on industrial lines, must take upon themselves the principal task of organizing production and restoring the shattered productive forces of the country."

The Second [All-Russian] Congress, in February, 1919,[22] declared that "in the process of practical collaboration with the Soviet government, directed toward the strengthening and the organization of the national economy, the trade unions have made the transition from control over production to the organization of industry by taking an active part in the management of individual enterprises, as well as of the entire economic life of the country." The resolution concludes as follows: "Directly participating in every sphere of Soviet activity by contributing to the formation of state institutions, the trade unions must, by enlisting both their own organizations as well as the broad masses of the workers, train and prepare them for the management not only of production, but also of the entire state machinery."

---

[22] *Desyatyy sezd RKP(b)*, pp. 716–25. The theses were first formulated on January 18, 1921.

[23] The Second All-Russian Congress of Trade Unions took place in January, 1919.

The Third Congress, which took place in April, 1920, approved the basic decisions of the two preceding congresses and gave a few specific instructions as to the manner in which the trade unions should participate in the organization of the national economy.

The clearest definition of the role of the trade unions and of their practical work is given in the Program of the Russian Communist Party, adopted by the Eighth Party Congress in March, 1919. In the chapter of the Program entitled "In the Economic Sphere," we find the following in paragraph 5: "The organizational apparatus of the socialized industry must be based primarily on a trade-union foundation. . . . [Omission in the text.] Since, according to the laws of the Soviet Republic and existing practice, they are already participating in all local and central organs of industrial administration, the trade unions must achieve a de facto concentration of the entire administration of the whole national economy considered as a single economic unit."

2. The transition from military tasks to economic construction uncovered a crisis of the trade-union movement, arising from the fact that the daily work of the unions was far removed from the tasks formulated in the [trade-union] congresses and in the Party program. During the past two years the Party and the state organizations were engaged in narrowing the sphere of operations of the trade unions and they have reduced the influence of the workers' unions in the Soviet state to zero. The role of trade unions in the organization and the administration of industry has been debased to that of an information and recommendation bureau. [Charges are made that the trade unions have no paper or printing facilities.]

3. The downgrading of the role and importance of the trade unions has been taking place at a time when the experience of the past three years of the proletarian revolution has shown that the unions had fully and consistently followed the Communist line, and have been leading the great masses of non-party workers in the same direction. [This downgrading of the trade unions has been taking place at a time] when it became clear to everyone that the realization of the program of the Russian Communist Party in our country, where the overwhelming majority of the population are small producers, required a strong, authoritative mass organization, accessible to the widest proletarian circles.

The downgrading of the role of the trade unions in Soviet Russia is an expression of bourgeois and class hostility directed against the proletariat and should be ended immediately.

The Present Tasks of the Trade Unions

4. The experience of the last three and a half years of Soviet construction has demonstrated that the successful accomplishment of a task was made possible only in the degree that there was mass participation of the workers in it. We should take account of this experience and direct our activity in a way that would attract the laboring masses to take part in the direct management of the country's economy.

5. Victory over disruption and the restoration of the productive forces of our country is possible, and can be attained only on condition that the existing system and methods of organization and administration of the national economy of the Republic are radically changed. The methods of administration which lean on cumbersome bureaucratic machinery preclude any creative initiative and independence of the union-organized producers. It is this bureaucratic system, operating over the heads of organized producers and employing appointed officials and dubious specialists, that has created a split in the administration of the economy, and is now leading to perpetual conflicts between the shop committees and plant administrations, between trade unions and economic organizations. This system must be repudiated unequivocally.

6. The present tendency to ignore the resolutions of the [Eighth] Party Congress on the role and objectives of trade unions in the Soviet state is direct testimony of the lack of confidence in the potentialities of the working class. The class-conscious and advanced elements of the working class and organized Communists should exert every effort to overcome this distrust and to resist the bureaucratic stagnation within the Party. . . .

7. The critical economic position of the country requires heroic measures to prevent the approaching catastrophe. The basic measures capable of raising productivity relate to the adoption of an economic policy that confers upon the industrial trade

unions a decisive voice in the state economic organizations. Management of the national economy is at the same time the management of the laboring masses. By introducing a system of national economic organization and administration based on the trade unions, a unity of leadership will emerge which will remove the opposition between the laboring masses and the specialists and create wide opportunities for the organizational and the administrative activities of men of science, theory, and practical experience.

8. Trade unions are workers' organizations, built on the principles of workers' democracy and accountability of every organ from the lowest to the highest. During the period of their existence the unions have gained a good deal of experience, and they include [in their membership] people with talents in the field of economic administration. Entire branches of our war-production, machine building, metallurgical industries and other industries are being administrated by workers. Hundreds of highly complicated industrial enterprises are managed by collegiums or by individual worker-administrators. But these administrators have no responsibility and are not accountable to the trade unions which placed them in these positions, and they are required to report only to the economic agencies.[24] The unification of industrial leadership with the trade unions in charge will remove this unhealthy state of affairs.

9. The transition from the existing system of bureaucratic administration of the economy, alienated from the initiative of the toiling masses, should be made in an orderly way and should begin with the strengthening of the nuclei of the trade unions, such as factory-shop committees, with the view of giving them the training needed for economic management. [A list of eight steps is given by which this objective can be attained.]

10. The entire work and attention of the trade unions should be transferred to factories, plants and institutions and concentrated on the development of the mentality of the worker. Therein lies the role of the trade unions as schools of communism. In developing the intelligence of the liberated producer, the trade unions should organize their work in such a way as to transform the laborer from a mere appendage of a moribund

[24] That is, the Supreme Council of National Economy.

economic machine into an intelligent builder of communism.
Every screw of the machinist, every thread of the weaver, every
nail of the blacksmith, and every brick of the bricklayer should
serve as a connecting link and foundation of the new production
relationships. Communist education must be built on this foundation.

The Administration of the National Economy

11. In its final and fully developed form, the organizational
structure of the economy, as well as the relationship of the various economic organs, should lead to the concentration of the
entire economic administration in the hands of the industrial
trade unions.

12. This administrative concentration of the unified economy
of the Republic can be achieved by establishing an organizational
framework under which all organs of national economic management, both central and local, are elected by the representatives of
the organized producers. In this way a unity of will is created,
which is essential to the organization of the national economy,
and which ensures a wide participation of the laboring masses in
the administration of our economy.

13. Organizing the administration of the entire national economy should be within the jurisdiction of an all-Russian congress
of producers, united in industrial trade unions, which will elect a
central organ to take charge of the management of the entire
national economy of the Republic.

a. All-Russian congresses of industrial trade unions representing individual branches of the economy are to elect organs for the
management of sectors and branches of the economy.

b. Oblast, guberniya, uezd, regional, etc., organs of administration are to be created by the corresponding local congresses of
industrial trade unions. In this way a fusion of centralized production and local initiative and independence will be achieved.
Oblast, guberniya, uezd, regional, etc., departments of economic
administration are to be established, in every case, by the trade
unions concerned.

14. Enterprises with related output are to be combined into

groups *(Kusty* and *Glavki)* to ensure the best utilization of technical means and materials. Similar enterprises located in the same city are to be combined under a common management created by the trade union. Administrations for consolidated enterprises located in non-contiguous territories are to be created by congresses of workers' committees of the given enterprises, at the initiative of the trade unions.

Organization of Workers' Committees

15. In order to bring about a more rapid organization of labor and production on socialist principles, all workers and employees in every enterprise and institution of the Republic, being members of trade unions, should participate in an active and orderly manner in the administration of the national economy.

16. All workers and employees, irrespective of their position or trade, who work for individual economic establishments, such as factories, plants, mines, in all transport and communication establishments, and in every variety of agriculture are the direct administrators of the property which is in their charge. They are responsible for the safeguarding and the rational utilization of this property before all the toilers of the Republic.

17. As participants in the organization of management for the various enterprises, the workers and employees in factories, plants, shops, institutions, in transport and communication services, as well as agricultural and other enterprises, elect a Workers' Committee which is the directing organ of a given enterprise.

18. The Workers' Committee is the primary organizational cell of the union of a given trade and is to be constituted under the supervision and control of the corresponding union.

19. The duties of a Workers' Committee consist in the management of a given plant or enterprise and include:

a. Directing the production activities of all workers and employees of the economic unit in question;

b. Taking care of the needs of the producers.

20. [This section states that the work program of an enterprise and its internal procedures are within the competence of the workers engaged in the enterprise.]

Organization of the Workers' Standard of Living

21. An indispensable condition for the improvement of the national economy is the need of introducing a system of wages in kind. This will raise the productivity of labor and improve the living conditions of the workers. The measures listed below should be made part of the wage agreements and included in the payments in kind.

  a. To abolish payment for the rations *(paek)* and for other articles of mass consumption rationed to the workers by the food organs;

  b. To abolish payment for meals distributed to workers and their families;

  c. To abolish payment for the use of bathhouses, street cars, theaters, etc.;

  d. To abolish payment for housing, heat and light;

  e. In localities where the housing problem is critical, it is necessary to reduce the quarters occupied by Soviet and military institutions in order to make available more housing space for workers;

  f. To organize the repair of workers' apartments at the expense of the industrial enterprises, on condition that the fulfillment of the basic production targets of the enterprise is guaranteed;

  g. To give a high priority to the construction of workers' settlements and communal living quarters, which should be included in the program of the Committee on Urban Construction during the nearest construction period;

  h. To place special trains and street cars in operation at the beginning and end of the work day;

  i. To give preferential treatment to workers in the distribution of consumer goods;

  j. To simplify and speed up the distribution of bonuses in kind, both basic and supplemental;

  k. To attach to factories or to establish shoe-repair shops and clothing-repair shops to serve the needs of workers of a given factory. These shops are to receive every assistance from the factory in securing necessary instruments and materials;

  l. If an enterprise has communal garden plots, these should be supplied with necessary implements and tools, to be paid for by the enterprise;

m. The expenditures connected with the above-enumerated measures should be included in the plant's budget.

A. SHLYAPNIKOV
*Chairman of the All-Russian
Union of Metal Workers*

In addition to Shlyapnikov, the Workers' Opposition platform was signed by five other members of the Central Committee of the Metal Workers' Union, four members of the Central Administration of Artillery Plants, eight members of the Central Council of the Miners' Trade Union, one member of the Party Control Commission, and a number of other leaders of various trade unions. In all, there were thirty-eight signatures.

In developing their position on the trade-union issue, the sponsors of the Platform of the Ten seem to have adopted a strategy of ambiguity. They approved the resolution of the Ninth Party Congress that the trade unions, as the organizers of the economy, must become "a component part of the machinery of the Soviet state" (Trotsky's position), but they opposed their rapid conversion into governmental agencies. They rejected the methods of compulsion in trade-union work, but they did not exclude the application of "the principles of proletarian compulsion." They advocated a democratic procedure in electing trade-union officials, instead of appointing them from the top, but they insisted that the elections had to be "under the supervisory control of the Party." These equivocations made the Platform of the Ten an easy target for attack by Trotsky and Madam Kolontay. At the same time, the evasions constituted an element of strength in the platform in that they engendered—in a good many Congress delegates—the hope of breaking away from the cruelties of the *Tsektran* era and avoiding the chaos of workers' control. The platform was adopted by the Congress and became the official Party program.

[Excerpts from the resolution adopted by the Tenth Party Congress, March 16, 1921][25]

The Role of the Trade Unions under the Proletarian Dictatorship

1. The general aims and the role of the trade unions during the dictatorship of the proletariat were adequately defined at the preceding congresses and conferences of the Party and the trade unions. Already the First All-Russian Congress of Trade Unions, which took place early in January, 1918, i.e., shortly after state power passed into the hands of the Soviets, stated in its resolution the following: "At the present moment, the center of gravity in the work of the trade unions must be shifted to the field of economic organization. Trade unions, being class organizations of the proletariat, organized on industrial lines, must take upon themselves the principal task of organizing production and restoring the shattered productive forces of the country. They should aim to participate most emphatically in the work of all centers regulating production, to organize workers' control and the registration and distribution of workers, to organize exchange between villages and cities, to participate most actively in the demobilization of industry, to fight against sabotage, to enforce the duty of universal labor, etc.

"In their developed form, after having been transformed by the socialist revolution which is now taking place, the trade unions will become instruments of state authority, working in subordination to other organizations for the realization of new principles in the organization of economic life."

[25] *Desyatyy sezd RKP(b)*, pp. 590–97. The platform took its name from the number of Bolshevik leaders who originally signed it. They were: V. Lenin, G. Zinoviev, M. Tomsky, Ya. Rudzutak, M. Kalinin, L. Kamenev, A. Lozovsky, G. Petrovsky, F. Artem (Sergeev), and J. Stalin.

Already our Party Program of 1919 called attention to the fact that "the organizational apparatus of the socialized industry must be based, first and foremost, on a trade-union foundation. Since according to the laws of the Soviet Republic and the existing practice, they are already participating in all local and central organs of industrial administration, the trade unions—so declares our party program—must achieve a de facto concentration of the entire administration of the whole national economy considered as a single economic unit. This will ensure the closest possible tie between the central machinery of state administration, the national economy, and the large masses of the toilers. In this way the trade unions will facilitate the widest possible participation of the toiling masses in the management of the economy."

Likewise, the Ninth Congress of the Communist Party (in 1920) resolved: "The tasks of the trade unions are mainly in the sphere of economic organization and education. In accomplishing these tasks, the trade unions are to act not as a self-contained and an organizationally isolated force, but as a component part of the basic machinery of the Soviet state under the leadership of the Communist Party." The [resolution of the] Ninth Congress further states: "Since the Soviet state is the widest organization which concentrates the entire social strength of the proletariat, it is clear that the trade unions, in the course of development of the proletarian consciousness and the growth of creative initiative of the masses, must gradually become transformed into auxiliary instruments of the proletarian state and not vice versa." [26]

The Second and Third All-Russian Congresses of Trade Unions, as well as the Fifth All-Russian Conference of Trade Unions, defined the general tasks of trade unions during the period of the proletarian dictatorship in the same spirit.

These definitions retain their full force at the present moment and stand in no need of any change. The problem facing the Tenth Congress is not that of finding new theoretical formulations of the role of trade unions during the epoch of the dictatorship

[26] The second part of this quotation differs substantially from the original version of the corresponding section of the Ninth Party Congress resolution on the organization of trade unions. See *Devyatyy sezd Rossiyskoy kommunisticheskoy partii*, Chapter II, section 1, p. 384. The original resolution also contained a section that stated that "no trade union should interfere directly in the work of an enterprise," *ibid.*, Chapter IV, section 2, p. 385.

of the proletariat, but rather one of determining the ways in which the theories already formulated are to be realized in life.

Position of the Trade Unions after Three Years of Civil War [27]

2. The critical conditions of the three years of civil war kept the trade unions from the successful discharge of their aims. The trade unions, like other workers' organizations, had to give almost all their forces to the front. Nevertheless, the unions played an important role in economic construction. Immediately following the November Revolution, the trade unions were the only organization which, concurrently with the introduction of workers' control, could take and had to take upon themselves the work of organizing production and managing industrial enterprises.[28] The state apparatus for the management of the national economy in the first period of Soviet rule had not yet been in working order, and the sabotage of factory owners and of the higher technical personnel presented in an acute form the problem of preserving industry and re-establishing the normal functioning of the country's economy.

In the next period, when the management of enterprises was being organized by the Supreme Council of National Economy, the trade unions worked side by side with the state economic organizations.[29] This parallelism was explained and justified by the weakness of the state [economic] organizations. The role of the trade unions in the organization of production was confined mainly to participation in the formation of *Glavki* and *Tsentry*. This work was of a sporadic nature, and what is more, it fre-

[27] In the original draft of the platform the caption for this part of the resolution read: "Not a Crisis but a Growth." After Trotsky's criticism of this caption (see p. 254 below), it was replaced by a new caption.

[28] The allegation that the trade unions had in fact taken over the management of industry is not supported by the evidence. Actually, the trade unions were kept from industrial management by the workers' control committees, on the one hand, and by the Party Central Committee, on the other. Lenin talked a good deal about trade-union management of industry, but at the same time he pursued a different line of policy, which aimed at creating a separate administrative agency to run the national economy. That agency was the Supreme Council of National Economy. See Chapter I, section D of this study, "Trade Union Management Proves an Illusion."

[29] The state economic organizations are the administrative bodies, such as *Glavki*, that were set up by the Supreme Council of National Economy.

quently led to situations in which the delegated workers lost touch with the trade unions which sent them [to the *Glavki*]. This, in turn, prevented the trade unions and their representatives in the economic organizations from influencing the work of these organizations. If the participation of workers in the operation of the economic organs is to become more effective, it is essential that the workers who are assigned [to the *Glavki*] by the trade unions should maintain uninterrupted contact with these unions and that the trade unions should participate more closely in the organization and the administration of production. . . .

The inauguration of a new period [with the end of the civil war] finds the trade unions in a rather weak position relative to the enormous tasks which the economic front is placing before them. The peculiarities of the present transitional period, as of every transitional period, create formidable difficulties for the trade unions. Nevertheless, what the trade unions are going through now is *not a typical trade-union crisis, not a breakdown, but the beginning of a new growth.*[30] In this respect the fortunes of the trade unions do not differ from those of the Party and of the Soviets.

The Trade Unions as the Prop of the Proletarian Dictatorship

3. The Russian Communist Party is maintaining the dictatorship of the proletariat in a country where the peasant population has a preponderant majority. However, since at this time the peasantry is no longer threatened with the restoration of the power of the landlords, the preservation of the proletarian dictatorship is bound to encounter new difficulties. The successful realization of this dictatorship is possible only when the trade unions are imbued with a unity of purpose and will and are functioning as mass organizations that are open to every proletarian, no matter what the level of his class-consciousness.

Trade Unions as a School of Communism

4. The most important role of the trade unions in Soviet Russia is their role as a *school of communism*. Only the trade

---

[30] Italics as in the original text.

unions, insofar as they are concerned with every aspect of a worker's life, can perform the task of giving the large masses of backward workers the rudiments of a political education. The predominant mass of trade-union membership (6,970,000 members, of whom about half a million are members of the Party)[31] consists of non-party men. Communism is built with the human material which we inherited from capitalism. The trade unions of Soviet Russia are gradually turning into organizations which include every worker. The trade unions are organizing toilers who under capitalism were alien to the proletarian family (store clerks, hospital attendants, art workers, etc.). Re-educating these vast masses, bringing them closer to the more advanced proletarian groups, and training them for the task of socialist construction constitute the most important objectives of the trade unions in their role as a school of communism. . . .

The half a million party men, who are now members of the trade unions, should by patient, continuous, and persistent effort win over to the side of our party the millions of non-party workers who at present constitute the majority in the trade-union movement.

The Fusion of the Trade Unions with the State

5. The rapid fusion of the trade unions with the state would be a great political mistake. At the present stage of development this would greatly interfere with carrying out the above-mentioned tasks by the trade unions. The present position of the trade unions vis-à-vis the state is unique. The trade unions at present are already discharging a number of functions of state organs. These Soviet state functions are bound to increase gradually. Nevertheless, the Congress is bound to state that any artificial speeding up of the fusion of the trade unions with the state,

---

[31] The figure of trade-union membership of nearly 7 million at the beginning of 1921 seems highly dubious (the original draft of the platform, which was published in January, 1921, gives the same figure). According to official data, the number of trade-union members in 1919 was 3.4 million (*Vestnik putey soobshcheniya*, No. 12, 1919, p. 18). On April 9, 1920, when the Third All-Russian Congress of Trade Unions was in session, the number of trade-union members was given as "over three million workers" (*Rezolyutsii III Vserossiyskogo sezda professionalnykh soyuzov*, p. 55). A doubling of trade-union membership in the course of nine or ten months, at a time when the industrial labor force was sharply declining, is highly improbable.

while contributing little to the improvement of the economic position of the Republic, would greatly hamper the role of trade unions as a school of communism. The main problem is to conquer the vast non-party masses.

Methods of Persuasion and Methods of Compulsion

6. The principal method of trade-union work is not the method of compulsion, but the method of persuasion. This does not in the least exclude the possibility that in case of necessity the trade unions should apply the principles of proletarian compulsion (compulsory mobilization of tens of thousands of trade-union members, disciplinary courts, etc.). Reorganizing the trade unions by orders from above is certain to defeat its own end. The methods of workers' democracy, which were so sharply curtailed in the three years of cruel civil war, should be re-established first of all, and on a wide scale, in the trade-union movement. It is necessary first of all to re-establish the system of electing officials for the various trade union organs, instead of appointing them from above. The trade unions should be built on the principle of democratic centralism. At the same time the most energetic struggle should be undertaken to ensure that centralization and militarized forms of work do not degenerate into bureaucracy and "standpatism." The recourse to labor militarization will be crowned with success only to the extent that the Party, the Soviets, and the trade unions succeed in explaining to the masses of toilers the necessity of these measures for the salvation of the country.

The Party and the Trade Unions

7. The Russian Communist Party, as represented by its central and local organizations, is unquestionably directing, as it did in the past, the ideological work of the trade unions. The Communist factions of the trade unions are wholly subordinate to the party organizations as defined by a special statute. At the same time the Tenth Congress of the Russian Communist Party warns, in the most insistent and categorical form, all party organizations, as well as individual comrades, against petty tutelage and excessive interference in the daily work of the trade unions. To be sure, the selection *(podpor)* of the leading personnel of

the trade-union movement must be under the supervisory control of the Party. But the party organizations [in exercising that control] must strictly adhere to the methods of proletarian democracy, particularly in the trade unions, where the selection *(otbor)* of leaders must be made by the organized masses themselves.[32]

In selecting leaders for the most important trade-union positions, the Party must make sure that the appointees are good managers who fully understand the significance attached to the production aims [of the trade unions]. The Party must also make sure that the above qualifications of the prospective leaders are combined with devotion to communism, a sense of discipline, and, especially, with experience in working with large masses of workers and skill in handling them. It cannot be forgotten, not even for a minute, that trade-union work requires great attention and sympathetic response to the minutest needs of the toiling masses.

The Trade Unions and the Political Departments

8. In the course of the civil war, the Party was forced, in exceptional cases, to sanction the organization of political departments which, to a certain extent, were replacing the trade unions. Such an exception was *Glavpolitput*.

The Ninth Party Congress, which adopted a resolution establishing *Glavpolitput*, underlined the temporary character of this institution.[33] In practice, however, *Glavpolitput* and its adjunct,

---

[32] The Russian terms, *podbor* and *otbor*, have almost the same meaning and are frequently used interchangeably, but there is a slight difference in their connotations. *Otbor* connotes a kind of selection, in which a natural or spontaneous process has been at work. Thus the English expression "natural selection" is rendered in Russian as *estestvennyy otbor. Podbor*, on the other hand, is used in the sense of a purposive selection, when, for example, a selection of books is made for a certain subject. *Podbor* would also be used in the selection of personnel with certain qualifications. It cannot be stated with certainty that the writers of the resolution had this distinction in mind, as there is no consistent pattern in the use of these terms in other documents of the period.

[33] There are a few inaccuracies in the last two statements. *Glavpolitput* was first established early in 1919, and at that time it made no attempt to replace the trade unions. It was only after Trotsky took control over the transport system, in March, 1920—i.e., at a time when the civil war was nearly over—that *Glavpolitput* replaced the trade unions. The Ninth Party Congress, however, approved Trotsky's policy of replacing the railway trade unions by *Glavpolitput* (see pp. 184–85, above).

Tsektran, manifested a tendency to break away from the trade-union masses and to oppose the trade-union organizations. This resulted in a deviation from the normal methods of trade-union democracy.

The Tenth Party Congress endorses the abolition of *Glavpolitput*, as well as the decision of the Party Central Committee which called upon *Tsektran* to give up its peculiar methods of work and to adopt the procedures of normal workers' democracy. . . .

[The remaining part of the Platform of the Ten enumerated the measures that would re-establish the methods of trade-union democracy. These measures can be briefly summarized as follows:

1) Participation of trade unions in the preparation of a unified economic plan and of a production program;
2) Participation in the formation of economic administrative organizations;
3) Control over production by assisting the economic agencies in carrying out the production plans;
4) Registration and distribution of the labor force;
5) Establishment of wage scales, both in money and in kind;
6) Production propaganda directed toward raising labor productivity and assistance in labor mobilization;
7) Enforcing labor discipline by means of disciplinary courts and the Committees on Labor Desertion.]

MADAM KOLONTAY CRITICIZES THE PARTY
LEADERSHIP

In the course of the controversy over the role of the trade unions in the Soviet state, the Workers' Opposition group found unexpected support from Madam Aleksandra Kolontay, a brilliant speaker and talented pamphleteer. In a pamphlet entitled *The Workers' Opposition*, which she published shortly before the meeting of the Tenth Party Congress, she delivered a fiery denunciation of the ruling group of the Party Central Committee. She accused both Lenin and Trotsky of having betrayed the revolution and declared that the only way to save communism was by transferring the administration of industry to the workers.[34]

THE PARTY LEADERSHIP AND THE WORKERS' OPPOSITION

[A critique by Madam Kolontay][35]

. . . The basic thesis of the Workers' Opposition states: "The organization of national-economic management is the prerogative of the All-Russian Congress of Producers, united in trade and industrial unions, which elect the central organ directing the entire national economy of the Republic" (Theses of the Workers' Opposition).

It is just at this point that the parting of the ways of the Workers' Opposition and the top Party leaders begins. *Distrust toward the working class* (not in the sphere of politics, but that of economics) is the quintessence of the "theses" which bear the signature of our top Party leaders. They do not believe that the framework of the Communist order can be created by the coarse hands of the untutored workers. All of them—Lenin, Trotsky, Zinoviev, and Bukharin—seem to think that industrial production is such an "ingenious thing" that it cannot be managed without "directors." First (they all seem to say) let the workers become educated and then, when they grow up, the teachers from the Supreme Council of National Economy will be removed and the industrial unions will be permitted to take over the management of the economy. All high Party leaders agree on one essential point: not to let the trade unions take charge of industrial production for the time being. They differ only in their views as to *why* the trade unions should be kept away from industrial management. . . .

In the theses of the Ten it is stated: "At the present time the center of gravity in the work of the trade unions should be shifted into the sphere of economic organization. The trade unions, as

---

[34] At the Congress, Kolontay charged that her pamphlet, which—according to the statement of the State Publishing House (*Gosizdat*)—was issued in 1.5 million copies, actually appeared in only 1,500 copies. "Three extra zeroes were added by *Gosizdat*," she observed sarcastically (*Desyatyy sezd RKP(b)*, p. 103).

[35] A. Kolontay, *Rabochaya oppozitsiya*, Moscow, 1921, pp. 25–29.

the proletarian class organizations, built on industrial lines, should take upon themselves the *principal work* [36] in organizing production." The expression "principal work" lacks precision, is rather vague and can be given numerous interpretations, but it produces the impression that the platform of the Ten gives more leeway to the trade unions in managing the national economy than Trotsky's system of *Tsektran* administration. Is this really the case?

The theses of the Ten go on to explain what is meant by *principal work:* "The most energetic participation in all centers regulating production, organization of workers' control, registration and distribution of the labor force, organization of exchange between cities and villages, active participation in the demobilization of industry, fight against sabotage, assisting in the general mobilization of labor, etc." This is all. Nothing new and nothing more than what the trade unions were doing before and which so far has failed to save our industry and to solve the problem of restoring the productive forces of our country. To remove any doubt that the trade unions will be given not a leading but a secondary role in production, the platform of the Ten states: "In their developed form (not now, mind you, but in their developed form) the trade unions will become the organs of the socialist state, working in subordination to other organizations for the realization of new principles in the organization of economic life."

Next comes the problem of trade-union *subordination* to the Supreme Council of National Economy. How does this differ from "the fusion" of Comrade Trotsky? The difference is only in the methods. The theses of the Ten strongly emphasize the *educational character of the unions,* mainly in the sphere of economic organization. On the question of the role and mission of the trade unions, our top party leaders have suddenly turned from politics to "pedagogy."

The problem of *how to manage the economy* has turned into the most curious controversy on the subject of how to bring up the masses. In reading the theses and the stenographic reports of the speeches of our top leaders, one is astonished by their pedagogical proclivities. Every creator of a set of theses proposes his

[36] Italics as in the original text.

own most perfect system of bringing up the laboring masses. All these "educational" systems, however, provide no room for the initiative of those who are being educated. As pedagogues our leaders are behind the times.

The trouble is that Lenin, Trotsky, Bukharin, and others view the problem of the trade unions not in relation to economic administration, nor in mastering production, but as a *means of educating the masses*. During the debates, some of our comrades thought that Trotsky stood for a gradual "governmentalization of the unions" and was prepared to assign to the unions the task of administering the national economy as is stated in our program. This point of view seemed at first to put Trotsky on common ground with the Workers' Opposition, at a time when the group represented by Comrades Lenin and Zinoviev, being opposed to "governmentalization," looked upon the principal mission of the trade unions as "a school of communism." Trotsky himself, it would seem, understands the tasks of the trade unions somewhat differently. In his opinion the basic work of the unions is to organize production. In this he is perfectly right. Comrade Trotsky is also right when he says that "to the extent that the unions are schools of communism, they become such schools not by carrying on general Communist propaganda (in that case they would simply perform the function of a club) or in mobilizing their members to requisition food [from the peasants] or serve in the army, but in the sense of *giving their members an all-round training for the participation in production* (Trotsky's report of December 30, 1920). All this is beyond dispute. Only one thing is left out: The trade unions are not only *"schools of communism"*; they are also the *creators of communism*.

The creativeness of the [working] class is being overlooked. Trotsky replaces it by the initiative of "the real organizers of production" inside the unions, the "leading Communists of the trade unions" whom the Party appoints to responsible administrative positions. Trotsky is frank. He does not believe that working masses are prepared to build communism and to create new production forms. He has expressed this openly. He has already carried out his system of "club education" of the masses to prepare them, by using the methods of apprentice schools, for the role of "masters" of *Tsektran*. It is true that by beating the apprentice on the head with a boot-stretcher, the student, when he becomes the master, is very likely to make a mess of the business, but so long as the teacher's club hangs over his head, he works and produces.

This appears to be the meaning of Trotsky's assertion that the center of gravity should be shifted "from politics to production problems." To raise productivity by any means is Trotsky's principal aim. But Lenin and Zinoviev disagree with him. They are "pedagogues" of a more modern trend of thought. "There has been [they say] much talk about the trade unions as schools of communism. But what does a school of communism mean? If we take this definition seriously, it means that in the school of communism it is necessary first of all to *teach* and to educate, and not to issue *commands.*" (A stone thrown into Trotsky's garden.) Comrade Zinoviev then adds: "The trade unions . . . [omission in the text] are performing an enormous task, both for the proletarian and the Communist cause. This is the *basic* role of the trade unions" (italics mine). It is essential to remember that these organizations have their own special tasks—not of issuing orders, not of being bureaucrats, and not of being dictators. Their task is first and foremost that of drawing the millions of working people into the channels of the organized proletarian movement.

Trotsky, the pedagogue, has gone too far in his system of education. But what does Comrade Zinoviev propose? He proposes to give the trade unions elementary lessons in communism "to teach them the elementary principles of the proletarian movement." But how? Through practical experience and practical creation of new economic forms (just what the opposition wants)? Nothing of the kind. The group led by Lenin and Zinoviev favors a system of education based on moral guidance through well-chosen examples. . . .

According to Lenin, the Party has taken in the "proletarian vanguard." The chosen Communists, in close cooperation with the specialists of the Soviet economic organizations, are searching by the laboratory method for the best forms of Communist economics. They are guided by the "good pedagogues" of the Supreme Council of National Economy and of the *Glavki* and *Tsentry.* The working masses and the trade unions can only look on. They must not touch the rudder of control with their hands.

They have not finished their education. Lenin is also of the opinion that the trade unions (i.e., the class organization of the workers) are not the creators of Communist economic forms. He believes that "the trade unions serve only as the connecting link between the vanguard [of the proletariat] and the masses. . . ." [Omission in the text.] This is not the "club system" of Trotsky; it is the German system of Froebel-Pestalozzi, based on "training by examples." The trade unions do nothing essential for the economy. They are merely engaged in *persuading* the masses and serve as a connecting link with the Party.

There is still the question as to which system is better. Trotsky's system, at any rate, is clearer and therefore more realistic. By examples alone, taken from virtuous [pedagogues], education does not greatly advance. This should be remembered, and remembered well. . . .

TROTSKY'S DEFENSE

The policy of outright labor militarization which Trotsky defended so stubbornly through 1920 was given a new emphasis in the platform which he and Bukharin presented for approval to the Tenth Party Congress. In this platform Trotsky made extensive use of the concept of "production democracy" as being the proper function of the trade unions and a means of ensuring workers' participation in the organization and management of industry. As a result his position appeared to be close to the platform of the Workers' Opposition. To counteract this impression, Trotsky delivered a vigorous defense of his attitude in which he made it clear that his idea of production democracy in no way dispensed with the need of the Party dictatorship. He poured ridicule on the program of the Workers' Opposition, on the one hand, and, on the other, on the platform of the Ten, whom he accused of making concessions to the Workers' Opposition. But Trotsky's verbal blasts had little influence on the Congress. In the minds of a good many Congress delegates, Trotsky's name was too closely associated with the high-handed methods of *Glavpolitput* and *Tsektran*; and Tomsky, the Chairman of the Central Council of Trade Unions, attacked him sharply on this score.

THE PRIMACY OF THE PARTY DICTATORSHIP

[From Trotsky's speech at the Tenth Party Congress,
March 14, 1921][37]

. . . The Workers' Opposition came out with dangerous slogans, in that they have made a fetish of democratic principles. They have placed the workers' rights to elect representatives for workers' organizations above the Party, as though the Party had no right to assert its dictatorship even in cases when that dictatorship clashes temporarily with the passing mood of the workers' democracy.

In Petrograd, Comrade Zinoviev declared, with some exaggeration to be sure, that if Shlyapnikov's "Congress of Producers" is allowed to assemble, 99 percent of it would be comprised of nonparty men, Socialist Revolutionists, and Mensheviks. This is a monstrous exaggeration and should be stricken immediately from the record. Was this said for the enlightenment of the [Third] International,[38] that our "workers' democracy" consists in 1 percent of the working class stifling the voice of the other 99 percent? This is a monstrous exaggeration! But even if we reduce Zinoviev's 99 percent by a large amount, there would still remain a substantial number [of dissatisfied people]. Information arriving from the provinces shows that local Communists are helpless in resisting the pressure of anarchic elements. We have lots of young people in our Party.

It is essential that we should become aware of the revolutionary-historical birthright of the Party, which is in duty bound to retain its dictatorship, regardless of the temporary vacillations of the amorphous masses, regardless of the temporary vacillations even of the working class. This awareness is essential for

---

[37] *Desyatyy sezd RKP(b)*, pp. 353–55.
[38] The Third Congress of the Third International was scheduled to meet toward the end of June, 1921.

cohesion; without it the Party is in danger of perishing at some turning point.

At any given moment, the dictatorship does not rest upon the formal principle of workers' democracy. To be sure, workers' democracy is the only method by which the masses can be drawn more and more into political life. . . . [Omission in the text.] This is a truism, and I agree that this truism has at times been forgotten. This has to be corrected and new methods of propaganda used, but on condition that the Party as a whole is united in its understanding that over and above the formal aspect [of workers' democracy] is the Party dictatorship which safeguards the basic interests of the working class even when the moods of that class are temporarily vacillating. Should the so-called Workers' Opposition fail to understand this, direst consequences would be likely to follow upon this failure.

I am bound to state that during the early period of our struggle, especially against Comrade Zinoviev who was the most eloquent champion of the platform of the Ten, he degraded the role of the Party in its relation to workers' democracy to a nonentity, and when I was trying to show that workers' democracy should be subordinated to the economic interests of the working class, Comrade Kamenev, who joined the platform of the Ten, declared that for Trotsky workers' democracy is a "contingent" idea. But if we look upon workers' democracy as something unconditional, as something which stands above everything else, then Comrade Shlyapnikov is right when in the first version [of his platform] he says that every plant should elect its own administration, that every regional congress should elect its administrative organ, and so on, until we come to the "All-Russian Congress of Producers." From a formal point of view this is the clearest line of workers' democracy. But we are against it. Why? . . . [Omission in the text.] Because, in the first place, we want to retain the dictatorship of the Party, and, in the second place, because we think that the [democratic] way of managing important and essential plants is bound to be incompetent and prove a failure from an economic point of view. We maintain that the economic interests of the working class are above the formal criterion of workers' democracy. This was the issue around which the basic contest was going on. But Comrade Lenin, to the extent that he was taking part in the discussion, remained extremely careful. He was merely making hints, so as not to confuse Comrade Zinoviev. This was the impression formed by comrades belonging to different camps and the impression was confirmed today.

Passing to the draft of the resolution of the Ten, I should like to remind you that it is not the speeches that will come up for a vote but the resolution itself, and I am bound to state that the resolution is in the highest degree imperfect. Comrade Zinoviev says: "We anticipated and now we are actually going through a crisis—not only a trade-union crisis but also a crisis of the revolution." But this turns the tables against you. I have the habit of submitting my proposals to the Central Committee in written form, and I could read you one of my statements in which I said that we are approaching a crisis, that the crisis within the Party and the trade-union crisis are not independent crises, but that they are reflections of a deeper crisis; that the concessions which Comrade Lenin has offered to the Workers' Opposition (together with the threat of removing certain elements of the Workers' Opposition) were in the right direction. I pointed out that our Party is the only party in the country and all dissatisfaction is being channeled through our Party, and that by broadening the base of our regime, both within and outside the Party, we would get a deeper comprehension of the dissatisfaction, because the problem is not one of finding a mode of coexistence with the Workers' Opposition, but is basically a question of changing the course of the Party, and through it that of the trade unions and of the working class, in the direction of economics.

Comrade Lenin accused me (he also accused Comrade Bukharin of eclecticism) of drawing an antithesis between economics and politics, whereas politics is merely the concentrated form of economics. What is there to say? . . . [Omission in the text.] There is politics that relates to small matters and there is politics affecting large problems. There is politics that is going on at the Congress and takes place in "two or three rooms" and is called a maneuver. There is also big politics which encompasses the relations between classes. I was maintaining, and still maintain, that the questions of inner party agreements, of making new approaches and compromises, especially of expanding the boundaries of workers' democracy, are highly important matters, but they all have to be subordinated to the economic criterion. I was, therefore, not forgetting about the relation between politics and economics. We anticipated the approaching crisis. Its symptoms were first visible in various spheres of work: Soviet, Party, and others. In the trade unions it expressed itself in the pressure of the consumer psychology of the working class. The working masses were not sufficiently imbued with the psychology of production and the crisis in the trade unions expressed itself in the increased pressure of the consumer's point of view, which pressure was much stronger on the lower trade-union levels than on the higher. On the lower level this pressure found no theoretical formulation, but on the higher it did find such a formulation. Comrade Zinoviev says that our crisis is not a trade-union crisis, but a general crisis. We, on the other hand, maintain that there is a trade-union crisis which is a special manifestation of the crisis of the revolution, a crisis which we are going to overcome but which is with us for the present. From this the surprising conclusion was drawn that we were wrong in affirming that there was a crisis. Their rejoinder was that what we are having is not a crisis but a . . . [omission in the text] growth. That's where the crux of the matter is! Comrade Zinoviev simply forgot the second half of his assertion; namely, that we have no crisis but growth. How can we say at this time that we have no crisis but growth? This is a monstrosity. . . . The chapter of your resolution, "Not a Crisis but a Growth," should be crossed out in its entirety.[39]

[Trotsky then analyzed the chapter of the platform entitled "Trade Unions as a School of Communism." He made the point that the chapter did not "say anything" because every Soviet institution was a school of communism, and, in addition, that the chapter was full of contradictions. He ended with the remark: "I am afraid that Vladimir Ilich [Lenin] did not write this part; it is not his hand." (Applause.)]

The next chapter, dealing with the "governmentalization" [40]

[39] The chapter was not crossed out, and only the title was changed—from "Not a Crisis but a Growth" to "Position of the Trade Unions after Three Years of Civil War" (see p. 240, above).

[40] Ibid., p. 357. Governmentalization of the trade unions, that is, making the unions part of the Soviet government, was a perennial issue of the period and was raised at every trade-union congress and in many resolutions. Not much, however, was done to implement these resolutions. (See pp. 36–38, above.)

of the trade unions, is not much better. It states that "the rapid governmentalization of the trade unions would be a grave error." What does "rapid" mean? How many miles an hour? This is absolutely superficial, obscure, and slovenly. . . .

Next comes the chapter [41] entitled: "Methods of Persuasion and Methods of Compulsion in Trade Unions." This problem lacks clear formulation, but on the whole is rather accurately stated. We have no objection against it. To avoid misunderstanding on this score we have fully taken it over into our theses. As regards the next section, "The Party and the Trade Unions," I am inclined to think that Lenin's hand has gone through it. (VOICE: "You are way off the mark!") [42] You say off the mark. . . . [Omission in the text.] Maybe it was not his hand, but a short telephone conversation. *(Laughter.)* It was not so bad. It improved the resolution. . . .

Next comes the chapter: "Trade Unions and Political Departments." No important principles were raised there, but the chapter is damaging from the point of view of the autobiography of the Party Central Committee. The chapter raises the question of *Tsektran*,[43] which played, as you know, a large role in our theoretical struggle. By this time, every village knows what *Tsektran* is. It is [pictured as] a kind of creature that takes away the grain, which carries a stick in its hand, does not allow the workers to breathe freely, and, when the toiler is worn out, it offers him vinegar in place of the milk which Comrade Zinoviev has at his disposal. *(Applause.)* Nonetheless, I would like to remind you of the conditions under which *Glavpolitput* was established. In the resolution of the Ninth [Party] Congress it is stated: "The Congress recognizes, at the same time, the absolute necessity of taking exceptional and extraordinary measures (martial law, etc.) necessitated by the frightful disintegration of the transport system, in order to prevent its complete paralysis and the ruin of the Soviet Republic."

Glavpolitput was thus created at the Ninth Party Congress for the purpose of saving our transport system. It was using the most cruel methods and provoked widespread discontent. But

---

[41] *Ibid.*, p. 358.

[42] The Russian expression is *"Popali paltsem v nebo,"* meaning "You hit the sky with your finger."

[43] Central Committee of the Transport Union.

Glavpolitput gained the greatest victory. Owing to the efforts of several thousand Communists who were thrown into this most difficult work, we achieved the first important successes.

[Trotsky then cited statistics showing that spectacular improvements of the transport system were a result of *Glavpolitput* and *Tsektran* activities; and he continued:]

There is no doubt that work in this field was conducted by cruel measures, but the Party was fully aware of this and could have stopped it at any moment. *Tsektran* was established on August 28 [1920]. Tomsky was against it, but Lenin, Zinoviev, Stalin (I was not in Moscow at the time, but was for *Tsektran*) voted against Tomsky. The members of *Tsektran* thus received their mission from the Ninth Party Congress, and they conducted a heroic struggle which was greatly successful and which led to the recovery of the transport system. Not to recognize this at the Party Congress, when it was fully acknowledged at the Eighth Congress of Soviets,[44] would be a great injustice. People are being persecuted for work which they are doing in accordance with your will. It would be a crime to carry out in relation to *Tsektran* and the political departments the measures proposed in the draft resolution of the Ten. . . .

AN ATTACK ON TROTSKY'S ARBITRARY METHODS

[Excerpt from Tomsky's speech at the Tenth Party Congress, March 14, 1921][45]

. . . I should like to say a few words to Comrade Trotsky. Comrade Trotsky complains that I attacked him for high-handedness, but that there was no such thing [as high-handedness]. [I affirm that] there was such a thing in connection with the

[44] The Eighth Congress of Soviets, which met toward the end of December, 1920, passed a resolution commending "the self-sacrificing effort of all honest and class-conscious workers that led to the improvement of labor discipline and a better organization of transport administration" (*Sezdy Sovetov Soyuza SSR, soyuznykh i avtonomnykh sovetskikh sotsialisticheskikh respublik,* Moscow, 1959, I, 151).

[45] *Desyatyy sezd RKP(b),* pp. 372–73. Tomsky was Chairman of the Central Council of Trade Unions.

appointment of railway commissars. Let me remind you, Comrade Trotsky, of your speech at the Fifth Conference of Trade Unions.[46] The stenographic report, which contains your clever catchword about "shaking up" *(peretryakhivanie)*, is before me. This is what it says in the well-known "first draft": "As regards Soviet economic institutions, we build, rebuild, break them up, and build again, selecting and checking up on workers in various positions. The trade unions stand almost entirely aside from this work, yet it is absolutely clear that if the trade unions are given the task of mastering the production process in the course of one, two, or three years, it is essential [right now to start reorganizing the unions by selecting, first of all, its leading personnel].[47]

It is not necessary to tell the Congress what all this means. Trotsky's error consists in the fact that he intends to treat non-party workers in the same manner, and we called Trotsky's attention to this error. One day he came to the Central Committee and said: "We did such and such things in *Tsektran* and the results were very good." But I had my doubts at that time and I am going to tell the Congress why I had my doubts. When *Tsektran* presented to me a draft [of a resolution] in which purely military methods were proposed, I did not approve the draft. In that draft it was stated: "The railway transport is militarized. Workers, repair-shop men, and employees,[48] because they find themselves on the most important economic front, are subject to the strictest military discipline.

"Believing that the trade unions must operate in strictly military ways and that responsible union officials should be accountable for their acts to an even greater degree than the rank and file membership, the Presidium of *Tsekprofsozh* [Central Commitee of the Railwaymen's Trade Union] hereby resolves to introduce the following disciplinary penalties: (*a*) personal reprimand, (*b*) official reprimand, (*c*) severe reprimand, (*d*) arrest [from 15 to 30 days], (*e*) confinement in forced-labor camps from one to six months."

[46] The conference took place in November, 1920 (*ibid.*, p. 870).

[47] The brackets are in the text, and the explanation that the enclosed part of the sentence was reconstructed on the basis of the original draft of Trotsky's theses, submitted to the Party Central Committee on November 9, 1920. The 1963 edition of the stenographic records of the Tenth Party Congress does not use the brackets in quoting Tomsky's speech.

[48] The Russian term, *sluzhashchie*, refers to office employees.

When such military methods are being introduced, we dissent. Trotsky seems to have a bungling and obstinate approach to workers' organization and non-party masses. . . .

The vote of the Congress was overwhelmingly in favor of the platform sponsored by Lenin and Zinoviev, which received 336 votes, as against 50 votes for the Trotsky and Bukharin platform, and 18 votes for the Workers' Opposition. Only two abstentions were recorded.[49]

To many delegates of the Congress, the platform of the Ten held out a prospect of greater trade-union independence than Trotsky's proposals. The platform of the Ten also seemed to offer an opportunity for the rank and file of the Party to make their influence felt in the formulation of Soviet economic policy. But on March 16, on the very last day of the Congress meetings, Lenin startled the delegates by introducing two resolutions, one on "The Unity of the Party" and the other on "The Syndicalist and Anarchist Deviation in our Party."

The second resolution was aimed primarily at the Workers' Opposition, which was condemned as a petty-bourgeois and an anarchist deviation "impeding the consistent development of the Party line and helping the class enemies of

---

[49] *Desyatyy sezd RKP(b)*, p. 402. The official count of the vote raises the problem as to the actual division of opinion within the Congress on the issue of trade-union policy. There were altogether 724 voting delegates to the Congress (*Desyatyy sezd RKP[b]*, pp. 764–65). Of the 193 participants in the Congress who were sent to assist in quelling the Kronstadt revolt, only 98 were voting delegates; the rest were either non-voting members or guests (*ibid.*, pp. 810–14). If we can assume that none of the voting delegates who were sent to Kronstadt returned to attend the March 14 session when the trade-union issue was being debated and voted upon, a total of 626 voting delegates must have been present at the session (724 − 98), since there is no record to indicate that another group of voting delegates was sent to Kronstadt. The official count shows that only 404 delegates voted (336 + 50 + 18). By adding the two abstentions we get a figure of 406. What became of the remaining 220 voting delegates?

The 1963 edition of the Proceedings of the Tenth Party Congress does not clear up the mystery of the missing votes. It reduces the number of missing votes from 220 to 156—still an impressive figure. See *Desyatyy sezd RKP(b)*, pp. 745, 767.

the proletarian revolution." It further warned that propaganda of the ideas of the Workers' Opposition was "incompatible with membership in the Russian Communist Party." [50]

The Unity of the Party resolution was of a more general but more drastic character in that it was directed against the formation of any group within the Party that challenged the general Party line. In the form in which this resolution was originally published, clause 7 was omitted,[51] but it was made public a few years later and was used as a basis for expulsion from the Party.

ENTRENCHMENT OF THE PARTY APPARATUS

[Resolution of the Tenth Party Congress, March 16, 1921][52]

1. The Congress calls the attention of all members of the Party to the fact that the unity and solidarity of its ranks, and the establishment of complete confidence among Party members, are particularly essential at the present moment, when, due to a number of circumstances, the vacillations among the petty-bourgeois elements of the country have increased.

2. Even prior to the general Party discussion concerning the trade unions there were signs of factionalism within the Party; i.e., the emergence of groups with separate platforms tending to create a group discipline of their own.

It is necessary that all class-conscious workers clearly realize the harm and the inadvisability of allowing any kind of factionalism, which must inevitably lead to the weakening of the friendly work within the Party and to the encouragement of those enemies who joined the Communists under false pretenses and are striving to use the disagreements [in the Party] for counterrevolutionary purposes. [The Kronstadt uprising was cited as an example of counterrevolutionary plotting by Mensheviks and Socialist Revolutionists.]

[50] *Ibid.*, p. 590.
[51] *Desyatyy sezd Rossiyskoy kommunisticheskoy partii*, p. 310, gives only six clauses of the resolution.
[52] *Desyatyy sezd RKP(b)*, pp. 585–87.

3. Propaganda on this question must consist in explaining fully the harm and the danger of factionalism from the point of view of Party unity and the unity of the will of the proletarian advanced guard, which unity is a basic condition for the success of the proletarian dictatorship. The propaganda must also explain the peculiarity of the newest tactics of the enemies of the Soviet power. These enemies are now convinced of the hopelessness of staging a counterrevolution under the white guard banner and are straining every effort to utilize disagreements within the Communist Party to push through a counterrevolution and to transfer power to groups externally resembling the Soviet government.

4. It is essential that every Party organization pay strict attention to the emergence of any just criticism of the Party's shortcomings or any analysis of the general Party line from the point of view of practical experience and with the aim of correcting mistakes. Care must be taken that this criticism is not discussed by separate groups adhering to one "platform" or another, but that it is submitted to the consideration of the Party as a whole. With this in view, the Congress directs that the Discussion Leaflet is issued at regular intervals. Everyone who criticizes [the Party] must bear in mind the position of the Party surrounded by enemies and must also, by direct participation in Soviet and Party work, strive to rectify the errors of the Party.

5. While instructing the Central Committee to abolish completely all factionalism, the Congress at the same time declares that questions which attract particular attention of Party members, such as purging the Party of non-proletarian and unreliable elements, combating bureaucracy, developing democracy and initiative of the masses, etc., should be studied with the closest attention and tested in practical work. All Party members should know that the Party is prevented from taking the necessary measures [to meet the above difficulties] on account of various obstacles, but that it will continue experimenting with new methods to fight against bureaucracy, to spread democracy and the initiative of the masses, and to expose and expel the [hostile] elements that joined the Party.

6. The Congress orders the immediate dissolution of all groups, without exception, which adhere to any of the platforms,

and authorizes all organizations to hinder all factional activity. Failure to carry out this resolution of the Congress carries with it the unconditional and immediate expulsion from the Party.

7. In order to enforce strict discipline within the Party and in the entire area of Soviet work, and to achieve the greatest unity, while at the same time eliminating every form of factionalism, the Congress authorizes the Central Committee to make use of every provision of Party penalties, including expulsion, for violation of Party discipline or the formation of factions. In case members of the Central Committee are involved, they should be demoted to the status of alternate members, or in extreme cases expelled from the Party. Whenever a member of the Party Central Committee, or an alternate member, or a member of the Party Control Commission is involved [in a violation], a Plenum of the Central Committee should be called, to which alternate members and members of the Control Commission should be invited. If the assembly of these most highly placed members of the Party decides by a two-thirds majority that it is necessary to demote a member of the Central Committee to the status of alternate member, or to expel him from the Party, such decision should be enacted at once.

The resolution of the Tenth Party Congress on the trade-union question had little immediate effect on the position of the Russian worker. On March 24, 1921, a few days after the Congress adjourned, the Central Committee for Compulsory Labor (*Glavkomtrud*) was abolished, but the system of compulsory labor remained intact. All decrees and orders of the *Sovnarkom* and *Glavkomtrud* on compulsory labor remained in force and all work connected with the registration, mobilization, and distribution of labor under the compulsory labor laws was transferred to the People's Commissariat of Labor, the People's Commissariat of Internal Affairs, and the People's Commissariat of War. These three commissariats were charged with the responsibility of co-ordinating the work of labor mobilization, the organization of labor battalions, the utilization of prison labor, and the transportation of those called up for compulsory labor to their place of work.[53]

The trade unions were now to be organized on "democratic" principles and they were to be converted into schools of communism. To ensure that the schooling was effective, the *Sovnarkom* issued a decree on April 5, 1921, that re-established workers' disciplinary courts and placed them under the supervision of the trade unions.

REVIVAL OF WORKERS' DISCIPLINARY COURTS

[Decree of the *Sovnarkom*, April 5, 1921][54]

For the purpose of improving labor discipline and raising productivity of labor to the highest possible limit, the Soviet of People's Commissars, by way of amending the previously published statute, decreed to enact the following:

1. Local Disciplinary Courts are to be established by the *Guberniya* trade-union councils and the *Uezd* trade-union bureaus. The jurisdiction of these courts is to extend over all enterprises and establishments of the R.S.F.S.R., over all workers and employees, as well as the administrative-technical personnel and higher officials.

2. The All-Russian Central Council of Trade Unions is placed in charge of setting up these courts, to determine their number, their staffs and their forms of procedure. The Disciplinary Courts are maintained at the expense of the Republic, which [expense] is included in the appropriations of the All-Russian Central Council of Trade Unions.

3. The chairmen of the local Disciplinary Courts and their deputies are elected by the *Uezd* trade-union bureaus and the *Guberniya* trade-union councils. Members of the Court and their deputies are elected—the former by the leading organ of the factory administration, the latter by the general assembly of

---

[53] *S.U.R.*, 1921, No. 30, Art. 164.
[54] *Ibid.*, No. 23/24, Art. 142.

trade-union members of the enterprise or institution [whose members] are on trial.

4. The *Guberniya* Disciplinary Court is attached to the *Guberniya* Council of Trade Unions and consists of a chairman elected by the *Guberniya* Council of Trade Unions and [two] members, one representing the *Guberniya* Council of National Economy and one, by rotation, from among the chairmen of local Disciplinary Courts. The sessions of the *Guberniya* Disciplinary Courts are attended in a consultative capacity by a representative of the *Guberniya* Council of the People's Court.

5. The chairman and the members of the Court are elected for a period of six months. However, if they are found unfit for their work, they may be recalled before the end of their tour of duty.

6. The sessions of the Disciplinary Courts are to take place at regular intervals after working hours, are open to the public, and their decisions are to be made public. . . .

Note: The sessions of the Disciplinary Courts, as a rule, take place at the factory, plant or enterprise involved.

7. The right to summon a person before the Court belongs to the trade union or to the central or local administrations of the factory or [state] institution. Individual members of trade unions may exercise this right only with the consent of the factory-shop committees or superior trade-union organs.

8. Disciplinary Courts have jurisdiction over the following offenses:

a. Late arrival, idling, and early departure from work without valid reasons;

b. Absenteeism without valid reason;

c. Activities which distract others from work and interfere with such work;

d. Neglect of duties, especially turning out defective output, as well as damage of materials, machinery and other losses;

e. Non-fulfillment of established norms of labor productivity, without valid reasons;

f. Neglect of established labor-safety precautions;

g. Doing extrinsic work during working hours;

h. Hooliganism, unbecoming behavior, and rudeness during working hours;

i. Non-compliance with work orders of superiors;

j. Refusal to do the work which has been assigned to the worker;

k. Rudeness and inattentiveness toward visitors;

l. Violation of existing regulations concerning wage agreements;

m. Laxity toward violation of discipline and failure to utilize the labor force in a rational way;

n. Small pilfering during work, if it is not of an organized and systematic character;

o. Violation of established rules of internal organization and other violations not listed in this statute.

9. Examples of punishments which may be imposed by the Courts:

a. Reprimand and warning of subsequent punishments;

b. Public reprimand;

c. Decrease of piece-rate bonuses or bonuses in kind, including their suspension during a certain period of time;

d. Making up for time lost after working hours or during holidays, either with or without overtime pay;

e. Sentencing to perform various kinds of work either during or after working hours;

f. Demotion up to three months with reduced pay;

g. Suspension for six months from promotion;

h. Suspension for six months from the plant or office;

i. Transfer to hard compulsory labor for a period up to six months without deprivation of freedom;

j. Confinement to a concentration camp for a period up to six months.

10. Disciplinary Courts are not precluded from imposing other forms of punishment, not in excess of those enumerated in Chapter 9 of this statute. They must always keep in mind, however, that the Disciplinary Court is a production-educational institution.

11. Decisions of local Disciplinary Courts can be appealed to a corresponding *Guberniya* Disciplinary Court within a three-day period.

12. If the offenses are of a character that they merit a harsher form of punishment, they should be transferred to the People's Courts.

13. Minors are subject to the disciplinary measures enumerated in points *a* to *g* of Chapter 9 of this decree. If the offense is of a more serious character, the case is forwarded to the Commission on Minors.

14. [The Courts may set free those sentenced to forced-labor camps before the expiration of their sentences.]

15. [In its investigating work the Court will use either Court members or the trade unions.]

16. [The Court has a right to demand that every institution and every official submit material and information required by the Court.]

17. General guidance and supervision over the Workers' Disciplinary Courts is exercised by the All-Russian Central Council of Trade Unions and the People's Commissariat of Justice.

18. [The All-Russian Central Council of Trade Unions, with the consent of the Supreme Council of National Economy, and the Commissariat of Justice formulates all procedural matters under which the Disciplinary Courts operate.]

V. ULYANOV (LENIN)
Chairman of the Sovnarkom

POSTSCRIPT

For several months after the Tenth Party Congress adjourned, compulsory labor laws remained on the books but the regime of labor compulsion was somewhat relaxed. The change of Communist policy in the field of agriculture affected every other sphere of Soviet economic activity, including labor. The resumption of free trade in agricultural products led to a limited revival of free enterprise in industry, and therefore to free employment. Large-scale industry remained in the hands of the state, but its administrative machinery was greatly decentralized and split into a number of trusts that were ordered to operate on the principle of *khozraschet*, i.e., economic cost accounting. This gave the trusts considerable latitude in the management of the plants under their jurisdiction, including the right to hire and fire workers independently of the centralized state machinery that had hitherto controlled the mobilization and allocation of labor on a national scale. One year after the promulgation of the New Economic Policy, much of the legislation that pertained to compulsory labor had been revoked.

Militarization of labor represents the culmination of an experiment in central economic planning that the Russian Communists consistently pursued during the years 1918–20. Its failure is part of a more general failure, which Lenin frankly acknowledged. In a statement made in October, 1921, Lenin said:

We expected, or perhaps it would be more correct to say that we assumed without sufficient calculation, that we would be able by the direct fiat of the proletarian state to establish state production and state distribution of goods on a communistic basis in a country of small peasants. Life has exposed our error. There was need of a series of transition stages . . . to communism." [55]

It was left to Lenin's successors to go through the necessary transition stages. When, under the First Five Year Plan, the drive for the socio-economic transformation of Russia was resumed, in 1929, the labor militarization model of 1920 was once again called into being.

[55] Lenin, *Sochineniya*, XXVII, 29.

BIBLIOGRAPHY

This bibliography does not purport to give all of the materials relating to the subject of this work, or even all of those consulted in its preparation. The list includes merely the sources that were cited in the foregoing pages, but it provides such annotations as are necessary to indicate the general character of the materials that are available in Russian.

LAWS AND STATUTES

Sbornik deystvuyushchikh postanovleniy, instruktsiy i telegrafnykh rasporyazheniy po provedeniyu trudovykh i guzhevykh povinnostey (Compilation of Acting Laws, Instructions and Telegraphic Orders Relating to the Enforcement of Labor and Cartage Services). Moscow, 1921.

Sobranie uzakoneniy i rasporyazheniy rabochego i krestiyanskogo pravitelstva (A Collection of Laws and Ordinances of the Workers' and Peasants' Government). Moscow, 1917, 1918, 1919, 1920, 1921.

CONGRESSES

Desyatyy sezd RKP(b) (The Tenth Congress of the Russian Communist Party [Bolshevik]). Moscow, 1933.
    There is also a 1963 edition of the Proceedings of the Tenth Congress.

Devyatyy sezd Rossiyskoy kommunisticheskoy partii, Stenograficheskiy otchet (The Ninth Congress of the Russian Communist Party, Stenographic Report). Gosizdat, Moscow, 1920.
    There is also a 1960 edition of the Proceedings of the Ninth Congress.

N-skiy. *Vtoroy Vserossiyskiy sezd professionalnykh soyuzov (The Second All-Russian Congress of Trade Unions).* Moscow, 1919.

Pervyy Vserossiyskiy sezd professionalnykh soyuzov, Stenograficheskiy otchet (The First All-Russian Congress of Trade Unions, Stenographic Report). Moscow, 1918.

Protokoly zasedaniy Vserossiyskogo tsentralnogo ispolnitelnogo komiteta 4-go sozyva, Stenograficheskiy otchet (Protocols of the Ses-

267

sions of the All-Russian Central Executive Committee of the 4th Convocation, Stenographic Report). Moscow, 1920.

Rezolyutsii III Vserossiyskogo sezda professionalnykh soyuzov (Resolutions of the Third All-Russian Congress of Trade Unions). Moscow, 1921.

Rezolyutsii tretego Vserossiyskogo sezda sovetov narodnogo khozyaystva (Resolutions of the Third All-Russian Congress of Councils of National Economy). Moscow, 1920.

Sezdy Sovetov Soyuza SSR, soyuznykh i avtonomnykh sovetskikh sotsialisticheskikh respublik (Congresses of Soviets of the Union of Socialist Soviet Republics, Union and Autonomous Soviet Socialist Republics). Moscow, 1959.

Tretiy Vserossiyskiy sezd professionalnykh soyuzov, Chast I (The Third All-Russian Congress of Trade Unions, Part I). Gosizdat, Moscow, 1921.
    Part II consists of the resolutions that were adopted by the Congress.

Trudy I Vserossiyskogo sezda sovetov narodnogo khozyaystva, Stenograficheskiy otchet (Proceedings of the First All-Russian Congress of Councils of National Economy, Stenographic Report). Moscow, 1918.

Trudy II Vserossiyskogo sezda sovetov narodnogo khozyaystva, Stenograficheskiy otchet (Proceedings of the Second All-Russian Congress of Councils of National Economy, Stenographic Report). Moscow, 1919.

VIII sezd Rossiyskoy kommunisticheskoy partii, Stenograficheskiy otchet (The Eighth Congress of the Russian Communist Party, Stenographic Report). Moscow, 1919.

Vosmoy sezd sovetov rabochikh, krestyanskikh i soldatskikh deputatov (The Eighth Congress of Workers,' Peasants' and Soldiers' Deputies). Gosizdat, Moscow, 1921.

Vtoroy Vserossiyskiy sezd professionalnykh soyuzov, Stenograficheskiy otchet (The Second All-Russian Congress of Trade Unions, Stenographic Report). Gosizdat, Moscow, 1921.

COLLECTIONS OF WRITINGS AND DOCUMENTS

Arkhiv Russkoy revolyutsii (Archives of the Russian Revolution). I. V. Hessen, ed. Berlin, 1921–34, 21 vols.

Bolshaya Sovetskaya entsiklopediya (*The Large Soviet Encyclopedia*). 1st ed., Moscow.

Bunyan, James. *Intervention, Civil War and Communism in Russia, April–December, 1918.* Baltimore, The Johns Hopkins Press, 1936.

Bunyan, James, and H. H. Fisher. *The Bolshevik Revolution, 1917–1918: Documents and Materials.* Stanford, Calif., Stanford University Press, 1934.

De War, Margaret. *Labour Policy in the USSR, 1917–1928.* London, 1956.

Dopolneniya k obzoru deyatelnosti narodnogo komissariata truda za 1921 god (*Supplement to the Review of the Activities of the People's Commissariat of Labor for 1921*). Moscow, 1921.

Lenin, V. I. *Sochineniya* (*Collected Works*). 3rd ed., 30 Vols. Moscow, 1928–37.

Stalin, I. V. *Sochineniya* (*Collected Works*). Moscow, 1946–55.

Statisticheskiy yezhegodnik, 1918–1920 (*The Statistical Yearbook, 1918–1920*). Moscow, 1920, 2 vols.

General

Anikst, A. *Organizatsiya rabochey sily v 1920 godu* (*Organization of the Labor Force in 1920*). Moscow, 1920.

    A review of labor militarization during 1920, written by a deputy chairman of the Central Committee on Compulsory Labor.

———. *Stati i doklady sa 1918–1920 po organizatsii raspredeleniya rabochey sily* (*Papers and Reports for 1918–1920 on Organizing the Distribution of the Labor Force*). Moscow, 1921.

———. *Organizatsiya rynka truda za dva goda sovetskoy vlasti* (*Organization of the Labor Market during Two Years of Soviet Rule*). Moscow, 1920.

Bergson, A. *The Structure of Soviet Wages: A Study in Socialist Economics.* Cambridge, Mass., Harvard University Press, 1944.

Bukharin, N. *Ekonomika perekhodnogo perioda* (*Economics of the Transition Period*). Moscow, 1920.

Carr, E. H. *The Bolshevik Revolution, 1917–1923.* Vols. 1–3 of *History of Soviet Russia.* 7 vols. New York, 1951–60.

Dan, F. *Dva goda skitaniy* (*Two Years of Wandering*). Berlin, 1922.

    Valuable comments on the Russian revolutionary scene by a

leading Menshevik who for two years traveled around the country and finally reached Germany in 1922.

Kolontay, A. *Rabochaya oppozitsiya (The Workers' Opposition)*. Moscow, 1921.

Krestyanstvo i trudovaya povinnost (The Peasantry and Labor Duty). Moscow, 1920.

Kritsman, L. *Geroicheskiy period velikoy Russkoy revolyutsii (The Heroic Period of the Great Russian Revolution)*. Moscow, 1924.

Lorimer, Frank. *The Population of the Soviet Union: History and Prospects*. Geneva, The League of Nations, 1948.

Contains an analysis of population changes in Russia in 1918–22, based on the Soviet population census of 1926.

Maysky, I. *Demokraticheskaya kontrrevolyutsiya (The Democratic Counterrevolution)*. *Gosizdat,* 1923.

Reminiscences of a member of the Samara government in 1918, who later joined the Bolsheviks.

Pankratova, A. *Fabzavkomy Rossii v borbe za sotsialisticheskuyu fabriku (Factory-Shop Committees in Their Struggle for a Socialist Factory)*. *Glavpolitprosvet,* Moscow, 1923.

Pasternak, Boris. *Doktor Zhivago*. Ann Arbor, University of Michigan Press, 1959.

Platonov, S. F. *A History of Russia*. New York, 1925.

Pravda o Kronstadte (The Truth about Kronstadt). Prague, 1921.

An account of the Kronstadt uprising, published by the Socialist Revolutionists.

Rozenfeld, Ya. S. *Promyshlennaya politika SSSR (Industrial Policy of the USSR)*. *Gospolitizdat,* Moscow, 1926.

Sarabyanov, V. *Ekonomika i ekonomicheskaya politika SSSR (Economics and the Economic Policy of the USSR)*. *Gosizdat,* Moscow, 1926.

This source provides extensive data on the decline of the Russian economy between 1918 and 1921.

Schapiro, Leonard. *The Origin of the Communist Autocracy*. London, 1955.

Vishnevsky, N. M. *Printsipy i metody organizatsionnogo raspredeleniya produktov (Principles and Methods of an Organized Distribution of Products)*. Moscow, 1920.

Gives a detailed account of the rationing system in Russia during 1918–20.

Periodicals

Byulleten moskovskogo potrebitelskogo obshchestva (Bulletin of the Moscow Consumers' Society). Moscow, 1919.

Byulleten narodnogo komissariata truda (Bulletin of the People's Commissariat of Labor).

The official organ of the labor commissariat.

Izvestiya glavnogo komiteta po vseobshchey trudovoy povinnosti (News of the Central Committee on Universal Compulsory Labor). Moscow, 1920, Nos. 1–7.

The official organ of *Glavkomtrud.*

Narodnoe khozyaystvo (National Economy).

The official organ of the Supreme Council of National Economy.

Professionalny vestnik (Trade-Union Herald).

Official organ of the Central All-Russian Council of Trade Unions.

Vestnik putey soobshcheniya (The Railways' Herald).

Organ of the railway workers' trade union.

Newspapers

Delo naroda (The People's Cause).

Organ of the Central Committee of the Socialist-Revolutionists of the Right.

Ekonomicheskaya zhizn (Economic Life).

A daily paper published by the Supreme Council of National Economy.

Izvestiya Vserossiyskogo tsentralnogo ispolnitelnogo komiteta sovetov rabochikh, krestyanskikh, soldatskikh i kazachikh deputatov (News of the All-Russian Central Executive Committee of Soviets of Workers', Peasants', Soldiers' and Cossacks' Deputies).

The official organ of the Soviet government.

Izvestiya tsentralnogo komiteta Rossiyskoy kommunisticheskoy partii (News of the Central Committee of the Russian Communist Party).

An information bulletin of the Party Central Committee, it was first published as a weekly supplement to *Pravda.* With

272 BIBLIOGRAPHY

issue No. 21, on September 4, 1920, it became a separate publication. In 1929 it became a periodical, entitled *Partiynoe stroitelstvo*.

Novaya zhizn (The New Life).

A newspaper, founded by Maxim Gorki, that was highly critical of Bolshevik policies.

Pravda.

The official organ of the Central Committee of the Communist Party.

INDEX

Abramovich, R.: denounces forced labor, 135–36

Absenteeism: measures to combat, 166–67; and decline of industrial production, 173–74

Administration of nationalized industry. *See* Industrial management

Administrative agencies: and depletion of labor force, 82–84

Agriculture: and bread war, 2; and barter, 81–82; conditions in 1920, 215; revolt against, 216, 217; and New Economic Policy, 218–19

Anarchosyndicalist deviation: imputed to Workers' Opposition, 258

Arakcheev regime: explained, 104*n*

Bagmen: explained, 82*n*

Barter, 81–82

Bonuses in kind, 176–78. *See also* Incentives

Bourgeoisie: and forced labor, 51–52, 64–65; Trotsky's proposals *re*, 55–56; drafting of, 57–67

Bourgeois specialists: employment of, 48–49, 86, 130–31, 195; three categories of, 196

Bread monopoly: and effect on food supply, 78–79; and changes in diet, 79–80; and illegal market, 81–82; explained, 94*n*

Bread rations. *See* Food distribution

Bukharin, N. I.: and "Buffer Resolution," 207–8; associated with Trotsky, 220, 221–29

Central Executive Committee: proclaims universal liability to labor, 62–64; establishes forced-labor camps, 72–75; decrees labor books for workers, 76

Cheka. *See* Counterrevolution, Extraordinary Commission to Fight

Committee management. *See* One-man management

Compulsory Labor, Central Committee on: establishment of, 112–14; and Commissions on Compulsory Labor, 114, 116; and Central Extraordinary Commission on Firewood and Cartage Duty, 155–56; and *Dezertirkomissiya*, 164 and *n*; abolition of, 261; mentioned, 98, 116

Concentration camps, 71–72

Councils of National Economy: First All-Russian Congress of, 18, 21–24; Second All–Russian Congress of, 27–29, 40–41; Third All–Russian Congress of, 105–9; mentioned, 101, 128. *See also* Supreme Council of National Economy

Counterrevolution, Extraordinary Commission to Fight: and forced-labor camps, 72; and *Glavkomtrud*, 114; and labor desertion, 165, 168, 169

Currency depreciation: and Workers' standard of living, 22–24, 84, 175, 179; and wage rates, 86, 180

Dan, F.: critical of labor militarization, 135; derides labor armies, 150–51

Democratic Centralists: and opposition to Trotsky, 121–23; mentioned, 129, 209, 243

Desertion, Central Commission to Fight against: establishment of, 165; operation of, 167–68

Dzerzhinsky, F.: appointed chairman of *Glavkomtrud*, 114; appointed chairman of *Tsechrezkomtopguzh*, 155; supported Trotsky's platform, 229

Economic dictatorship: and labor discipline, 67, 68–70. *See also* Militarization of economy

Epidemics, 67, 172*n*47, 173*n*

"Every worker a soldier," 119–21

Factory-shop committees: and workers' control, 8–11, 14; criticized by Lozovsky, 12

Famine, 67, 172*n*47, 173*n*

Financial policy: and currency *emission*, 180

Food detachments: explained, 95*n*

Food distribution: "class principle" of, 54–55; and labor productivity, 67, 89, 173; and food monopoly, 78–79; and illegal market, 81–82; and "armor-clad" rations, 171; Lenin's ideas on, 176

Food-requisition cordons: activity of, 82

Forced-labor camps: establishment of, 72–73; regulations of, 73–75; mentioned, 67

French Assignats: and Russian rubles, 179–80

273